ADVANCE PRAISE FOR

Dramatism and Musical Theater:
Experiments in Rhetorical Performance

"Kimberly Eckel Beasley and James P. Beasley deliver rivetingly insightful approaches to Burkean Dramatism as a heuristic for creating and sustaining effective rhetorical performances. Framed within the timespan of the early days of the divisive Trump administration and concluding toward its demise, the book artfully examines how musical theater is especially capable of creating choratic spaces of potential for unity. *Dramatism and Musical Theater: Experiments in Rhetorical Performance* seems to be made for this moment, yet it also illuminates a return to the interdisciplinary value of writing, rhetoric, and theater pedagogy. The convergence of these scenes of rhetorical activity manifests a kairotic resacralization of the rhetorical canon of delivery.

The book does more than simply explain 'the pentad' and imagine rhetors will know what to do with it. Instead, by sharing a sense of who Burke was and the range of his hopes, Beasley and Beasley offer Kenneth Burke's pentadic pedagogical approach in ways that reasonably reframe both written and theatrical performances as acts. When seen as acts through the pentad, we are better able to explore motivation and situatedness from within scenes of our performances, our lives, all toward increasingly choratic, and therefore at least momentarily 'unified,' participation in rhetorical performances, in life."

—Dr. Bonnie Lenore Kyburz, Independent Scholar; Author of Cruel Auteurism: Affective Digital Meditations Toward Film-Composition

"As a former Director of Forensics, who has judged a lot of Rhetorical Criticism and Communication Analysis rounds, and as an Equity Actor and Professor of Dramatic Arts, I am fascinated by the approach of this text. *Dramatism and Musical Theater: Experiments in Rhetorical Performance* is an innovative, insightful, and informed approach to the practice of performance."

—Jeff Green, Professor and Department Chair, Theatre, Communication, and Media Arts, Georgia Southwestern University

Dramatism and Musical Theater

This book is part of the Peter Lang Media and Communication list.
Every volume is peer reviewed and meets
the highest quality standards for content and production.

PETER LANG
New York • Bern • Berlin
Brussels • Vienna • Oxford • Warsaw

Kimberly Eckel Beasley
and James P. Beasley

Dramatism and Musical Theater

Experiments in Rhetorical Performance

PETER LANG

New York • Bern • Berlin
Brussels • Vienna • Oxford • Warsaw

Library of Congress Cataloging-in-Publication Data

Names: Beasley, Kimberly Eckel, author. | Beasley, James P., author.
Title: Dramatism and musical theater: experiments in rhetorical
performance / Kimberly Eckel Beasley, James P. Beasley.
Description: New York: Peter Lang, 2021.
Includes bibliographical references and index.
Identifiers: LCCN 2020033405 (print) | LCCN 2020033406 (ebook)
ISBN 978-1-4331-7284-7 (hardback) | ISBN 978-1-4331-8134-4 (paperback)
ISBN 978-1-4331-7285-4 (ebook pdf) | ISBN 978-1-4331-7286-1 (epub)
ISBN 978-1-4331-7287-8 (mobi)
Subjects: LCSH: Acting in musical theater. | Musicals—Production and
direction. | Burke, Kenneth, 1897–1993.
Classification: LCC MT956 .B43 2021 (print) | LCC MT956 (ebook) |
DDC 792.6—dc23
LC record available at https://lccn.loc.gov/2020033405
LC ebook record available at https://lccn.loc.gov/2020033406
DOI 10.3726/b17556

Bibliographic information published by **Die Deutsche Nationalbibliothek.**
Die Deutsche Nationalbibliothek lists this publication in the "Deutsche
Nationalbibliografie"; detailed bibliographic data are available
on the Internet at http://dnb.d-nb.de/.

Table of Contents

List of Figures

Acknowledgments

Writing this together with James, I'd first like to thank him for including me in his scholarship and in the vision he has had for more than a decade of researching Kenneth Burke and Burke's theory of dramatism and using it to elevate the writing of a writer, the acting of an actor, and the performing of a performer. That Jim has always been inspired by Burke's theory, encouraging me as a director to utilize it in production, has changed the way I approach a show with my cast—my students. Thank you to my fellow design colleagues at Jacksonville University who have tirelessly seen my productions through from start to finish. Thank you to my fellow voice colleagues at JU, whose teaching of singing is sound and solid as we together support each other and our students in their craft. Thank you to the Kurt Weill Foundation for their College/University Performance grant that helped make *Street Scene, an American Opera* possible. Thank you to the cast, crew, and musicians of every production featured in this book. Without the combined efforts of on stage, back stage, and under the stage, none of this is a reality. And special thanks to the cast of my first musical at JU, *Little Women*, the first to experience Kenneth Burke's pentad and go with the flow. You are all "astonishing"!

Writing this together with Kimberly, I'd first like to thank her for including me in her scholarship and in the vision that she brings to each production she directs. Her attention to detail is an inspiration to her students and to the audiences that have been able to attend her productions. Thank you to our families for their support, and thank you to Peter Lang Publishing for their guidance in the editorial process, and we are grateful for the support of Peter Lang Publishing for bringing these stories to life.

Grateful acknowledgment is made to the following for permission to reproduce material in this book:

Astonishing
Fire Within Me
from the Broadway Musical LITTLE WOMEN
Music by Jason Howland
Lyrics by Mindi Dickstein
Copyright (c) 2005 BMG Sapphire Songs (BMI), Howland Music (BMI) and Little Esky Publishing (ASCAP)
All Rights Administered by BMG Rights Management (US) LLC
International Copyright Secured All Rights Reserved
Reprinted by Permission of Hal Leonard LLC

AIN'T IT AWFUL THE HEAT
From the Musical Production "Street Scene"
Lyrics by Langston Hughes, Music by Kurt Weill
TRO-© Copyright 1948 (Renewed) Hampshire House Publishing Corp., New York, NY
and Chappell & Co., Inc., Los Angeles, CA
International Copyright Secured Made In U.S.A.
All Rights Reserved Including Public Performance For Profit
Used by Permission

LONELY HOUSE
From the Musical Production "Street Scene"
Lyrics by Langston Hughes, Music by Kurt Weill
TRO-© Copyright 1948 (Renewed) Hampshire House Publishing Corp., New York, NY
and Chappell & Co., Inc., Los Angeles, CA
International Copyright Secured Made In U.S.A.
All Rights Reserved Including Public Performance For Profit
Used by Permission

Introduction

On February 26, 2017, the Academy of Motion Picture Arts and Sciences presented awards for the best films of 2016. It was the first Academy Awards Ceremony since Donald J. Trump had been elected president, and it was not even two months into the new administration. In those two short months, however, Trump's administration had already banned citizens from several Muslim countries, creating chaos in the immigration system and on travel infrastructures. Many actors had condemned President Trump for his policies, and even more for his demagoguery toward people of color at home and abroad. Even the host, Jimmy Kimmel, began his opening monologue by saying, "This broadcast is being seen by over 200 million people in over 200 countries. All of them who now hate us."[1] Yet, just before the broadcast began, Justin Timberlake entered the auditorium singing, "I got this feelin/inside my bones/," the beginning verse of his smash hit, "Can't Stop the Feeling."[2] For the first five full minutes of the broadcast, everyone in the auditorium was standing and singing along, a *chorus* of dance and emotion. The moment brought together everyone in the room, as if they needed to exhale for a bit and just enjoy that moment. When I use the word "chorus" here, I do so in its classical sense, coming from the Greek word *chora*, which implies a gathering together, and *chora* is one of the most important concepts in the larger meaning of rhetoric. While rhetoric comes from the Greek word *rhetra* or "a bargain (between two people)," there cannot be a bargain between people without those people "coming together," without *chora*. In this sense, Justin Timberlake at the Academy Awards becomes what Kenneth Burke called a "representative anecdote,"[3] as his song and the audience's participation created a choratic moment, a coming together. In the same way, we fully acknowledge that there is much to worry about in the present moment. As we write this, the Trump administration is defying a Supreme Court decision to ask a citizenship question on the 2020 census. Are there more important issues to write about in this present moment? Yes. Are there more important uses of rhetoric in this present moment? Yes. However, we choose to write about rhetoric and music theater at this moment because it is our way to "gather together," to show how music, movement, drama, and rhetoric can make our world a closer place.

How to Use This Book

This book is intended for three audiences: students in advanced writing courses, students in advanced theater or music theater courses, and directors of university musical theater productions. For the students in the advanced writing course, we hope that this book makes the rhetorical theory of Kenneth Burke very approachable through examples of the dramatistic pentad in popular musicals. For the advanced theater or music theater students, we hope that this book gives you a method of characterization through staging, giving you more ownership over the roles you are inhabiting, whether your director tells you what they want or if they do not. For the director of university theater, we hope that this book provides tools to give you more ownership over the choices you make on your production, from choice of musical, to using limited resources, to articulating this intellectual work to university administrators, and to empowering the students you work with on the stage.

Dramatism

Chances are that many of you have never heard of Kenneth Burke or the concept of "dramatism" before. However, there is a very good chance that your teachers have heard of him and/or have used his concepts of literary theory in their teaching. Kenneth Burke dropped out of college twice, once when he was a first-year student at Ohio State in 1918 and later at Columbia University. In New York, he began hanging out in Greenwich Village with a group of writers such as John Dos Passos, Hart Crane, and his childhood friend, the critic Malcolm Cowley.[4] In the magazine *The Dial*, he became known for writing literary criticism of modernist authors such as T. S. Eliot and Ezra Pound. But writing about literature wasn't all he did. He went out on the town, and when he did, it was to go to concerts at the symphony or the theater. At the time Burke was living in New York, he turned his attention to writing music and theater criticism, and his good opinion was one of the most sought after in those intellectual circles. While writing about the literature, music, and theater of New York, however, Burke kept his eye on world politics and affairs, and at the beginning of the 1930s, he would turn his talents to these broader concerns.[5] In the 1930s, Europe was experiencing a revolution, with demagogues finding footholds in Spain, Italy, and of course, in Germany. Burke was always intrigued at the writer's, musician's, or the actor's purpose and how that purpose would impact the audiences they wrote, performed, or acted for. In turning his attention to political rhetoric, Burke sought to analyze how communication in the two realms, literature and life, were not separate but were part of what he called "the human barnyard."[6] Over the next twenty years, Burke devoted his study to bridging the gap between "literature and life," and the resulting theory that Burke developed would later become known as "dramatism."

In *A Grammar of Motives* (1945), Kenneth Burke outlined his conception of what he would call "dramatism": a method that readers can use to identify the rhetorical nature of any text or act, opening it to multiple perspectives.

ACT: what was done?
SCENE: When and where was the act performed?
AGENT: Who did it?
AGENCY: How and with what was the act performed?
PURPOSE: What motivated the act?[7]

While these questions might seem simplistic, how we answer these questions quickly becomes complicated. Ask two people to describe a traffic accident, and you will not get the same answer, but beyond this cliché lies a simple truth, "It's more complicated than that,"[8] as Burke used to say. Burke's questions were not unique to him, of course, since it was Aristotle who asked similar questions in his famous treatise, *On Rhetoric*, in the 3rd century BCE. Burke's application of these questions was unique to him, however, in that these questions became that bridge between "literature and life" that he was searching for. Think about it for a minute; you write a paper for a class; what kinds of response do we usually get? Something like the following: "You need a stronger thesis statement," "You don't have a counterargument here," or even "You don't repeat your thesis in your conclusion." In other words, we often think of our own writing and the writing of others as an object, a piece of art, or a piece of garbage. Burke encouraged thinking of our own writing and the writing of others as an act, not pieces of art or garbage, but as actions made to achieve specific purposes. If we think about writing that way, it changes our orientation to what is valuable. If we think of writing as an object, we focus on its *intrinsic* characteristics: intro, thesis, supporting points, counterargument, or conclusion. But if we think of writing as an act, we focus on its *extrinsic* characteristics: who wrote it, under what conditions, by what means or method, and for what purpose. There are no "norming" characteristics, common denominators that all writing must have, but there is an accounting for differences in writers, conditions, and purposes. We began this introduction with an apology of sorts for not taking on the issues confronting our country, but in a way, we have come back around to it here. Burke's pentad makes allowances for writers of different countries, religions, backgrounds, and educational levels. As Asao Inoue has written:

> Reading to correct, or reading to compare to an ideal text in our heads, always means that readers never really read each other as intellectuals, never respect the labor and effort that goes into drafting even a messy draft, never engage well with the writer as thinker, never engage well with their ideas, and certainly never critique the very discourse the writer is attempting to learn and perhaps change. What happens is that we read to look for deficits, not differences.[9]

If the word *rhetoric* comes from the Greek word for "a bargain (between two people)," then what also happens when we only read for those intrinsic characteristics is that we ignore its rhetorical capabilities. We will have several opportunities for students to practice this "pentad" throughout this book, and we hope that students enjoy getting to "read each other as intellectuals," respecting "the labor that goes into messy drafts," engaging "with other writers," and ultimately enjoying the ways to "interpret the interpretations."

Dramatism and Theater

Congratulations! You've just been cast as the lead in your favorite musical. You know the music by heart, and you've been rehearsing everything from your favorite moments to your curtain bows. There's nothing else to do, right? "It's a bit more complicated than that," Burke used to say, and he would be correct. While everything is perfect in your world right now, chances are that your director is feeling less confident. Chances are that she chose this particular show not just for your acting and singing ability, but because it somehow meets other expectations or requirements. Perhaps the sets are already in storage, so this particular production would cut costs; or maybe the director has conducted archival research on the production and is needing more qualifications for tenure and promotion. Whatever the reason, your director is presenting this production as an academic opportunity for students and an addition to her scholarly activity.

As you and your director collaborate, there are many challenges, and the first challenge is "musical theater" itself. As musical theater bridges both the interpretive focus of theater and the contextual focus of musicology, it often brings together two very divided disciplines. For example, while there is broad latitude in how characters and their dialogs can be interpreted from the theatrical world, there are fewer interpretive options for the musical performer. In addition to the original material, musical lyrics operate in an intermediary role between acting and singing. Therefore, not only are there lyrics to be analyzed, but there is music accompanying and underscoring those lyrics that also inform an actor's performance.

This dilemma is precisely why a developed theory of musical theater interpretation and production is significant, especially within the context of collegiate education. Musical theater forms are much more closely tied to popular culture than "straight" theater. Musicals create their own drama, yet the drama is understood to be ironic. We will talk more later about Burke's "psychology of information" in literature and the "psychology of form" of music a bit later, but the important point to note here is that music and literature are operating in two distinct, competing, epistemologies, or "ways of thinking." For example, even though Elle Woods does not know how she will win the case in the musical *Legally Blonde*, the audience knows she will. Kenneth Burke called this "dramatic irony" when the audience knows more than the characters, resulting in a kind of persuasiveness. The form helps us predict the outcome. If the form helps the audience predict the outcome, then what is a performer to do to keep the audience thinking? How can you keep yourself from "phoning in" your own performance?

Burke has an answer for that, too, and that answer is in the purpose of his method of dramatism. Another way to think about might be to think of it as dramatizing, taking a situation that doesn't seem to be that complicated and revealing how fraught with difficulty it actually is. Burke writes, "A perfectionist might seek to evolve terms free of ambiguity and inconsistency...what we want is not terms that avoid ambiguity, but terms that clearly reveal the strategic spots at which ambiguities necessarily arise."[10] As a musical theater performer, you understand, maybe more than anyone else, the importance of having the audience feel that your character is in trouble or that your situation is beyond resolution, just before you save the day. In order to find those moments of ambiguity, we need to dramatize them, or bring the drama into the drama, so to speak. Dramatism is the invitation to "consider the matter of motives in a perspective that, being developed from the analysis of drama, treats language and thought primarily as modes of action."[11] Words move, they circulate, they range, they pierce, they hurt, they give pleasure, and they sting. Most importantly, for Burke, they reveal motives. How we describe any act reveals more about us than it does about that act. "You must have a description that names the act (describes what took place in thought or deed), and another that names the scene (the background of the act, the situation in which it occurred); also, you must indicate what kind of person (agent) performed the act, what means or instruments were used, and the purpose."[12] By describing the act, the scene, the agent, the agency, and the purpose, we are able to "interpret our interpretations." In other words, we are able to discover what we think or feel before we realize why we even think or feel that way in the first place.

Here's an example: where we live in Florida, we have experienced a phenomenon known as "red tide," a form of algae that has taken over many of Florida's most beautiful beaches, but also has devastated the fish and shellfish industry in the Gulf Coast. This last sentence, in essence, is a description of an "act," a "description that names the act (describes what took place in thought or deed)." Second, we would go about describing the "scene," so how about describing the scene as *the protected coastal areas of the Gulf Coast known for fishing, swimming, and wildlife?* Third, we would describe the "agent," or the "person or object which performed the act." Let's describe the agent which has performed the act of "experiencing red tide" as *human polluters who do not care for clean water.* So, you start to see how this is revealing our interpretations on who is responsible for the act, right? Fourth, let's describe the "agency," or the "means by which the act was accomplished" as *state policies which allow corporations to dump harmful pollutants in coastal waters.* Fifth, let's finish up by describing the purpose of the act as *in order that corporations will give campaign contributions to state lawmakers that allow them to dump harmful pollutants in coastal waters.* In this example, our answers might differ from someone else that does not believe that human pollution is causing red tide. But what about our interpretation? We indicated that it was "polluters" that were causing red tide, but based on our description of "agency," we start to see that it might be the politicians that are more to blame, right? That's where this work gets fun. You find out other characters' motives for their actions. The more detailed the description, the more you and your audience will get out of it, and we'll have plenty of time later on to practice these descriptions in some of the accompanying study guides.

Burke's analysis doesn't even really stop here, either. Up until this point, we've been discussing Burke's dramatism as a way to develop the interpretive possibilities at your disposal. But what about the potential for Burke's dramatism as a way of theatrical staging? One of the newest textbooks on musical theater acting, Joe Deer and Rocco Dal Vera's *Acting in Musical Theatre: A Comprehensive Course*, treats staging in the following manner: "When we see a dynamic or deeply affecting performance, we rarely remember the staging, unless it is highly choreographed or unless it gets in the way of the performer."[13] We will use the theories of both Burke and Debra Hawhee to develop a memorable method of dramatistic staging, one that features the symbolic act as "a mind helping a body think."[14] In this way, Burke's dramatism demonstrates how "the whole body may become involved in this attitudinizing of the poem."[15] By using Burke's dramatistic pentad, you will be able to realize how your own motivations can become the basis for theatrical staging. When we say that Burke described dramatism as a "mind helping a body think," we are applying Jaclyn S. Olson's description of Burke's emphasis on "the productive forces of the body, that maintain a logical parallel to our patterns of thinking"[16] to the staging process in musical theater production.

As you will read throughout this book, we want to constantly challenge traditional theater interpretation and staging methods with Burke's dramatism. To do so, we will contrast some of the most closely held practices in the fields of theater and drama with our applications of Burke's essential concepts: dramatistic pentad, identification, trained incapacities, and perspectives by incongruity. For example, one of the sharpest contrasts we make between Burke's "dramatism" and Stanislavski's "Given Circumstances" is described in the second chapter on Burke's "scene ratio." As a perspective by congruity, Burke's dramatism serves a "mind helping a body think," and this perspective by incongruity turns the tables, so to speak, on traditional staging methods. Jaclyn S. Olson explained how this process could work:

> Our having hands, Burke argues, results in hand thoughts, which might allow us to use language of grasping, a particular idea to invoke the physicality of the gesture. In this formulation, the body becomes the primary vehicle for engagement with the environment and others—even the symbolic structures the mind erects are guided by the potentialities of its physical form.[17]

While traditional methods of interpretation and staging concentrate on the "magical If," or "How would I behave 'as if' I were this character?" Burke's dramatism engages the body as the bridge between the actor and their character. But not just a bridge between the actor and their character, however, since Burke's body-gestures are not just guided by the environment of the character, but by both the actor and the character together, an experiment we conducted on scene ratio and scene-agent will be described in the second chapter. As inhabitants of a particular location, student actors are receptive to the sensations of a particular scene. Olson has described this process that we attempt to apply to scene-motivated staging in chapter two as well: "By inhabiting an environment, all organisms impose meanings on it, making and remaking its significance through the names we give and our physical activity—our demands—within it."[18] In other words, we hope to demonstrate how our physical activity on the stage became a kind of "perspective by incongruity," changing the meanings of these productions *as they were happening*, not through thinking about themselves "as if" they were their characters, but through their bodies responding to their local circumstances, what Kenneth Burke might call their "as was."

Musical Theater Production

While arts programs are under increased scrutiny as viable academic programs, collegiate theater directors have little margin for error. The academic director must weigh several considerations among students, departments, and institutions. Will this production help students receive acting nominations? Will this production ensure that the department can remain solvent? Will this production bring new prospective students to campus? Therefore, most collegiate directors of musical theater are constantly working toward taking popular crowd pleasers that will bring in ticket sales or prospective students and demonstrating how these productions deserve scholarly, artistic attention.

There are many differences between collegiate musical theater production and professional production, most specifically, the dual roles of everyone involved: the performers are both actors and students, and the director is both dramaturg and professor. For the academic department, the musical is both ticketed performance and graded class, and for the university at large the ticketed performance is both budget conscious and recruitment driven. These tensions express themselves in outcomes: teachers want to have their course objectives met, while students want award nominations from organizations such as BroadwayWorld.com and the Kennedy Center Theater to add to their resumes. Music or Theater Departments want ticket sales to add to the budget, while universities are looking for increases in new applications. The academic director must weigh these considerations against one another. Will my learning objectives also help students receive acting nominations? Will my learning objectives ensure that the department production isn't a "flop"? Will my learning objectives bring new prospective students to campus? The tensions that exist in these dualities, therefore, are at the heart of collegiate musical theater production. In many cases, decisions are made to push or pull in one or several of these directions, leaving the director with many zero-sum choices. In collegiate production, these choices carry risks for tenure and promotion, as well as tenuous interdepartmental relations in securing funding, increasing recruitment, providing assessment data, and departmental or institutional accreditation.

If the academic musical theater must negotiate among all these given motives, then it is necessary to understand systems that address the complexity of competing motives. Kenneth Burke's *Grammar of Motives*, his *Rhetoric of Motives*, and parts of his *Symbolic of Motives* have all provided methods and tools for this complicated situation. Because musical theater forms are much more closely tied to popular culture (entertainment) than "straight" theater (art and literature), musicals generally do not challenge audiences to create their own drama. C. Ronald Kimberling writes on dramatism's ability to challenge the inherent limitations in popular art's predictable forms:

> The Burkean model provides a tentative answer to the frequently posed question as to whether popular art reflects or engenders social values and mores. Dramatism would suggest that it does both. Popular art reflects social values because it presents universal patterns of experience, patterns that the audience must recognize if it is to understand the work. It engenders values by presenting dramatic scenarios placing ordinary values in conflict situations demanding that some hierarchy of values be established, and by stimulating audience identification with the processes of value formation.[19]

As musical theater bridges both the interpretive focus of theater and the contextual focus of musicology, disciplinary boundaries are often violated and simultaneously observed. Therefore, while there is broad latitude in how characters and their dialog can be interpreted from the theatrical world, there are fewer interpretive options for the musical interpreter. While Kimberling focuses on the importance of dramatism's ability to combine both art and entertainment, Debra Hawhee describes how this is accomplished: through movement. Hawhee wrote, "Burke's model of musical rhetoric involves a certain giving over of oneself on the part of the audience member, and that giving over seems to happen at the level of bodily perception."[20] Hawhee's theory of Burkean movement serves as a method of musical theater performance, and this book describes how utilizing Burke's dramatistic pentad in the staging process of collegiate musical performance creates a new idiom for student actors. What Burke and Hawhee and provided in theory, however, this book attempts to do in practice. Each of the four chapters in this book describes how teaching Burke's dramatistic pentad to student performers in collegiate musical theater production helps directors see where to push or pull among these competing purposes. In other words, in the same way that Burke's dramatistic pentad help critics "interpret their interpretations," academic directors can not only see how each feature of a production is "in motion," but also see how to use that motion for their rhetorical effects on student character analysis and staging, on university resource allocation, and on community engagement.

This book is divided into five chapters. In chapter one, we begin by examining dramatism and its application in musical theater production. In this chapter, we introduce many of the current texts in use for musical theater interpretation and production, and we describe how utilizing Burke's dramatistic pentad offers students more complex methods of interpretation. In other words, we consider this chapter analogous with Burke's description of an ACT, as this chapter is our description of what we believe has happened and is happening in musical theater production. In our example of a production of Jason Howland's *Little Women*, we describe how students used pentad work in order to determine how, where, when, and why they should move on stage in every scene. In addition, this chapter also includes some theorization on the cross-disciplinarity of music and theater as a collaborative example for faculty development. This chapter ends with some basic pentad work for students in the writing or theater classroom.

In chapter two, we begin by examining how Burke's dramatism has informed current theories of context analysis. We consider the chapter analogous to Burke's description of SCENE, and through a description of performing Elton John's *Aida*, we describe how students used pentad work in order to determine not only how, where, when, and why they should move on stage, but also how the set itself should move in every scene. For the musical theater director, we detail how utilizing Burke's dramatistic pentad for set design improved resource allocation between music and theater departments, but we also theorize some differences between Stanislavski's and Burke's techniques, particularly how to motive staging when there are minimal set pieces. This chapter concludes with exercises in focusing on the SCENE-ACT ratio for self-directed staging.

In the third chapter, we begin by examining how Burke's dramatism has informed current theories of sociolinguistic difference. We consider this chapter analogous to Burke's description of AGENT, and through a description of the performance practice of Kurt Weil's *Street Scene*, students used pentad work to examine how linguistic differences between cultures informed how they characterized and responded to differing immigrant groups. In this example, students can use pentad in order to not only determine how, where, when, and why they should move on stage, but also how the immigrants themselves moved in and around New York City's Lower East Side. For the musical theater director, utilizing Burke's dramatistic pentad for teaching the history of immigration achieved specific learning goals. This chapter concludes with exercises in focusing on the AGENT-ACT ratio for self-directed staging.

In chapter four, we begin by examining how Burke's dramatism has informed current theories of AGENCY, or how or by what means the act occurred. In our example of Stephen Sondheim's *Into the Woods*, students can use pentad work not only to determine how, where, when, and why they should move, but also how the objects should move on stage in every scene. For the musical theater director, we detail how utilizing Burke's dramatistic pentad for props and their movement on stage creates new ways for audiences to think about the role of art. This chapter concludes with exercises in focusing on the AGENCY-ACT ratio for self-directed staging.

In the final chapter, we begin by examining how Burke's dramatism has informed current theories of a writer's PURPOSE. In our example of performing Steven Swartz's *Children of Eden*, students can use pentad work not only to determine how, where, when, and why they should move, but also to evaluate the purposes of revising origins and origin stories. For the musical theater director, we detail how using Burke's dramatistic pentad for purpose creates new ways for directors to orient their directing work. This chapter concludes with exercises in focusing on the PURPOSE-ACT ratio for self-directed staging.

As the Curtain Rises

In each chapter, we begin with the student writer and how Burke's dramatism can help reorient student writers around the extrinsic factors that motivate their writing situations. We then move outward to how Burke's dramatism can aid the student actor in developing their characters, and finally to academic directors and how dramatistic staging can exert influence on their resource allocation and their learning objectives for their students. At the end of each chapter, we provide worksheets for use in the classroom or in scene preparation, and at the end of the book, we provide some tables and resources for further study, particularly as it involves the use of archival research in character development, scene preparation, and options for staging. We hope that these resources provide teachers and students with enough support material as we all challenge our "trained incapacities" by means of these "perspectives by incongruity" for the purpose of "earning our increment."

Kimberly Beasley
James Beasley
St. Johns, Florida

Notes

1 Jimmy Kimmel, *89th Academy Awards*, produced by Michael De Luca and Jennifer Todd, aired February 26, 2017.

2 Justin Timberlake, "Can't Stop the Feeling." May 16, 2016. Compact Disc Single. Performed for the *89th Academy Awards*, produced by Michael De Luca and Jennifer Todd, aired February 26, 2017.

3 Kenneth Burke, *A Grammar of Motives* (Berkeley: University of California Press, 1950), 59–61.

4 Ann George and Jack Selzer, *Kenneth Burke in the 1930's* (Columbia: University of South Carolina Press, 2007), 11.

5 Ibid.

6 Kenneth Burke, *A Grammar of Motives* (Berkeley: University of California Press, 1950), 442.

7 Ibid., xv.

8 Kenneth Burke, *Rhetoric of Religion* (Berkeley: University of California Press, 1961), 277.

9 Asao Inoue, "A Grade-Less Writing Course That Focuses on Labor and Assessing," in *First Year Composition: From Theory to Practice*, ed. Deborah Coxwell-Teague and Ronald Lunsford (Clemson, SC: Parlor Press, 2014), 87.

10 Kenneth Burke, *A Grammar of Motives* (Berkeley: University of California Press, 1950), xviii.

11 Ibid.

12 Ibid.

13 Joe Deer and Rocco Dal Vera, *Acting in Musical Theatre: A Comprehensive Course* (New York: Routledge, 2008), 260.

14 Jaclyn S. Olson, "Our Bodies and the Language We Learn," *Rhetoric Review* 38 (2018): 262.

15 Kenneth Burke, *Philosophy of Literary Form: Studies in Symbolic Action* (Berkeley: University of California Press, 1973), 9.

16 Jaclyn S. Olson, "Our Bodies and the Language We Learn," *Rhetoric Review* 38 (2018): 262.

17 Ibid.

18 Ibid., 263.

19 C. Ronald Kimberling, *Kenneth Burke's Dramatism and Popular Arts* (Bowling Green, OH: Bowling Green University Press, 1982), 84.

20 Debra Hawhee, *Moving Bodies: Kenneth Burke at the Edges of Language* (Columbia: University of South Carolina Press, 2009), 24.

Bibliography

Burke, Kenneth. *A Grammar of Motives*. Berkeley: University of California Press, 1945.

_____. "As the Curtain Rises." *The Centennial Review* 10, no. 5 (1966): 279–282.

_____. *Philosophy of Literary Form: Studies in Symbolic Action*. Berkeley: University of California Press, 1971.

_____. *The Rhetoric of Religion*. Berkeley: University of California Press, 1961.

Deer, Joe and Rocco Dal Vera. *Acting in Musical Theatre: A Comprehensive Course*. New York: Routledge, 2008.

George, Ann and Jack Selzer. *Kenneth Burke in the 1930's*. Columbia: University of South Carolina Press, 2007.

Hawhee, Debra. *Moving Bodies: Kenneth Burke at the Edges of Language*. Columbia: University of South Carolina Press, 2009.

Inoue, Asao. "A Grade-Less Writing Course That Focuses on Labor and Assessing." In *First-Year Composition: From Theory to Practice*, edited by Deborah Coxwell-Teague and Ron Lunsford, 71–110. Clemson, SC: Parlor Press, 2014.

Kimberling, C. Ronald. *Kenneth Burke's Dramatism and Popular Arts*. Bowling Green, OH: Bowling Green State University Press, 1982.

Kimmel, Jimmy. "89th Academy Awards." Produced by Michael De Luca and Jennifer Todd. Aired February 26, 2017.

Olson, Jaclyn S. "Our Bodies and the Language We Learn: The Dialectic of Burkean Identification in the 1930's." *Rhetoric Review* 38, no. 3 (2019): 258–270.

Timberlake, Justin. "Can't Stop the Feeling." May 16, 2016. Compact Disc Single. Performed for "89th Academy Awards." Produced by Michael De Luca and Jennifer Todd. Aired February 26, 2017.

CHAPTER ONE

Acts in Motion: Dramatism in Jason Howland's *Little Women*

Drama and Its Isms

We begin this chapter where we began our use of Burke's dramatism. It was Memorial Day, 2003, and we were having dinner at one of our favorite restaurants. We began talking about Kimberly's upcoming auditions for Little Women: The Musical. As we began to talk about the motivations of the characters, we started to draw Burkean pentad on the paper tablecloth. We started with Jo's refusal of Laurie's proposal, describing the scene of this refusal, describing what kind of agent Jo is by refusing the proposal, describing the means by which she refuses his proposal, and finally, describing the purpose for refusing his proposal. But then we thought, what if Jo accepts Professor Bhaer's proposal? Is that a different scene, a different agent, a different agency, and a differing purpose? So, we drew that pentad on the white paper tablecloth. This white paper tablecloth began the journey of utilizing Burke's dramatism as a way to help the student actors understand their motivations. However, as we worked more and more with the pentad, we began to see how this work could help them see dramatism as a method of dramatistic staging. In other words, when an actor knows her purpose for performing the act, knows the agency by which she will accomplish the act, and knows who that character is when they accomplish the act, then that actor's movement and that actor's motion itself are embodied motives. Our work with Jason Howland's *Little Women* is our first attempt at this method of self-directed staging. We will first discuss Burke's concept of the act, then Burke's act-scene ratio for the writing classroom.

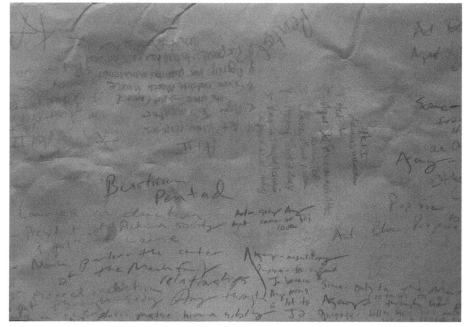

Figure 1.1. Pentad table work. Photo credit: James Beasley

We will then address the use of Burke's pentad as part of the musical theater classroom and in the performance practice of Jason Howland's *Little Women*. We conclude with some director's notes on why *Little Women* was chosen for pentadic analysis and some in-depth staging analysis for classroom performance.

Act Ratios

In an analysis of the dramatistic pentad, Burke begins with the Act, or "what was done." The most famous example is to have more than one person describe a car accident. There will be as many descriptions of what happened as there are witnesses. In order to begin to understand the motivations involved in these descriptions, it is necessary to name the act. But even Burke understands this is not so simply done. In *A Grammar of Motives*, Burke wrote, "We have said that a fully rounded vocabulary of motives will locate motives under all five aspects of our pentad. Yet, there is a paradoxical tendency to slight the term act, in the very featuring of it. For we may even favor it enough to select it as our point of departure; but by the same token it may come to be a point of departure in the sense of the term that is left behind."[1] In other words, we look to describe the act in order to begin describing the other parts of the pentad. Burke encourages us not to be so hasty, however. He wrote, "We see this temptation in the search for an act's motives, which one spontaneously thinks of locating under the heading of scene, agent, agency, or purpose, but hardly under the heading of act."[2] What is apparent, then, is that how one describes the act will determine the course of the rest of the dramatistic pentad. However, if we see how the act itself may reveal motives, then how we describe that act changes the way in which we view the importance of motivation itself. Take for instance the writing of an academic paper. In the Introduction, we introduced the concept of intrinsic criticism as opposed to extrinsic criticism. Most students are familiar with intrinsic criticism, the grading of the intrinsic features of their writing: thesis statements, grammar error, counterarguments, conclusions, etc. However, if one views a student's paper as an Act, then the entire orientation of that paper changes. What was done here? What happened? The possibilities are endless since we could describe a student paper with the phrase "a student followed directions," but we might just as easily describe the student paper with the phrase "a student bravely shared their opinions." If we describe the paper as "a student follows directions," we imply that the paper should be judged by the completion of those directions. However, if we describe the paper as "a student bravely shared their opinion," then we open up the possibility for responding to the paper with the student's own purpose in mind. The point is that the difference between "a student followed directions" and "a student bravely shared their opinions" is a difference in motives, and for Burke, how a description of the act changes the way in which we view the importance of motivation itself. In other words, we do not need to look for motives or motivations; they will find us.

This is why Burke invites us to linger on the act, since the act is not a means to an end, but because the description of the act has material consequences for the teaching of writing itself. Clayton Lewis wrote, "By over-privileging agency, much of contemporary writing pedagogy implicitly undermines what is, in Burke's view, more important—the student's natural ability to act with language."[3] In fact, the very ability for students to act with language is dependent on one's writing pedagogy, for, as previously stated, most students encounter the intrinsic writing process, not through Burke's extrinsic pentad. This ability to act with language is precluded when students must "check the boxes" of the features of a text, but is made possible when writing students and teachers are able to see through the paper as an act. Earlier we used a statement by Asao Inoue to illustrate what happens when teachers "compare a student text to an ideal text in their heads," but the last part of Inoue's statement seems to connect to the student's "ability to act with language" here. For Inoue, being able to stand outside the text allows students to "certainly never critique the very discourse the writer is attempting to learn and perhaps change." In other words, if you want your students to become change agents in their writing and ultimately in society, it will be difficult through "comparing student writing to an ideal text in your head." But even more specifically, moving past "what occurred" just to get to "the means by which it occurred" prematurely truncates the act of students engaging in the discourse "the writer is attempting to learn and perhaps change." Lingering on the act, students begin to value acts as symbolic action, identify important symbolic actions in society, and create paths for their own change actions in society.

If we examine Lewis's claim a bit longer, we can see how it not only affects the teaching of writing but how we teach several popular genres of writing. Lewis sees writing pedagogy as under-privileging the act in every type of writing task, which makes sense if these writing tasks are based in intrinsic writing pedagogy, as in, for example, the features of specific forms or genres. For Lewis, different writing genres are not merely agencies, that is means to a specific end, but they are acts in themselves. Lewis starts with personal writing and demonstrates how an overemphasis on the agent could prevent students from seeing themselves as actors. "The other major strand of contemporary writing pedagogy, that of the expressionists, over-privileges the agent-writer and thereby undermines that writer's capacity to act with language. In the pentad, Burke very clearly separates agent from act."[4] Mere autobiography, for example, de-emphasizes the act, to put all the focus on the agent's actions, not the actions of the agent. The difference is subtle, but it is worth noting here in order to develop into the examples of music theater that we will use a bit later on. The difference is also important in noting the effects of intrinsic autobiographical writing and an extrinsic one. Lewis wrote, "There is a great difference between writing autobiography, doing expressive writing, and an autobiographical act which transforms one's conception of the self—even one without clear form—into another conception of the self. Being act-centered, the latter is based in Burke's dramatistic view of language."[5] While Lewis is correct, we wonder if the act-agent ratio serves as a bridge. For example, there is also a difference between a student seeing that an act can be accomplished, "red tide can be prevented," and a student seeing that an act can be accomplished by them, "red tide can be prevented by me." In this way, the act is important for students to realize that change can occur, but this comprehension provides the fulcrum by which students can realize that they themselves can effect this change.

Secondly, Lewis turns his attention to persuasion and persuasive discourse and the consequences of using persuasion as one of the many agencies rather than as an act in itself. He wrote, "Similarly, our view of reader-based discourses is changed. Persuasion and direction cease to be modes of discourse and become particular forms of action which aim to transform the audience's attitudes and ideas. The discourse ceases to be an agency and becomes dynamic, an act."[6] Since persuasion is one of the most often-assigned projects in writing classes, viewing persuasion as an act changes the nature of assigning this project as well. If we describe a student paper as "following an assignment," then the means by which this occurred could be "a persuasive essay." However, if we describe a student paper as "persuading others to take action against red tide," then the agency could run in several directions that center on the language use of the corporate polluters, the legislators, the environmental activists, or even the students themselves.

By what means are we persuaded? For the academic paper, the answer is usually some kind of argument by authority, one of Aristotle's four topics. However, if argument itself is described as an act and not as an agency, students are then able to question the efficacy of arguments themselves in the persuasive motive. Inoue concluded that comparing a student text to "an ideal text in our head" will not engage with the "very discourse the writers are trying to learn and perhaps change," and this is a specific example of how the efficacy of the very discourse, in this case argument itself, could be "examined and changed." Lewis wrote, "And content-based discourses, such as argument, analysis, synthesis, become acts of ordering and reordering; one organization or lack thereof, becomes through the act of language transformed into another which presumably is more useful, generative, and comprehensive."[7] By what means are we persuaded? By making argument an act instead of an agency, students can question the instances in which argumentation is actually persuasive or not. Lewis concludes, "I suggest then, that all of the traditionally conceived discourses are vitalized by the Burkean act and are themselves transformed from agencies, with stative and prescriptive qualities, to acts, with dynamic and interactive qualities."[8] In our example of red tide, therefore, students understand that they cannot exert change by arguing about red tide, but that they can exert change because those who are not able to change red tide use argument as an agency and not an act.

Changing discourse from an agency to an act serves as a bridge for the students wanting to be act agents. Lewis wrote, "Our writing student, Burke suggests, has the capacity to act within the symbolic orders which constitute his identity and reality. Put another way, he is part of the verbal motion of the world while he also retains the ability to act, to make a difference, with language."[9] These act agents who are part of the world's "verbal motion" are otherwise known as actors, and as such, acting describes how "verbal motion" is characteristic of the act-agent ratio. We could rewrite Lewis's sentence the following way: "Our drama student, Burke suggests, has the facility to act within the symbolic order which constitutes his identity and reality." While the "writing student" has the "capacity" to act within the symbolic order, it is the drama student that has the facility to "act" within the symbolic order through the "verbal motion" of the play. Lewis describes it in this way:

> Motion might be described as a variety of action without an authentic agent; that is, motion is the operation of pure agency. Still another way to observe identities between the two terms is to recall that Burke's action is rooted in dramatism which is in turn, rooted in the fundamental nature of language. Thus, all uses of language have at least vestiges of action—even those we might call motion.[10]

An actor, whose motions on the stage are the "means by which" an act occurred, is then similar to our writing student, whose use of argument is a "means by which" a persuasive essay is written.

Writing pedagogies that act, that delay or postpone the "will to agency" have at least the potential to effect change. An important result of this change is the ability to change the student's writing realities. Lewis describes this process, as well:

> The writing student may act; that is she may symbolically act through language to make a difference—to transform discordances, disharmonies, perceived chaos and disorder, conflicts or other signs of difference into newly created orders which, in turn, will irrevocably change her view of herself, change her audience, and possibly change reality itself.[11]

For Lewis, however, the change in perspective is confined to the writing classroom: the student herself, the audience of her writing, and the writing situation of the classroom. We propose that if language performs this important function, then the stage is set for a performance, and as such, the act-agents of this performance can affect social change. It is Debra Hawhee who connects Burke's dramatism to physical motion when she wrote, "Burke's use of Paget reveals an early insistence on the body's role in communicative practices and a resulting bodily poetics: the body both models and performs the physical movements to produce speech, and in doing so, almost literally breathes life into words."[12] While the writing student has the potential for change, the drama student has the facility for change. While it is possible, in Hawhee's words, for the writing students to breathe life into words in the writing classroom, the stage offers the facility for Burke's dramatism to realize its full potential. "The pentad (act, scene, agent, agency, purpose), Burke's dramatistic tool par excellence, so frequently tends to produce two-dimensional, flat analyses when it could, if historically reconnected with Burke's use of Paget's bodily theories, become so much more lively."[13] For Hawhee, bodily movement plus language equals the most fully developed form of dramatism. But what if bodily movement as choreography, and staging, and singing were added to language? If dramatism cannot be fully developed without bodily movement, would bodily movement, choreography, staging, and singing constitute a kind of hyper-dramatism? If so, would music theater constitute a kind of hyper-act?

We propose that the music theater student has the necessity to affect a kind of hyper-change, "in herself, her audience, and reality itself." The writing student has the potential to work as a change-agent, but for Lewis, the path to becoming this act-agent is by merely interpretive moves in the writing classroom. For our purposes, we want to propose an even further revision of the sentence, "Our music theatre student, Burke suggests, has the necessity to act within the symbolic order which constitutes his identity and reality." We suggest that through the verbal-motivated act, music theater students not only have the capacity and facility to act within the symbolic order, but also have the necessity as well. In this sense, the act-agent, or the actor, forms attitudes and performances that are not merely the work of an agent, but of an act-agent, a performer. What if music theater is not an agency, not a "means by which" the act occurred, but an act itself? What if we begin not with how music theater can be applied to dramatism, but with how dramatism can be applied to music theater? That is what we will attempt to demonstrate in the next part of this chapter.

Dramatism as Musical Theater[14]

While Burkean applications of dramatism to the world of dramatic theater are easily seen, here we attempt to utilize Burkean identification as a method of char-acter analysis in musical theater production. Since musical theater, as a popular art form, crosses many disciplinary boundaries, it is often difficult to demonstrate its scholarly purposes. We demonstrate that an analysis of Burkean motives can be more successful in musical production than current interpretive applications through its mystification of popular forms, its ability to promote identification, and its ability to offer Burke studies new directions in the arena of performative rhetoric.

As part of musical theater production at a regional, liberal arts university, the scholarly attention to interpretation is a necessary facet of each student's learn-ing experience. To demonstrate how even the production of a popular musical demands scholarly attention, directors have often resorted to focusing on literary interpretation or even archival research methodologies in this educational environ-ment. To this end, it is important to maintain a transparent connection to literary theory, and specifically its manifestations in musical theater characterization and production. As musical theater bridges both the interpretive focus of theater and the contextual focus of musicology, disciplinary boundaries are often violated and simultaneously observed. Therefore, while there is broad latitude in how characters and their dialog can be interpreted from the theatrical world, there are fewer interpretive options for the musical interpreter. This dilemma is precisely why a developed theory of musical theater interpretation and production is significant, especially within the context of a liberal arts education.

In the development of musical interpretation in academic environments, there are three major textbooks which model interpretive strategies for musical theater: *The Third Line* by Daniel Helfgot, *Acting for Singers* by David Ostwald, and *Acting in Musical Theatre: A Comprehensive Course*, edited by Joe Deer and Rocco Dal Vera. While all three offer comprehensive acting for singing techniques, none of them allow for how those techniques influence each other, requiring actors in musical theater to utilize only one perspective. This study demonstrates the significance of being able to understand how interpretations actually influence each other and how Kenneth Burke's dramatistic ratio, "how the what influences the what," is a much more successful hermeneutic practice in musical theater interpretation due to its contextual focus, and that contextual focus is also a characteristic of musical disciplinarity.

Daniel Helfgot's *The Third Line* (1993) was the first and is the oldest systematic approach to interpretation in music theater production. In *The Third Line*, Helfgot comes at acting for singing specifically for the operatic performer. The "park and bark" stigma associated with opera is a thing of the past, as contemporary opera must contend with the vivacity of music theater style acting, and opera singers are now more beautiful and spontaneous than ever on the stage. This is reinforced through several of Helfgot's chapters, such as "The Opera Performer as Actor," "Movement and Expression," and "Auditioning, Competitions and Recitals." The "third line" specifically refers to Helfgot's three-pronged structure of "Focus, Attitude, and Gesture." The third line is the singer's interpretation of the other two lines—the music and the text. The third line encompasses the music analysis, the textual analysis, the dramatic intent, and the expressive interpretation of the music.

David Ostwald's *Acting for Singers* (2005) improved on Helfgot by highlighting competencies such as using improvisation, improving concentration, analyzing dramatic structure, fashioning objectives and super objectives, subtext, and rehearsing and auditioning. Its focus is both opera and music theater, using examples from *Carmen* as well as *West Side Story*. Ostwald incorporates theme statements for the entire production, involving everyone from the Director to the Actor in a fascinating study of motivated character development.

The newest addition to musical theater interpretation and production is *Acting in Musical Theatre: A Comprehensive Course* (2008) by Joe Deer and Rocco Dal Vera. The emphasis on musical analysis in this text is important for the music theater actor, in contrast with the operatic performer who usually needs more analytical acting support. Therefore, the chapters include topics such as foundational acting techniques, musical analysis, elements of storytelling, character analysis, the journey of the song, intensifiers, stylistic elements, as well as auditioning and rehearsal process techniques.

Musical Theater Interpretation and *Little Women, The Musical*

When it came time to produce a musical theater show in a liberal arts educational setting, Kimberly began with these three interpretative textbooks in mind. Since students in this regional, liberal arts voice program had not previously been required to analyze their characters much in the past, the choice of interpretive approach would be significant. Would students be open to such character work? Kimberly's own favorite directors by far have been those that have encouraged her own delving into her character and then forcing that research to reveal itself in rehearsal. Characters whose objectives were handed to her by a director have been forgotten, shallow characters. Of the three textbooks available, *Acting for Singers* by David Ostwald was originally chosen to achieve the kind of character development the director thought she wanted, enabling the actors' own interpretations, actions, and directions.

The musical that was chosen for production was Jason Howland's *Little Women, The Musical* (2005). As a Broadway musical, it ran for five months before touring nationally for over a year, and it featured musical theater megastars Maureen McGovern as "Marmee," and Sutton Foster as Jo March. Because the story of *Little Women* is so well known, the director did not want the students copying what they had seen in the movies, specifically the most recent adaptation by Gillian Armstrong, the one with which they were all most familiar. Since *Little Women, The Musical* is based on the Louisa May Alcott novel, the character analysis work would also have the added dimension of literary analysis. As the director and actors read through the script day for the first several days, super objectives were the first tool each actor utilized in developing their character.

> If you have already developed your superobjective, you can fashion your objectives by asking yourself, 'How does my character pursue his superobjective in this scene?' You will find the concept of strategic means to be a good clarifying device. Invoke it by saying to yourself 'I,…am working toward… by means of…. Fashion your answer depending on what you feel the music, text, and the stage directions suggest.[15]

In rehearsal, as the director had them journal about the super objective of their own life that helped them apply this concept to their *Little Women* character, the students' super objectives began to come together: "I (character's name) and working toward (fill in the blank)." Some examples of some of the students' super objectives were the following:

- I, Professor Bhaer, am working toward starting my life over again in America.
- I, Jo, am working toward using my writing to provide for my family.
- I, Meg, am working toward finding an eligible young man.
- I, Beth, am working toward making every day beautiful.
- I, Marmee, am working towards raising my daughters to find their place in the world.
- I, Aunt March, am working toward preserving the March family name.
- I, Mr. Laurence, am working toward putting up with my neighbors.

The super objectives of the other characters all helped to give them an overarching motivation for the entire show. But this was only the beginning since breaking down each scene only continued to enhance the largesse of the super objective, making this a very important first step. The super objective for Aunt March really helped the actor give life to her number, "Could You," in which she attempts to whip Jo into shape by manipulating her to change, telling her she might take her to Europe: "I believe you could captivate the world…If you could change there is so much you could achieve…someone full of dreams like you…gracious living will make you sublime." This number was a highlight from the show, and this super objective gave Aunt March in her limited stage time, a strong motivation for her entire character every time she was on stage.

In a move similar to Kenneth Burke's dramatistic ratios, Ostwald connects the purpose of an act with the means by which the act is accomplished. In Ostwald's grammar, these means are called "beats." Ostwald wrote the following:

> A character will try anything that is consistent with her moral code and personality to get what she wants. If her objective in a particular scene is 'I want to keep my beloved from leaving,' she might begin with flattery. If that doesn't work, she might try reasoning, cajoling, threatening, seducing, bribing, or even blackmail. We call these various strategies acting beats. Acting beats are mini-objectives that clarify the relationship of your character's individual thoughts and actions to her objectives.[16]

Discovering the "acting beats" for the ball at the Moffats was essential, since in the musical these scenes combine several balls and outings from the novel and the film adaptations into one. Because many dynamics are altered within this one section of Act I in the musical version, the scene objective/beat work on the getting ready for, attending, and recovering from the ball at the Moffats would make this scene pivotal for motivating the rest of the production. In the following charts, the director has provided examples of how utilizing Ostwald's objectives and beats lead the actors into an understanding of their motivations:

Getting Ready for the Ball

Characters	Objective: I am working toward	Beat(s): by means of
Marmee	Making sure her girls get every chance available to them	Getting Meg to her first ball.
Beth	Living through my sisters	Helping Meg get ready
Jo	Becoming a lady like AM says I have to	Going to this ball with Meg.
Meg	Finding an eligible young man	Attending the Moffat's ball.
Amy	Equality with my sisters	Getting ready for the ball, too.
Delighted	The girls helping Meg feel comfortable	Appealing to Meg's vanity and romantic tendencies
OVERALL	This scene works towards dividing the sisters and their places in life	By placing Jo and Meg outside their normal environment and leaving Beth and Amy at home.

At the Ball

Characters	Objective: I am working toward	Beat(s): by means of
Amy (in transition to this scene)	Putting Jo in her place for not letting me go to the ball.	Burning her story.
Jo	Not getting frustrated by all this becoming a lady stuff	Trying to be polished and elegant, remembering the reward in the end (Europe)
Meg	Making a good impression to the Moffats	Making sure Jo behaves herself
Laurie	Avoiding having to meet important people	Getting away from meeting important people.
Brooke	Not getting fired by Mr. L	Finding where the hell Laurie is

Characters	Objective: I am working toward	Beat(s): by means of
Take a Chance: Laurie	Laurie: Getting Jo to like him	Telling her how unique she is. Trying to get her to dance. Making jokes. Appealing to her love of adventure. Appealing to her as a friend. Being willing to box her. Convincing himself it will happen.
	Jo: distracting Laurie from liking her	Using humor. Making excuses. Scolding him. Being unladylike. Being competitive.
Take a chance transition (music)		
OVERALL	This scene works towards establishing how much Jo is determined to write and provide for her family	By revealing how much Laurie likes her despite her repeated rejections of him.

After the Ball

Characters	Objective: I am working toward	Beat(s): by means of
Beth	Helping Meg feel better	Asking her about the ball
Marmee	Welcoming her girls home	Helping Meg and making Amy apologize
Brooke	Proving he can take care of a woman	Helping Meg home
Meg	Letting John know she likes him	Letting him help her
Jo	Downplaying her conflicting emotions	Complaining about the whole evening
Amy	Doing what Marmee wants her to	Apologizing to Jo
Better Reprise: JO	Recovering from Amy burning my story	Going to my attic to vent
OVERALL	This scene works towards heightening Jo's conflicting emotions about who she is	Destroying her story and stirring up emotions over Meg and Brooke and her and Laurie

As can be seen from these charts, Ostwald's discussion of "beats" is extremely similar to Burke's concept of dramatistic "agency." Ostwald wrote, "You can fashion your acting beats, whether for operas, musicals, songs, art songs, or lieder, most effectively by once again using the device of means. Say to yourself 'I want to carry out my objective by means of...' Or you can ask, 'What do I do in this scene to achieve my objective?'"[17] While getting student actors to understand what they do in a scene to achieve their character's objective is important, what is missing from Ostwald's description is to what extent the act, agent, scene, agency, and purpose are acting on each other simultaneously, and this is the understanding that Burkean dramatism enables actors to accomplish, the ability to identify the degree of influence. In other words, while the pentad helps us understand "how the what influences the what," utilizing the pentad in musical theater productions helps us understand "to what degree the what influences the what," and this seems the most important result of this application for Burke studies at large.

Many adoptions of the pentad focus on the pentad's use for juridical rhetoric, or an examination of past "acts," whether it be Ronald Reagan's invasion of Grenada (Birdsell, 1987) Plato's rhetoric (Abrams, 1981), or even corporate picnics (Walker and Monin, 2001). Utilizing pentad for musical performance fundamentally changes the usefulness of Burke's thought from past events, to their adaptation for deliberative, or future events, i.e., an upcoming musical performance. Utilizing the pentad allowed actors to immediately see the degree of effect of their changing interpretations in real time. This ability to see the immediate variation of those changing interpretations is a potential new direction for Burke studies, and opens Burke scholarship from examinations of past acts, to new methodologies for studying rhetoric as future performatives.

Dramatism and *Little Women, the Musical*

The first goal in utilizing dramatism in the production process of *Little Women, the Musical* was to achieve a greater depth of character analysis than found in Ostwald's "beats" method. To achieve this goal, a brief introduction to Kenneth Burke's dramatism was given by a Burke historian. In his workshop, he presented students with the following:

> In *A Grammar of Motives* (1945), literary theorist Kenneth Burke outlined his conception of what he would call "dramatism": a method that readers can use to identify the rhetorical nature of any text, opening it to multiple perspectives.

> ACT: what was done?
> SCENE: When and where was the act performed?

AGENT: Who did it?
AGENCY: How and with what was the act performed?
PURPOSE: What motivated the act?

After readers answer these statements based on their interpretations, the next question focuses on the influence one may have on another. "How does the _____influence the _____?"

The director, therefore, took the worksheet above and had the students examine the "purpose-agency ratio" to determine what influence they had on each other, whether or not the purpose determined the agency, and vice versa. In the cases above, the students could see that Amy's burning of Jo's story was one of the most significant purpose-agency ratios of that entire sequence of the show, and therefore the staging of that scene would get more attention than other purpose-agency influences. The most significant implication from using Ostwald's "beats" before engaging in a discussion of the Burkean pentad was to see how limiting Ostwald's "beats" actually was on dramatic interpretation. Since Ostwald's beats were only one out of a possible twenty ratios that could be utilized, students immediately began pentading other scenes in which they were singing. For example, Jo is proposed to twice in the musical, once by Laurie and once by Professor Bhaer. Burke's dramatistic ratios immensely helped the actor who played Jo in finding her motivation for rejecting one and accepting another. By only using Ostwald's "beats," Laurie's antics take center stage in his being refused, but through pentading Professor Bhaer's proposal, a new reason for Laurie's rejection emerged:

- Act—Bhaer proposes
- Agent—mentor to Jo, represents "the Other," represents "not-Concord"
- Scene-outside the March house
- Agency—through her published book
- Purpose—to tell her he's missed her and loves her

In this pentad, it is Bhaer as "the Other," the fact that he is "not-Concord" that the actor who played Jo identified as having the most effect on Bhaer's acceptance, and therefore since Laurie is the next door neighbor, the one who most specifically represents Concord, the actor who played Jo was able to exploit this tension between the two men.

Directorial Intent, Actors, and Identification

The second purpose for utilizing Burkean pentad was to help shape the director's own interpretive focus. Since the director did not want to dictate the staging, the pentad helps students identify with the directorial interpretations as they creatively participate in the creation of the meaning of the performance. As part of the preparation for the production, the director conducted archival research in the Louisa May Alcott papers in the Houghton Library at Harvard University. What surprised her was that there was no evidence in the Alcott letters that would indicate that Louisa and "Beth" were very close in real life. There were no letters in Louisa's collection from "Beth," but many letters between "Beth" and "Marmee."[18] The director began to wonder whether Louisa's portrayal of Jo in the novel is what she merely wished her relationship had been with her sister "Beth" in real life. In the novel, they are very close; thus, every adaptation of the novel portrays them as very close. Based on her reading of the Louisa May Alcott letters, then, the director tried to capture a bit more of this dynamic in the scene "Some Things Are Meant to Be." This scene is normally staged with Jo's overwhelming sadness of Beth's impending death. Based on a new possible interpretation from the Alcott letters, the director wanted to stage Jo not as a grieving sister, but in denial over what is happening, so much so that she cannot even give Beth her full attention in this scene. By staging Jo as calloused to her sister's illness, though, the director could encourage the audience to identify with her need to change, to collectively hope this is not the Jo we are left with at the end of the story. When Jo does realize that her home is truly important, her recent denial then becomes an even more significant motivation for her writing and submitting her great novel in the first place.

In order for this alternate interpretation to not be merely handed down to the actors to obey, utilizing the pentad allowed the actors to come to these conclusions on their own, as they creatively participated in arriving at similar interpretations. In *A Rhetoric of Motives* (1950), Kenneth Burke wrote, "Longinus refers to that kind of persuasion wherein the audience feels as though it were not merely receiving, but were itself creatively participating in the poet's or speaker's assertion. Could we not say that, in such cases, the audience is exalted by the assertion because it has the feel of collaborating in the assertion?"[19] To demonstrate to the actors that they, too, might have alternative motivations than merely what is written in the novel, the actor playing Jo and the actor portraying Beth wrote their own pentad:

Pentad: Beth dies

Character	Jo	Beth
Act	Beth dies	Beth comforts Jo
Agent	Beth—sister who has no aspirations	Myself—I love home.
Scene	Beach—life goes on	Beach—I'd rather be back in Concord

Character	Jo	Beth
Agency	Hummels, Concord-frustration	Hummels, Concord-fulfillment
Purpose	Reminder of how awful Concord is	Jo's success

While they did not necessarily arrive at the same conclusion, the fact that they could arrive at similar conclusions allowed them to understand the staging and see how many other interpretations were possible, i.e., "if not this one, then why not that one?" The pentad also balanced this artistic freedom with the need to stay as close to audience expectations as possible as a feature of the musical theater genre. Dennis Brissett wrote the following on Burke's connection to dramatistic analysis:

> Dramatism gives one no criteria for such smug demarcations of one's own virtues and the vices of all others. We are not talking about some simplistic notion of demystification as an unmasking, a revelation of the truth; rather we are offering dramatism as a technique of analysis of human interaction and also as a method for assessing social theories of human conduct.[20]

The students could see that while there was no one single correct interpretation, there were limitations on how interpretive we could be. While the pentad helped create those interpretations, they simultaneously allowed the students to examine them:

> The demystification of action that can be achieved by reclaiming neglected pentadic elements has its counterpart in the critique of theories of action that similarly neglect elements of the pentad. And here, unlike other theories of action, dramatism provides the method of demystifying and criticizing itself. It is possible, therefore, to produce a dramatistic account of some situation, and, without shifting one's ground, equally possible to analyze that account.[21]

This analyzing of student interpretations is not allowed by Ostwald's "beats" method. The students only supplied what they thought were the agencies by means of which for their purposes, but they never considered why they believed that until they utilized Burke's dramatistic ratios. This is why filling out the charts for Ostwald's acting beats seemed like homework to many of the students, but creatively participating in persuading the audience that Jo March needed to change did not seem like homework at all.

Dramatism, Musical Theater, and Popular Art

These interpretative choices that involve the audience in the creative participation of Jo March's transformation, their identification, have an even greater implication for the genre of musical theater at large. Because musical theater forms are much more closely tied to popular culture than "straight" theater, musicals generally do not challenge audiences or create their own drama. Kimberling wrote on dramatism's ability to challenge the inherent limitations in popular art's predictable forms:

> The Burkean model provides a tentative answer to the frequently posed question as to whether popular art reflects or engenders social values and mores. Dramatism would suggest that it does both. Popular art reflects social values because it presents universal patterns of experience, patterns that the audience must recognize if it is to understand the work. It engenders values by presenting dramatic scenarios placing ordinary values in conflict situations, situations demanding that some hierarchy of values be established, and by stimulating audience identification with the processes of value formation.[22]

Again, the ball scene is an example of how dramatism can be used not only to reflect social values, but to engender values by demanding that the audience establish a hierarchy of those values. By utilizing Ostwald's "beats" in the previous charts, one can see how students supplied fairly formulaic means to their purposes, i.e., Meg wanting to make a good impression on the Moffatt's by making sure Jo behaves herself. However, since pentad allows students to both simultaneously produce and analyze their dramatistic accounts, the ball scene can be used to not only reflect social values, but to also engender conflicting values. To engender these conflicting values, however, some additional work is required by the actors than merely identifying the acting "beats." In other words, the actors must "earn their increment" through developing new pathways for conflicting values to operate. One of these pathways is the subject of Burke's *Language as Symbolic Action:*

> There is a further step in our outward direction: and it is the one we most need for our present inquiry. Insofar as a poem is properly formed, suppose you were to ask yourself what subtitle might properly be given to each stanza. Or suppose you were to break up each chapter of a novel into a succession of steps or stages, giving titles to such parts of a chapter, then to chapters, then to groups of chapters, and so finally to the whole work. Your entitling's would not necessarily agree with any that the author himself may have given, since titles are often assigned for fortuitous reasons. And of course, other readers might not agree with your proposed entitlings. But the point is this: Insofar as the work is properly formed, and insofar as your titles are accurate, they mark off a succession of essences.[23]

What Burke identifies as "subtitles," acting preparation generally calls "subtext." While "subtext" is a pretty common way for actors to find meaning in the script, it becomes even more significant the more the director wants the audience to establish hierarchies of values. For musical theater productions, with their inertia already tilted towards merely reinforcing cultural norms and values, subtext is essential in producing dramatistic pathways for audiences to consider these competing values. This is how the concept of subtext was introduced to the actors for *Little Women: The Musical*:

> Subtext now becomes useful specifically for the songs you sing. Subtext is the main source of your internal dialogue, the chatter of your inner voice expressing how you feel about what is happening. When you fashion subtext for each phrase of your text and complete it with internal thoughts for all the places where you don't sing, you make your character into a multi-level communicator like a real person, and you take a giant step toward being believable on stage.[24]

The focus on creating "internal dialog" to form a "multi-level" communicator has its roots not only in the "unending conversations" taking place, but also in the creation of multiple pathways of action. Will the characters act in predictable ways that reinforce social norms, or will characters surprise audience members by their resistance to formulaic behaviors? Using the example of the student analysis of the ball scene again, the creation of subtext created some surprising opportunities for presenting audiences with conflicting values to examine. Using Ostwald's acting "beats," the actor playing Meg indicated that her purpose was to make a good impression on the Moffatt's by making sure Jo did not embarrass them. However, through subtext of the same scene, other values are revealed. As Meg is approached by Mr. Brooke at the ball, she pulls Jo away from the dancing to calm her down, dropping her own dance card in the process. Mr. Brooke has come to get Laurie to take him home. They are center stage and Jo and Laurie are listening and observing them intently:

Meg: Sir! You've taken my dance card![25]
I need it but I don't want to have to ask.[26]

Brooke: Your dance card? – Oh! Is this yours? Sorry. So – you're Margaret March?
What? I'm an idiot. Who is this? She's pretty!

Meg: Yes, I am.
He's handsome!

Brooke: It's – a splendid party, isn't it? –
I am wowed by you!
Meg: Yes, it is. Quite - "lovely." So you're from Boston?
I don't know what to say...

Brooke: Actually Maine.
I can't stop staring at you!

Meg: I've never been to Maine.
Why did I just say that?

Brooke: You should go. It's beautiful country. Very primitive
You should come with me!

Meg: I like primitive.
Why did I say THAT?

Brooke: Really?
Does she like me?

Laurie: Mr. Brooke is a romantic.
Ooooo (sarcastic)

Meg: Is that true?
He has something I like.

Brooke: Well, no, no. I read Sheats and Kelley. I mean Keats and Shelley.
Shut up, Laurie, and let me talk!

Meg: So do I.
I understand you.

Brooke: You read Keats and Shelley?
This girl is way too cool for me.

Meg: All the time.
I actually know those guys.

In the ball scene, Meg's subtext reveals other purposes than just not embarrassing herself in front of the Moffatt's, which reinforces the social norms. When Meg responds to Mr. Brooke saying, "I like primitive," and her subtext for that line was "Why did I just say THAT?" she is both "producing a dramatistic account of some situation, and, without shifting one's ground, making it equally possible to analyze that account." Meg is reinforcing social norms, i.e., getting married to the handsome male lead character of a musical theater production, and simultaneously engendering social values, i.e., the legitimization of a distinctively different culture than that of the extravagant ballroom in which the attractive male lead character of a musical theater production and the attractive female lead character of a musical theater production will fall in love.

Motion, Action, and Staging

To "block" the production, the director wanted the actors to know why they were moving when they were, and to initiate their own movement rather than just being told to move when the director wanted. After all, the actors have done the character work for themselves more precisely than even the director, so their suggestions are often quite inspired. The addition of Burkean dramatism in the subtext process suggests blocking options to the actors that they can feel on their own, complicating how the audience believes the characters should be behave in response to social norms. Again, this complication is anachronistic for the musical theater genre, but dramatism opens musical theater up to such possibilities, while itself staying true to form. Kimberling wrote, "Burke would view [Kaplan's aesthetic theory] as dehumanizing. The reaction mode of Kaplan would find its place, in Burkean terms in the world of motion, not action. The world of human thought and language, however, necessarily implies action, since it is a dialectical process of giving wings to motive, transcending the linear stimulus response realm of mere motion."[27] Insomuch as subtext is an interior dialog, it participates in the dialectical process of "giving wings to motive," making staging much more meaningful than merely identifying "acting beats" only. In the ballroom scene, therefore, when Mr. Brooke says that Maine is "very primitive," he has many choices. He can reinforce social norms by delivering the line with disdain in comparison to the extravagant ballroom of the Moffatt's, or he could engender social values by deliver the line with pride, as an almost aside away from the other characters in the ballroom scene. When Meg replies, "I like primitive," she can reflect social norms by being embarrassed about valuing the primitive, or she can engender social values by shouting that out for all in the ballroom to hear.

The staging process, therefore, is based upon a deep understanding of the characters and their motivations for relating to other characters and their scenes independent of the individual objectives for each scene, the overall objective that the audience understands from each scene, and how a group of scenes relates to the entire act. Since no one character could both reflect and engender social norms at the same time, the director utilized a system of scene "leaders" and "followers" for each scene. While each scene demands its own leader, it is the balance of leaders to followers that both simultaneously reflects and engenders social values. The leader in a scene would be center stage more often than not; a follower in a scene would be more upstage rather than downstage. The leader could reflect a social norm, and the audience could witness that effect on the follower, or the leader could engender a new social value, and the audience could witness that effect on the follower.

In this way, motion becomes action, since the movement is motivated by "human thought and language."

In a society where television productions such as *Glee* or *Smash* portray musical theater production as frivolous pursuits of vanity devoid of scholarly attention, the significance of Burkean dramatism is vital to a reinvigoration of this popular art form. Brissett wrote, "It is only in the social scientific use of dramatism—seeing to give due weight to all elements of the pentad in the explanation of human conduct—that we can find an implicit commitment to the demystification of any single-minded explanatory scenario.[28] Dramatism reconnects musical theater to the contextualized field of musicology, while simultaneously distancing itself from pure aesthetic value conflict. The pentadic ratios, therefore, simultaneously provide the substance of interpretive material for musical theater production in the characterization, blocking, and staging phases of production, and the means by which to examine characterization, blocking, and staging without "shifting one's ground," creating exciting opportunities for the scholarly attention to this popular art form.

Director's Notes

Why This Show

While we have already discussed that *Little Women, The Musical* was my first to utilize Burke's pentad in its staging, I would like to speak to the particular circumstances surrounding this choice. First, the fact that *Little Women* is an ensemble cast also informed my use of pentad for the show. Because there is no leading lady or leading man, each character is on an equal plane from the beginning. Ensemble casts are challenging in this respect, since all the character work in the world by the actor will not facilitate both everyone's relationship to each other and the story being told. Therefore, using the pentad was extremely helpful in bringing an ensemble cast together in their focus. Because of the variable of telling the story with an ensemble cast, the Act of each scene became a logical focus for the show. This kept the story the focus, not any particular actor because the audience could see the actors reacting to the act and each other's reactions. This gave the audience so much more to watch.

The second reason pentad was chosen for *Little Women, The Musical* was in order to collaborate with the JU Orchestra in the pit, a collaboration that had not been attempted at JU in a long time. The score to *Little Women* is accessible, contemporary, and varied. Students would be collaborating with a full orchestra along with the characters on stage. As one of my first directing assignments, I wanted to emphasize the music in music theater, emphasizing the role that the music department had in the production of musicals. We have already noted how musical theater bridges both the interpretive focus of theater and the contextual focus of musicology. Dramatism in musical theater production seems to extend beyond mere interdisciplinary approaches, however. Debra Hawhee explained the issues inherent in interdisciplinarity:

> Interdisciplinarity is marked by disciplinary affinity—closely allied fields such as history and literary studies or gender studies and rhetorical studies sharing methods and cross listing courses—whereas transdisciplinarity is marked by shared interest in a particular matter or problem but often draws together radically different approaches. The difference is a matter of sharing methodologies verses broadening perspective, one of the main goals of transdisciplinarity.[29]

Therefore, while there is broad latitude in how characters and their dialog can be interpreted from the theatrical world, there are fewer interpretive options for the musical interpreter. This dilemma is precisely why a developed theory of musical theater interpretation and production is significant, especially within the context of a liberal arts education.

Table Work

Little Women, The Musical was an ideal place to begin work with the pentad, since I already knew the story so well, yet the musical version of the story had been its most recent adaptation.[30] *Little Women* is a well known and beloved as a story about the March family, specifically the coming of age of Jo March as an author, very much a man's world at the time. *Little Women* is told through of course the book, a few different movies, an opera, and finally a musical. Whenever you work with a well-known story that has been reimagined several different times and several different ways, research must be done, which puts all of those renditions into perspective. For me that meant going to the Alcott archives at Harvard University. As I read letters by Louisa to her mother, her father, her sisters, Walt Whitman, Thoreau, Abraham Lincoln, and more, I realized that these letters gave the story of *Little Women* even more meaning than it already had. And what was especially rewarding about this sort of research was the ability to take it back to the students in the form of pictures and documents. As this chapter walks through the production of this show, the reader will understand decisions that were made about staging and interpretation that directly related to what was discovered in the research process.

Additional table work with the students included not only sharing the photographs from the archival research, but talking about the theme. This demands a lot of conversation from the entire cast about conflicts, plot summary, important characters, the title, the last scene, and the other renditions of the story. The books and the movies are chronological, whereas the musical is in flashback. Jo starts out in New York, describing one of her stories in the form of an operatic tragedy. Only then do we go back in time to Christmas in Concord two years earlier.

The basics of theme work are presented clearly and expertly in Ostwald's book. One should not overlook this part of the process, especially when working with a group of college students. They are learning how to be part of a process at this stage in their performing lives, and theme work is a great way to bring the cast together in a common cause. Ostwald encourages asking several questions and considering many angles. My summary of his exercise applied to *Little Women* looked like this:

August 24—Fashioning a Theme Statement

1. Developing a theme requires several components
   a. Consider the title of the work
   b. Consider all the characters
   c. Consider the actions and conflicts in the plot
2. Some of the research we have already done will help, but additional research may be needed (Louisa Alcott papers at Harvard)
   a. Is this work based on another source such as a play, novel, or poem?
   b. What do we know about Louisa May Alcott? When did she write? Why did she write this story?
   c. What are some of the issues of the day? What effect does the Civil War have on the March family? Who is president? What are some external conflicts as a result of this situation? What are some internal conflicts for the March's?
3. Let's find the theme for *Little Women*:
   a. Review our list of conflicts and explore what is at stake in each one. Are the same stakes at issue more than once? When do conflicts escalate in intensity? What feelings become more intense? What issue(s) generate the feelings? Is there a pattern to the kinds of choices the major characters make when they are in conflict?
   b. Write out a plot summary labeling the characters with their functions and relationships. Is there a moral to the plot? Could this be the theme?
   c. Make a list of the four or five most important characters. How do they relate to each other? What connects them? Class? Family? Money? Politics? Religion? Love? Hatred? If there are characters that don't relate to each other, why are they in the same piece?

      d. Look at the title. Why this title? Why not something else (i.e., *The March Family*, or *Life and Love during the Civil War*)?

      e. Examine the last scene to see how conflicts are resolved.

      f. There is a book as well as movies and a play. What came first? How does this affect our study of the musical? How is the musical different than these other adaptations? What scenes are the same? What scenes are different? What scenes have been deleted in the musical version? Would all the themes be the same for each expression of the story? (look at Tour Reviews)

  4. Write a theme statement for *Little Women*.

After discussing all of these angles, we started tossing around some concepts, key words, and ideas:

- Civil War
- Transcendentalists
- Unitarians
- Alcott herself wanting to be a mystery writer
- Book and Movies move chronologically, musical is flashback
- Conflicts:
  - Jo and Laurie
  - Brooke and Laurie
  - Laurie and Mr. Laurence
  - Jo and Meg
    - Meg is tired of child's play and wants to fall in love
    - Meets Mr. Brooke and marries
  - Jo and publishing
    - Jo wrote to support her family
    - Uses writing to establish independence
  - Beth's health
    - Loves to be at home while others do not
  - Marmee's loneliness
    - Father is at war, she is raising the girls alone
  - Aunt March
  - Amy
    - Has trouble at school
    - Gets to go abroad with Aunt March
- Finales:
  - Meg marries and has twins
  - Jo gets engaged and starts a school

- ➤ Beth dies
- ➤ Amy marries Laurie
- ➤ Marmee gets everyone near her
- ➤ Mr. Laurence helps out
- Key words
  - ➤ Love
  - ➤ Writing
  - ➤ Proposing
  - ➤ Conformity
  - ➤ Independence
  - ➤ Inspiration
  - ➤ Dreams
  - ➤ Risk
  - ➤ Destiny
- Key ideas
  - ➤ Conformity equated to sacrifice
  - ➤ Finding love through loss
  - ➤ Novel vs. story
  - ➤ Family vs. home
  - ➤ Secure and stagnant vs. insecure and growing
  - ➤ Flashback as participatory, an opening, a journey

From ideas came some complete sentences:

1. *Little Women* celebrates the rewards of risking your own dreams in the hopes of finding something better and discovering love is all you need [what you were looking for].
2. *Little Women* celebrates the journey to realize a dream.
3. *Little Women* is a journey of loss and love, being true to oneself while staying open to change.

Until we arrived at:

> *Little Women inspires us to embrace change along the path to discovering our destiny.*

The totality of this theme work took the first week of rehearsal. Interspersed with music rehearsals, the student started to lock in to the story we were telling, our collective story. The next step for Ostwald is Super Objectives. I like this step as it starts to focus the actors inward a little bit, setting up their own Purpose in their own pentad for the show, and I will repeat them here:

- I, Professor Bhaer, am working toward starting my life over again in America.
- I, Jo, am working toward using my writing to provide for my family.
- I, Meg, am working toward finding an eligible young man.
- I, Beth, am working toward making every day beautiful.
- I, Amy, am working towards equality.
- I, Marmee, am working towards raising my daughters to find their place in the world.
- I, Mr. Brooke, am working towards proving my loyalty to the people I love.
- I, Laurie, am working towards acceptance.
- I, Aunt March, am working toward preserving the March family name.
- I, Mr. Laurence, am working toward putting up with my neighbors.

Super Objectives place the character in the story. However, I always like to have the actors consider themselves and how they feel about playing their characters. How are they the same as their character? How are they different? In subsequent chapters, we will consider this more; but for the moment, I provide the following chart that the leads in the show completed prior to staging.

Role (actor)	Personality of character	Physicality	Plays against	Plays with
Laurie (Ross)	Fun loving	Loose	My Jacksonville, FL location	My playfulness
	Defensive/nervous	Talks a lot and fast		
	Caring	Eye contact		
	Lazy	Slow		
Amy (Jet)	Particular/bossy	Fingers and hands	I am the oldest	I am sensible
	Affected/spoiled	Vocal lilt		
	Proper/vain	Ladylike, hair		
	Youngest/insecure	Inserts, interrupts		
Meg (Maggie)	Self-controlled	Speaks and listens in balance	Marriage and family	My birth order
	Polite	Vocal lilt		
	Traditional	Caretaker/mom instincts		
	Vain	Sighs		

Role (actor)	Personality of character	Physicality	Plays against	Plays with
Brooke (Erick)	Patient	Deliberate	My talkativeness	My relationship with my girlfriend
	Calm	Soft		
	Thoughtful	Listener		
	Loyal	Stands close		
Marmee (Keisha)	Strength	Posture	My age	My independence
	Passionate	Vocal color		
	Caring	Hugs and kisses		
Aunt March (Claire)	Formal	Posture	My sweet personality	My responsibleness
	Assertive	Interrupts, speaks deliberately		
	Cross	Vocal color		
	Irascible	Head and gestures		
Mr. Laurence (Alec)	Stern	Rigid	My age	My vocal color
	Easily bothered	Gestures/body placement		
	Defensive	Vocal volume		
Bhaer (Stephen)	Professional/ authoritative	Vocal color	My background	My scholarly aspirations
	Awkward	Restless/nervous		
	Arrogant/ knowledgeable	Head and posture		

As we will discuss in later chapters, Burke's pentad not only helped actors ask about the specifics of their character, they helped the characters ask the same questions about the actors themselves. Once theme work and super objectives were completed, work on individual scenes gets underway. We look at objectives and beats per character, but also talk about what the scene is there to accomplish. I assigned a leader to each scene in this show. Marmee and Jo took the lead with four apiece, but everyone getting at least one scene as the leader, save Mr. Brooke.

Although it is a progressive part of the story, Mr. Brooke and Meg getting engaged is very much from the perspective of Meg—which is fine since the title of this story is *Little Women*. At the point of each of the girls getting engaged, they are the star of the scene. Poor Mr. Brooke just doesn't have any scenes that command leadership as compared to Laurie and Mr. Bhaer. However, the scenes he does have, with the ball being one of the major ones, he is endearing and pivotal to our story of Meg. So each actor knowing they had a scene to lead led us into the final stretch—pentad.

This show being my first show using pentad was ideal, for I could both "interpret my interpretations," my long-held beliefs about the importance of this story, and I could use the pentad to reveal new interpretations that I did not realize could be possible. As such, pentad was an ideal way to bridge the gap between what I thought I already knew and what I had not anticipated being able to know, let alone demonstrate on stage. I will demonstrate the use of pentad through the two proposals, Beth's death and Jo's climax, "The Fire within Me," to the end of the show.

Jo is proposed to twice in the musical, once by Laurie and once by Professor Bhaer. Burke's dramatistic ratios immensely helped the actor who played Jo in finding her motivation for rejecting one and accepting another. By only using Ostwald's beats, Laurie's antics take center stage in his being refused, but through pentading, Jo's reactions to both proposals establish why Laurie would never be accepted and Professor Bhaer would.

In the proposal by Laurie, we find ourselves in the attic of the March house. The attic as the setting is important; traditionally a safe place for Jo, Laurie's proposal forever changes that. For Jo, not much is happening that she wants to happen. She still isn't in New York City writing, and Meg and Mr. Brooke just got engaged. For Laurie, he has been in Boston and is discouraged by his grandfather enrolling him in school. Laurie is perfectly content to stay in Concord near Jo. Too much action frightens him, but Jo can't get enough. She is excited for Laurie at the same time she is somewhat jealous of his opportunity. However, her insistence on speaking to him in her most casual, silly banter is a defensive posture for Jo to keep Laurie from falling in love with her, from proposing. Jo establishes the Act as well as becomes the Agent in this scene. Jo is driving the action at the same time her reactions to Laurie's lines in this scene as motivated by her defensive posture is engaging to watch. Even though Laurie is the one doing the kissing, the proposing, Jo's actions in reaction to his news and his advances lead the scene. She is the "who" who renders the act possible—Laurie isn't going anywhere until she tells him to leave. We started with the following objectives and beats:

Characters	Objective	Beat(s)
Jo LEADER	Eliminating Laurie's distracting attentions	Encouraging him to go to college. Being sarcastic. Telling him college is something she wants to do. Acting disinterested. Scolding him.
Laurie	Following through on his feelings for Jo.	Appealing to what Jo calls. Telling her he's going to college. Referring to her as his "best friend." Telling her he doesn't want to leave. Kissing her. Proposing to her like Brooke did to Meg.

Once the scene was analyzed traditionally, the pentad became a new layer of options for our expression of the scene physically. The pentad becomes a motivation for the subtext and subsequently the subtext motivates the staging. Our final pentad for this scene looked like this:

- Act—Jo refuses Laurie
- Scene—March attic
- Agent—Jo
- Agency—casual language, physical distance
- Purpose—to deter Laurie

Jo as the Agent was chosen as the scene leader. Applying leadership to one element helps focus the scene on what you want the audience to notice, and they aren't even sure why, they just know who to watch. Even though Laurie is the one proposing and could easily take over the scene, establishing Jo as the one who is refusing is much more interesting and plays into the theme of the show as a whole. However, even while establishing Jo/the Agent as the scene leader, the subtext is still influenced by other elements of the pentad. The Act and the Scene are prescribed in our story. This is the part where Jo refuses Laurie, and she does it in the attic. What is interesting about the attic, though, in regards to what we will see in the subtext and staging, is that there is not much space in the attic which in turn plays a role in the Agency—there is not much room for physical distance—which makes the Purpose more difficult to achieve and something very interesting to observe Jo try to accomplish.

Before going into staging, I want to share with you the set design for this production. Our attic was above and upstage of the living room, which was down and downstage. This is important as we work through the discussion of the scenes. I really enjoyed the Broadway production in its use of light in defining the setting, something I would sort of emulate because I admired it in some of my later productions. But my set designer and I had decided on a more literal set, which was fine with me—and he won a BroadwayWorld.com award for it! It was beautiful.

ATTIC WINDOW

TRUNK   DESK

                                                           EXIT

STAIRS

Once Jo enters the scene through the attic window, as the leader, she remains physically in control of the staging, establishing herself center stage. I have provided the actors' subtext in italics for clues as to how they decided to move and gesture, indicated in brackets.

JO: Laurie! Laurie, Laurie, Laurie! Christopher Columbus, it's so good to see you! You've not been here in weeks. [They hug – this is not a direction in the script, but one we decided to add. Jo is not suspicious yet of what Laurie has in mind and this friendly, casual behavior is typical of them so far in the story. It is not that Jo doesn't love Laurie, only that she doesn't love him in the way he wants her to.]

LAURIE: I was in Boston. I have dreadful news.
Calm down and listen to me. [Laurie initially walks away from Jo. He is nervous about what he wants to say – the Scene of the attic is also helpful to the drama of Laurie's news. Physical action and gesture can react to the limited space available and heighten the expectations.][31]

JO: What news?
I can take the time to listen. [Jo sits on the trunk to give him her full attention – Jo is comfortable in this space right now, something that will change later so the contrast at this point in the scene is important.]

So far we have addressed elements of the pentad regarding Scene and Agent – so far Jo has been very much in charge of setting the mood and calming Laurie down. As Laurie proceeds to tell Jo about Grandfather enrolling him in school, Jo responds with subtext that starts to hint at elements of Purpose – Laurie leaving helps facilitate her Purpose.

JO:	That's wonderful news!
	He needs to fall in love with someone else. [Jo has never been naïve about the potential of Laurie to fall in love with her. She just has always known she could handle it, convince him to move on, maintain control. Her super objective has ruled her motivations from the beginning – she is going to be a writer to provide for her family.]
LAURIE:	What's wonderful about it? Leaving the best friend I've ever had?
	What are you talking about?
JO:	I can't imagine life in Concord without you: Not seeing your silly grin every day –
	Please don't get romantic on me. [Jo needs to use what I call "buddy" language – casual, throwing Laurie off the track. Her gestures also portrayed this subtext in the same way.]
LAURIE:	I don't want to go.
	I can't leave yet. [Laurie knows he has to get to the point of his visit – to propose. A stage direction I added was to have him pacing as far as Jo's desk, only a few feet away, and nervously start playing with her papers.]
JO:	But you've got to go. This is an incredible opportunity. College – I'd go in a minute. I'd study everything.
	I need to convince him this is a good idea. [Jo is still sitting on the trunk – important to allow Laurie the limited space of the attic to try and find his balance and stay on task and for Jo to appear to maintain stability and control.]
LAURIE:	What do you need of schools? You're going to be a famous writer.
	You don't need school.
JO (laughs, doubting):	Famous?
	Stop playing with my pages. [This subtext of Jo's was in direct reaction to Laurie's actions, but Laurie has turned to her and closed the gap in space, taking away her ability to stand up and physically stop him from touching her papers.]
LAURIE:	I need to tell you something.
	Here I go. [Laurie sits on the trunk next to Jo and takes her hand. Jo does not make room for him to sit down, forcing Laurie to sit to her right. This is the first shift of control in the scene. Jo is now trapped next to him on the trunk in a small space and where she will have to cross in front of him to exit the attic down the stairs. We now have our scene leader/Agent in a reactive state as opposed to an active state, the Agency, Scene, and Purpose of the pentad becoming tenuous along with Jo's imbalance, bringing those elements into a sort of equality and drawing attention to the element of the Act – a "here it comes" moment we have been anticipating.]

Laurie begins to reminisce about the first time they met, the cherry tree Jo chopped down that belonged to his Grandfather, that that is the day he fell in love with her. Jo's subtext is translated by her physical demeanor as she becomes anxious about where this is going. Laurie's kiss finally drives her into action.

JO (pulling back):   What was that? [Jo immediately stands up. Her dilemma is that the stairs to exit the house are to her right, an escape harder to make having Laurie also to her right.]
Oh, no! [Jo's subtext motivates her physical alarm.]

LAURIE: A kiss.
What's wrong? [Laurie stands to meet her. This encourages Jo's fight or flight state.]

JO: I know it was a kiss.
I need to get away from him. [Now Jo is the one pacing. She has to get some space between her and Laurie. What if he tries to kiss her again? Once he starts singing to her, that becomes a certainty.]

LAURIE: It was my first kiss. I've thought about it a long time –
I saved it for you.
WE COULD LIVE A MILLION DREAMS,
Look, it's coming true,
BUT ONLY IF WE DARE.
You love adventure! [Laurie tries to appeal to her sense of adventure to bring her around to his advances. Again, subtext motivates the staging as he crosses to her.]
WE COULD GO TO SUCH EXTREMES.
THERE'S SO MUCH WE COULD SHARE.
Please have me.
(He comes at her again)

JO (holding him off):   What's got into you?
It's not working. [Laurie is blocking the stairs. All Jo can do is retreat to her desk on stage left. The limitation of the small space adds to the sense of anxiety.]

Laurie has Jo cornered and seizes the opportunity to present her with his ring. As Jo's desperation intensifies, she loses control and speaks the words she has been thinking in her subtext and exemplifying in her physicality the entire scene.

JO: No. No. No, find someone else! Find – find some accomplished girl!
Scold him.

LAURIE: I don't want an accomplished girl. I want you.
But it's you that I want.

JO: Well, you can't have me!

No one can. [Jo at this point can only turn away, avoid eye contact with Laurie and hope that he starts to give up.]

Laurie unsuccessfully tries to reason with Jo, but she is resolved and Laurie predicts for Jo what we all know will happen.

LAURIE:	You'll marry.
	I know you will.
JO:	I won't!
	Please…
LAURIE:	You will. Just not me. That's what you're really saying. You'll find someone –
	I'm not stupid.
JO:	Go away! I thought you understood me.
	… that I want to be a writer, not a wife. [Jo makes it very difficult for Laurie keeping her back turned, hiding her facial expressions and emotions.]
LAURIE:	You knew all along how I felt. Everybody knew!
	I have been so obvious!
JO:	You knew all along who I am – what I want. I bared my soul to you, Laurie. Go away.
	What I did is more special than love. [Jo finds the stage left corner of the attic. She has achieved all the physical space she can in the small attic. She will not look at Laurie and he realizes he has lost her.]

I had Laurie exit through the house rather than the attic window, the entrance he typically used when he was there to see Jo. But after Laurie's kiss, the attic is no longer a safe place for Jo or a welcome place for Laurie. He runs stage right down the stairs, and through the living room out the front door—where every other normal guest enters the home. What commences is the song this show is known for and that every mezzo-soprano musical theater major sings, the song "Astonishing." The mantra that actors "sing at the point they can no longer speak" their feelings, "Astonishing" initially dwells on Jo's final subtext from the dialog being a question and her position on the stage as off-center, off-balance.

JO:	
	WHO IS HE, WHO IS HE WITH HIS 'MARRY ME,'
	WITH HIS RING AND HIS 'MARRY ME'?
	No one has ever felt like this about me.
	THE NERVE, THE GALL.
	Are you kidding me?
	THIS IS NOT, NOT WHAT WAS MEANT TO BE,

HOW COULD HE RUIN IT ALL WITH THOSE TWO WORDS?
You are so stupid, Laurie! Now this is going to be awkward forever!
[Jo paces, distraught. The attic is feeling small and confined. The contrast of this song with the song "Fire Within Me" later in the show needs to be highlighted here. In "Astonishing," Jo is trying to control, avoid, and run from her problem while later she confronts, understands, and embraces it. The subtext above and throughout this song motivates her physically.]

I THOUGHT I KNEW HIM, THOUGH THAT HE KNEW ME.
I don't know this Laurie.
WHEN DID HE CHANGE, WHAT DID I MISS?
Was he giving me signs? I tried to discourage him.
A KISS? WHEN I THOUGHT, ALL ALONG,
THAT WE WERE MEANT TO FORGE FRONTIERS.
HOW COULD I BE SO WRONG?
How could he do this to me?
[Jo sits back on the trunk, trying to retrace what she missed. The scene of the attic only provides the trunk or her desk chair for sitting. Maybe if she revisits the trunk, she can rationalize what just happened.]

AND I NEED, HOW I NEED MY SISTERS HERE,
IF I CAN'T SHARE MY DREAMS,
WHAT WERE THEY FOR?
I don't know what to do.
I THOUGHT OUR PROMISE MEANT THAT WE WOULD
NEVER CHANGE AND NEVER PART.
This is beyond my control.
I THOUGHT TOGETHER WE'D AMAZE THE WORLD!
HOW CAN I LIVE MY DREAMS OR EVEN START
WHEN EVERYTHING HAS COME APART?
How will I recover from this?
[Jo initially rises and paces again, finally ending up on her knees center stage. Her loss of control, evidenced in her subtext, leads her to wander, looking and searching, finally surrendering to the fact that she and Laurie were never on the same page. The only place to collapse in this small space is on the floor, center stage, between her desk and the trunk.]

Subsequent lines of subtext throughout this song continually highlight Jo's Agency and Purpose having failed. Something we often did in rehearsal was simply read the subtext of the song and not the song lyrics themselves, getting away from the memorized aspects of having rehearsed the music and tapping into the spontaneity and naturalness of subtext which was motivated in the first place by elements of the pentad for this scene.

I have to leave.
It's not the same anymore.
Why did you do this, Laurie?
I should leave.
Am I am good enough?

I need more than this simple life.
I have to do this by myself.
I can imagine this new life.
When? Where? [At this point Jo finally rises, looking for what to do next.]

Home is not here.
I need the challenge.
I don't need any help.
[Jo uses the rhythm of the music in the bridge to find the stairs and make her way to downstage center]

I won't give up.
Just try to stop me.
Don't tell me what to be.
You haven't seen the last of me yet.
I won't stop until I get what I want.
I will be famous.
[curtain]

What is so great about this song is the journey that Jo takes as she sings. While we often think of the dialogue doing most of the advancing of plot and development of action, "Astonishing" dwells on the emotion at hand as well as advancing plot and developing action. The Jo the song starts with is not the Jo at the end. Not that every musical theater number doesn't advance the actor emotionally; this is just a special example of how this is done especially well.

Beth Dies

Research really inspired the dramatism in this show. Based upon my reading of the Louisa May Alcott letters, I tried to capture a bit more of this dynamic in the scene "Some Things Are Meant to Be." By staging Jo as calloused to her sister's illness, though, I encouraged the audience to identify with her need to change, to collectively hope this is not the Jo we are left with at the end of the story. When Jo does realize that her home is truly important, her recent denial then becomes an even more significant motivation for her writing and submitting her great novel in the first place.

Let's recall the pentads of Jo and Beth from earlier in this chapter:

Character	Jo	Beth
Act	Beth dies	Beth comforts Jo
Agent	Beth—sister who has no aspirations	Myself—I love home.
Scene	Beach—life goes on	Beach—I'd rather be back in Concord
Agency	Hummels, Concord-frustration	Hummels, Concord-fulfillment
Purpose	Reminder of how awful Concord is	Jo's success

This pentad provides several options—to actors and directors—for how this scene can be led. If the Act leads this scene, both characters have conflicting responses that can work against each other—denial and acceptance. If the Scene drives this scene, there is not a focus on Beth dying, which makes it all the more sad when we don't see her again. If the Agent drives this scene, Jo is reminded of her dissatisfaction with life while Beth expresses her pride in Jo and what she will accomplish. If the Agency leads this scene, both girls are frustrated with trying to pretend. If the Purpose leads this scene, it establishes Jo's denial of Beth's condition. Jo's denial is portrayed physically by her pacing on stage.

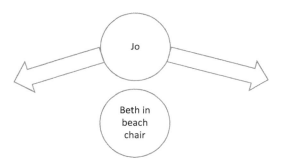

Bottom line, Beth cannot die on stage in this scene. The next scene in the show is a total shift in mood, but only after the beautiful postlude to "Some Things Are Meant to Be" provides us with the transition we need to understand that Beth does indeed die, but in the presence of a Jo who isn't in denial, distracted, and frustrated. This is the scene that gets us to not seeing Beth anymore, not the scene where she actually leaves.

"The Fire within Me"—the Writing of *Little Women*

We find ourselves back in the attic after Beth has died. Jo hasn't been up there in months. Marmee finds her there and sings "Days of Plenty," an intense power ballad about surviving and persevering in spite of heartache and defeat. Marmee is always the leader of her own song scenes, "Here Alone" being her first one. She is definitely the Agent that propels Jo to commit to the Act of the rest of the scene; because, once Marmee leaves, Jo is left alone, and this is where "it" happens:

- Act—the writing of *Little Women*
- Scene—the attic
- Agent—Jo
- Agency—embracing, not rejecting, the memories
- Purpose—"the four of us together—here at last."

This scene being Jo alone on the stage really highlights the act of writing. Pacing in the space, back and forth between her desk and the rest of the room, physicalizes her mental state, and though she feels the room is empty, it really isn't. As she removes the white sheets that were placed over everything when she left for New York City, the memories start to become inspiring, and she begins to embrace them rather than avoid them. She discovers the pentad element of purpose through the agency. One more note: my lighting designer and I used lighting to emphasize the hollowness of Jo's feelings in this scene by taking the light off the cyclorama, creating a colorless opening to the scene. It was one of my favorite moments of the set design, lighting design, and emotion coming together in the show.

JO:

HOW DO I GO ON?
JUST AN EMPTY ROOM.
I need to distract myself from all these feelings. [The room isn't empty at all, but Jo has closed herself off to any memories of this space. The pentad element of scene looms large in this song. Jo's subtext is evidence of her internal knowledge that what she is singing is not what she is thinking. This manifests itself in pacing and gestures with nervous energy.]

ALL I HAVE IS MEMORIES.
I am numb.
I NEED A TASK TO DO.
SOMEONE GIVE ME A TASK TO DO
I NEED A---
Someone please help me feel something else.

[Jo is aimlessly and rapidly pacing. Again, the attic is a relatively small space, so she can't go far. The scene forces her see things and confront her memories. Jo eventually slows down and walks toward her writing desk. She sits, and...]

(She finds the shell that BETH gave her)

I THOUGHT THAT SOMEHOW
WE WOULD ALWAYS HAVE FOREVER.
How did we come to this?
I THOUGHT THE PROMISES WE MADE
WOULD HAVE A DIFFERENT END.
Why did you leave?
I THOUGHT THE LOVE WE SHARED
WOULD KEEP US AS WE WERE.
Was I not good enough?
IT WAS THE FIRE WITHIN ME.

[She stands again as she begins to conjure up the memories, that she and her sisters were happy once. She begins to lean into the element of purpose in this pentad, using the agency of embracing the memories to accomplish that. As previously, I will demonstrate the ability of the subtext to stand on its own in highlighting the elements of the pentad.]

This was our home. [Agency]
[Jo makes center stage, the only open floor space the attic allows for – Scene.]
I thought it was strong enough.
I don't think I can do this alone.
[Jo takes in the entire space as she sings. Her traversing of the width of the attic as far as she can demonstrates an acknowledgement of what she knows this space needs to become for her again. She can't avoid it forever.]
Why couldn't I save you?
Not anymore, not ever again.
Did I not do enough?
I have obviously failed.

At this point, the stage directions have Jo pulling off the white sheets that have draped the attic furniture since Beth's death. Light pours into the space and Jo gets her idea. We start to hear in voice over the voice of Jo as she begins to write. She quotes her sisters, Meg first, then Amy and Beth. As she embraces the agency of the pentad and understands that the agency fulfills the purpose of this pentad, the tune and lyrics of "Astonishing" remind the audience of the last time we heard this song, bringing back the feelings of that moment, but for an entirely new purpose:

[Jo stands on her trunk – the same one where Laurie proposed. Although not noted before, this director had Jo stand on the couch in the living room at the end of Astonishing when she shouts "Christopher Columbus," a boyish, "I am going to be a writer and provide for my family even though I am a woman" moment. Having her stand on the trunk in the attic now, reminds the audience of that previously triumphant moment for Jo.]

HERE I GO AND THERE'S NO TURNING BACK:

Writing is all I have left. [Act]

MY GREAT ADVENTURE HAS BEGUN.

My life begins right now.

I MAY BE SMALL BUT I'VE GOT GIANT PLANS

TO SHINE AS BRIGHTLY AS THE SUN.

Thank you, Marmee, for helping me see! [Act and Agency]

HERE IN ALL THE SMALLEST DETAILS OF THE PAST

HERE IN THIS ATTIC, SUDDENLY LIFE IS SOMETHING VAST.

This is just the beginning. [Scene]

THE FOUR OF US FOREVER HERE AT LAST.

This is the story I have needed to write. [Act facilitating Purpose]

AS UNEXPECTED AS CAN BE.

It was always here in front of me, [She has made her peace with the Scene, the attic. This is where this book has to be written. No more running. No more hiding. No more white sheets covering up the memories.]

ASTONISHING.

I just never saw it.

[Jo sits to resume writing]

All that is left for Jo to discover lies in the hands of this manuscript. It is the catalyst for the last proposal in this show. In the proposal by Professor Bhaer, we find ourselves outside the March house. Let's now contrast the proposal from Act I from Laurie and this proposal in Act II from Mr. Bhaer: Proposal #1 from Laurie:

- Act—Jo refuses Laurie
- Scene—March attic
- Agent—Jo
- Agency—casual language, physical distance
- Purpose—to deter Laurie

Proposal #2 from Professor Bhaer:

- Act—Jo accepts Professor Bhaer
- Scene—outside the March house
- Agent—Jo
- Agency—writing the book he told her to write
- Purpose—to provide for her family

In this pentad, it is Bhaer as "the other," the fact that he is "not Concord" that the actor playing Jo identified as having the most effect on her acceptance; therefore since Laurie is the next door neighbor, the one who most specifically represents Concord, the actress who played Jo was able to exploit this tension between the two acts: refusal and acceptance.

"Small Umbrella in the Rain"

In this song, Jo and the Professor determine their differences will be what makes them compatible, that disagreeing once in awhile is not the end of the world, and that they are meant to be together because they love each other. This director used the back and forth of this eventual determination in the staging, drawing the pair apart and bringing them back together again several times until the final stanza.

Through objectives and beats, Jo was again established as the scene leader. She is embracing new changes all around her: accepting Aunt March's house, accepting that this new form of writing is what will make her successful, accepting Bhaer's proposal. That her book is the thing that brings the two of them together keeps the theme of this story and of the heroine front and center.

The now engaged, published Jo, has fulfilled her destiny, bringing full circle our theme for this show. While these lyrics also appear in "Weekly Volcano Press" at the beginning of Act II, Jo herself never sings these exact words:

"Volcano Reprise"

JO:

I got everything…

...Finally.

I didn't give up.

AND THE WORLD IS---

--Yours to claim when someone else feels the flame you always knew was there. [As an actor you always fill in what a lyric does not finish and this is how my actor playing Jo decided to finish her thought, using that opening of Act II moment to reconnect her dots as a character. I loved it!]

The addition of Burkean dramatism in the subtext process suggests blocking options to the actors that they can feel on their own, complicating how the audience believes the characters should behave in response to social norms. Again, this complication is anachronistic for the musical theater genre, but dramatism opens musical theater up to such possibilities, while itself staying true to form. While Burkean applications of dramatism to the world of dramatic theater are easily seen, this first chapter documents the process to utilize Burkean identification as a method of character analysis in musical theater production. Since musical theater, as a popular art form, crosses many disciplinary boundaries, it is often difficult to demonstrate its scholarly purposes. The authors demonstrate that an analysis of Burkean motives can be more successful in musical production than current interpretive applications through its mystification of popular forms, its ability to promote identification, and its ability to offer Burke studies new directions in the arena of performative rhetoric.

Notes

1 Kenneth Burke, *Grammar of Motives* (Berkeley: University of California Press, 1945), 65.
2 Ibid.
3 Clayton Lewis, "Burke's Act in the Rhetoric of Motives," *College English* 46, no. 4 (1984): 374.
4 Ibid.
5 Ibid., 375.
6 Ibid.
7 Ibid.
8 Ibid.
9 Ibid.
10 Ibid., 371.
11 Ibid., 376.
12 Debra Hawhee, "Language as Sensuous Action," *Quarterly Journal of Speech* 92, no. 4 (2006): 333.
13 Ibid.
14 This section, pages 9–29, was originally published as "Dramatism, Musical Theatre Interpretation, and Popular Artistic Production," *KB Journal: The Journal of the Kenneth Burke Society* 11, no. 2

(2016), Online at www.https/kbjournal.org/beasley. Licensed under a creative commons attribution non-commercial license.

15 Daniel Helfgot, *The Third Line: The Opera Performer as Interpreter* (New York: Schirmer Books, 1993), 112.

16 David Ostwald, *Acting for Singers: Creating Believable Singing Characters* (New York: Oxford University Press, 2005), 120.

17 Ibid.

18 Louisa May Alcott, "Personal Correspondence," Houghton Library Special Collections. Harvard University, Cambridge, MA.

19 Kenneth Burke, *A Rhetoric of Motives* (Berkeley: University of California Press, 1950), 57–58.

20 Dennis Brissett, et al., *Life as Theatre: A Dramaturgical Sourcebook* (Piscataway, NJ: Transaction Publishers, 2005), 336.

21 Ibid.

22 C. Ronald Kimberling, *Kenneth Burke's Dramatism and Popular Arts* (Bowling Green, OH: Bowling Green University Press, 1982), 84.

23 Kenneth Burke, *Language as Symbolic Action: Essays on Life, Literature and Method* (Berkeley: University of California Press, 1966), 369–370.

24 David Ostwald, *Acting for Singers: Creating Believable Singing Characters* (New York: Oxford University Press, 2005), 128.

25 All song lyrics and text are excerpted from Jason Howland, *Little Women, The Musical* (New York: Cherry Lane Music, 2005).

26 All subtext appears in italics and is the work of the students that portrayed these characters.

27 C. Ronald Kimberling, *Kenneth Burke's Dramatism and Popular Arts* (Bowling Green, OH: Bowling Green University Press, 1982), 70.

28 Dennis Brissett, et al., *Life as Theatre: A Dramaturgical Sourcebook* (Piscataway, NJ: Transaction Publishers, 2005), 336.

29 Debra Hawhee, *Moving Bodies: Kenneth Burke at the Edges of Language* (Columbia: University of South Carolina Press, 2009), 3.

30 At the time of this writing, Greta Gerwig's 2019 film adaptation had not been yet released.

31 All stage directions in brackets are the work of the director. These are differentiated from the stage directions centered and in parentheses which are part of the original script.

Bibliography

Abrams, Judith. "Plato's Rhetoric as Rendered by the Pentad." *Rhetoric Society Quarterly* 11, no. 1 (1981): 24–28.

Alcott, Louisa May. "Personal Correspondence." Houghton Library Special Collections. Harvard University, Cambridge, MA.

Beasley, Kimberly Eckel and James P. Beasley. "Dramatism, Musical Theatre Interpretation, and Popular Artistic Production." *KB Studies: The Journal of the Kenneth Burke Society* 11, no. 2, 2016. Online.

Birdsell, David. "Ronald Reagan on Lebanon and Grenada: Flexibility and Interpretation in the Application of Kenneth Burke's Pentad." In *Methods of Rhetorical Criticism: A*

Twentieth-Century Perspective. 3rd rev. ed., edited by Bernard L. Brock, Robert L. Scott, and James W. Chesebro. Detroit, MI: Wayne State University Press, 1987.

Brissett, Dennis, Charles Edgly, and Robert Stebbins, eds. *Life as Theatre: A Dramaturgical Sourcebook.* Piscataway, NJ: Transaction Publishers, 2005.

Burke, Kenneth. *A Grammar of Motives.* Berkeley: California University Press, 1969.

_____. *A Rhetoric of Motives.* Berkeley: California University Press, 1969.

_____. *Language as Symbolic Action: Essays on Life, Literature and Method.* Berkeley: California University Press, 1966.

Deer, Joe and Rocco Dal Vera, eds. *Acting in Musical Theatre: A Comprehensive Course.* New York: Routledge, 2008.

Hawhee, Deborah. "Language as Sensuous Action." *Quarterly Journal of Speech* 92, no. 4 (2006): 331–354.

_____. *Moving Bodies: Kenneth Burke at the Edges of Language.* Columbia: University of South Carolina Press, 2009.

Helfgot, Daniel. *The Third Line: The Opera Performer as Interpreter.* New York: Schirmer Books, 1993.

Howland, Jason. *Little Women, The Musical.* New York: Cherry Lane Music, 2005.

Kimberling, C. Ronald. *Kenneth Burke's Dramatism and Popular Arts.* Bowling Green, OH: Bowling Green State University Press, 1982.

Lewis, Clayton. "Burke's Act in the Rhetoric of Motives." *College English* 46, no. 4 (1984): 368–376.

Ostwald, David. *Acting for Singers: Creating Believable Singing Characters.* New York: Oxford University Press, 2005.

Walker, Robyn and Nanette Monin. "The Purpose of the Picnic: Using Burke's Dramatistic Pentad to Analyse a Company Event." *Journal of Organizational Change Management* 14, no. 3 (2001): 266–279.

CHAPTER TWO

Scenes in Motion: Dramatism in Elton John and Tim Rice's *Aida*

In the first chapter, we focused on the act ratio and its use in writing, in interpretation, and in musical theater staging. In this second chapter, we focus on Burke's scene and the scene ratio. Where or when did the act occur? Again, this might seem like a simple task, but describing a time and a place is more difficult that it first appears, for the focus is on a description, not the literal date and place. How we describe "when and where the act occurred" has important consequences on how we view student writers, how actors can create motivations for interpretation, and how directors can motivate scene-directed staging.

Scene Ratios

In an analysis of the dramatistic pentad, Burke continues with *scene* or "where and when the act occurred." For example, President John F. Kennedy was assassinated on November 22, 1963 in Dallas, Texas. That is the specific date and place, but how we describe that time and place is needed for our ability to interpret our interpretations. If we describe November 22, 1963 in Dallas, Texas as a "conservative hotbed of anti-democratic sentiment," then that is different than describing November 22, 1963 in Dallas, Texas as a "sympathetic region to Democratic appeasement of the Soviet Union." One description of the scene supports a "lone-gunman," while the other supports a "government conspiracy" of President Kennedy's assassination. How we describe a scene sets us forth on our journey of understanding the act.

It is not now November of 1963, but November of 2019. As Floridians, we have been affected this fall by yet another series of hurricanes and tropical storms, as has much of the eastern U.S. coastline. You may be reading this book for a class in the fall of 2020, and you might be under the same threat of hurricanes or storms yourself. You might be reading this book in California, under the threat of wildfires, as many counties in California are right now. In this fall of 2019, there is also a buildup to impeachment proceedings in Washington. If you are reading this book for a class in the fall of 2020, then a presidential election is right around the corner. Who is running? Who will win? What will *happen*? *When and where* will it happen? How you answer these questions reveal how you interpret your place and time within this history. This is a "journey worth the taking," and if you follow along for a bit, you'll see how high the stakes are for not just the teaching of writing or theater but for the very future of the arts themselves.

As a student, you might be thinking about the next assignment you have for a class, maybe this class. Does this assignment ask you to think about the situation that you are writing in, or does it pretend that there is no outside situation? That there isn't an election going on? That wildfires aren't raging around you, or that you've had to evacuate your dorm or home because of a hurricane threat? Context matters, and it is sometimes difficult to have an assignment for class that ignores the circumstances of your writing situation. While we often want our students to think about their circumstances in the acting situation, it is worth considering how little practice students have had in describing the time and place of their writing acts. How many times have students been asked to think of the "extrinsic" factors involved in the writing process? How often are students writing conditions taken into account in our writing assessments? In his personal letters, Burke often asked the question, "When in the world are we?" and in order to help our actors prepare for their roles, we can prepare them by considering their own time and place whenever they attempt an assignment. Let's start by considering Burke's analysis of "scene."

Burke often wrote on what he called the "scene-agent" ratio, or how the scene affected the actions of the agent. He writes, "A literary critic who spoke of the 'literary situation,' for instance, meant not the 'objective conditions' under which a writer writes, but the motives peculiar to a writer's medium. What looked 'scenic' was actually 'pragmatic,' since the writer's medium is an agency."[1] For Burke, the "literary situation" was much more than just motives, but those objective conditions, as they are part of the scene-agent ratio. For our purposes, we are interested in how the objective conditions of student writers affect their purposes in writing. For example, a student whose frustration is boiling over about the inadequacy of responses to inhumane policies on immigration may have difficulty adhering to error-counting rubrics on state mandated writing assessments, as they reinforce an "acculturationist" view of the writing situation, meaning that they force non-native speakers of English to conform to a specific standard, rather than allowing for differences in language use. This is just one example, but it sheds light on how "When in the world are we?" matters to student writers.

It also might be worth discussing among both students and teachers the conceptions and misconceptions of these "objective conditions" under which students write. I know that many faculty members assume that students can write in isolation, without distractions from home, roommates, media, etc., but that is not the case. The myth of the "writer writes alone" serves as what Burke calls a "representative anecdote," or perhaps a "super or hyper" anecdote, if you will. Linda Brodkey writes, "Simply put, such an anecdote functions as a proposition that at once organizes and analyzes experience through the processes of reflection, selection, and deflection. For Burke, the telling of such anecdotes is simply what people do. And while some may do it more formally than others, his interest, and ours, concerns their ideological functions."[2] In other words, the writer writes alone is a "terministic screen," a term (alone) that prevents (screens) us from thinking beyond it, or in addition to what is possible and more probable, i.e., the un-alone writer. Brodkey explains:

> In much the same way that using writing as a punishment teaches the wrong kind of lesson about writers and writing, this representative anecdote of writing as reading or reception can be counter-productive with respect to writing and writing pedagogy, insofar as the scene dampens (reduction) even as it stokes the desire (scope) to write.[3]

So, for instance, suppose we describe the student writing a paper act as "a student follows directions." If we do so, then we then seem to believe that the student has no interest in the paper, no personal connection to its outcome. If we then next turn to scene, how would we describe that? Does it make it easier or more difficult to imagine this "direction-following student" alone or with others? If the student writer is detached from the writing assignment, it is not hard to describe her writing scene as also alone and detached. However, if we describe the act of a student paper more extrinsically, such as "a student follows her interest in social justice on immigration," then it is harder for us to describe the scene as the lone writer writing, for example.

Let's extend this demonstration further. Instead of describing the writer's act as "following directions," let's describe the writer's act as "advocating for immigrants oppressed by the current White House administration." Then, if we describe the writer's *scene* as the "last days of the Trump administration," then the immediacy of action comes to the forefront. Brodkey's discussion of the lone writer writing demonstrates the narrowness of the "lone writer writing" representative anecdote.

> The parlor: Discuss with your class how the "where and the when" affects you as a student. Are there opportunities for you to use those situations in your writing? How?

We've been discussing the scene in relation to the writer's situation, but what about scene as it relates to the rhetorical situation? The rhetorical situation is defined as the moment in time and place when discourse operates. You may have even read about the rhetorical situation and the two competing definitions: Lloyd Bitzer and Richard Vatz. For Bitzer, the speaker steps into a situation, but for Vatz, the speaker creates the situation. This dichotomy has been taught as if there are no other ways to think about the rhetorical situation, but according to Cynthia Sheard:

> Within Burke's analytical scheme, then, language itself is 'scenic' to the extent that it is, in his words, 'the critical moment' at which human motives take form. We could describe Burke's notion of scene as *kairotic* to the extent that the "scenic" element of rhetoric is comprised of both temporal and spatial parameters or "contexts."[4]

In other words, the rhetorical situation is neither the speaker's presence nor the opening the speaker creates, for it is language itself. Sheard's description shows how language can do what Bitzer and Vatz's versions of the rhetorical scene cannot. For Sheard, "*Kairos*, then, is the scene of Burke's rhetorical theory."[5]

You may have heard of the term *kairos*, as well, or even utilized it in your writing. When *kairos* is defined as the "opportune moment," or "right time," for speaking or writing, then it is being treated as an object, like when our student paper is treated like an object. When student papers are treated like objects, it is easier to describe them by their deficits, rather than their differences. When student papers are treated as acts, then it is more difficult to describe them by their deficits and we can see them as different. Similarly, when we think of *kairos* as an act, the way that Burke and his dramatism invite us to do, then *kairos* is in motion, it influences not just a specific time and place, but many times and many places. Sheard writes the following:

> If *kairos* grounds all action in the discursive elements of the scene in which those acts take place, it therefore includes all those scenic or contextual elements of both time and place that circumscribe and delimit moments of discursive exchange: from the culturally transmitted opinions and attitudes that inform audiences orientations to and expectations of the discourse, to the exigence of the occasion itself and the conventions of that are dictated by that occasion at that time and place.[6]

Using *kairos* as an act, not an object, leads to the multiplication of possible times and places, rather than their addition or subtraction. If *kairos* is an object susceptible to an examination of its deficits, then a *kairos* "rubric" could be conceived. "The *kairos* the writer identifies is original, authentic, and productive" might get a score of "5" on such a rubric, while "The writer does not identify his or her *kairos*" might get a score of "0." However, when *kairos* is considered as an act, there are no additions that need to be made, only multiplications that can be made. Sheard writes, "In short, *kairos* denotes the infinite combinations of consubstantial, scenic, elements that exist as potentialities of discursive acts. As such, it can never be pinned down or reduced to a single one of its components without risk of finding them branching out again."[7] This irreducibility inherent in Burke's concept of *kairos* through the dramatistic pentad has important consequences for the stage actor, and as we will attempt to demonstrate, significant potential in the staging of time travel productions, such as Elton John's *Aida*.

Scene Change

In the same way that we are often not attuned to the student's writing scene in our reading and responding to student writing, we are often not attuned to the difficulty of the implications of "being in the moment" for work with student actors. *For the actor,* you might not have acting situations that are devoid of the where and the when, but you might have acting situations that are given to you or that you research. The most often utilized "method" is Stanislavski's "Given Circumstances." Ostwald writes, "The most efficient way to enter your character's reality is by using the Magical if. Developed by the great Russian acting teacher Constantin Stanislavski, this amazing tool is no more than the provocative phrase 'I'm going to behave as if...' Although these words may seem innocuous, they can powerfully stimulate your imagination. They can lift you directly into your character's world and help you generate believable actions that express your character's feelings."[8] If you are reading this as a student actor, then you are probably familiar with Stanislavski and the approach called "method acting." However, we want to listen carefully to how Ostwald describes Stanislavski's method, by describing it as the "most *efficient* way," and it can "lift you *directly* into your character's world." Here, the emphasis is on efficiency and directness. While this is often the case in student-acted performances, it is also anachronistic to the philosophy of teaching student actors and the emphasis on process and learning over time. Ostwald describes Stanislavski's method in determining the when and where of a particular scene: "Because the creators of the piece supply it, this information is commonly called your Given Circumstances. Answering the following six questions as your character and in the first person will enable you to extract the essence of those circumstances from the wealth of material in a score. When are the events taking place? In history? In her own life?"[9] The scene works that Stanislavski requires are *answers* to these questions. These answers can be found either through preliminary research or if it is not known, they are provided by the actor themselves. For example, if an actor were to answer these questions based on Stanislavski's "Given Circumstances," they might identify the literal time and place, but without your descriptions of these times and places, however, these situations remain the world of objects and not as acts. For Burke and dramatism, the most important part is how the actor describes the "Given Circumstances," not what they actually are. Burke's dramatism works against efficiency and directness, favoring slowness and misdirection. In fact, because Stanislavski's "Given Circumstances" is so prevalent in theater pedagogy, it may serve as a "trained incapacity," how our success blinds us to other methods for other circumstances. For the music theater director, Burke's dramatism ensures a commitment to method, to student's "earning their increment," or earning their own learning. By describing the "Given Circumstances," the actor can determine how they are interpreting their interpretations, and we will discuss how this specifically happened in our discussion of Elton John's *Aida*.

Another element that we specifically want to point to in our discussion of *Aida* is not just how "scene" can inform an actor's performance, but also how the sets themselves motivate staging. An actor's typical relationship to the set is along the lines of "Make sure you don't trip on that," or "We'll put some glow tape on that," or "Remember you have three stairs there," or "that wall sticks out three feet, so you'll need to make your path wider." Current textbooks in musical theater reiterate this gap, so perhaps this is a symptom of Stanislavski's "Given Circumstances." Deer and Dal Vera write, "No matter what the degree of realism or stylization, the staging of a song should be a physical expression of the song's dramatic action. And it's your job to create that physical expression. In the following units we'll discuss some frequently used tools and techniques for expressing that journey."[10] According to Deer and Dal Vera, the dramatistic action precedes the staging, and in this way is most similar to Lloyd Bitzer's concept of the rhetorical situation, the speaker or writer steps into the space created by the situation. This is also similar to the way in which Ostwald describes an actor's answers to Stanislavski's questions; the situation exists prior to the speaker's presence. We have already discussed how Burke's concept of the rhetorical situation is different, but this example helps define and explain how. If the situation exits prior to the speaker and it is their task to fill that situation, then that speaker's "scene" will remain "in place," so to speak. However, situations are not always static, situations change, they *move*. If these rhetorical situations move, we need a conception of the rhetorical situation that moves along with them. We have already discussed how Sheard's understanding of Burke's *kairos* involves "both temporal and spatial parameters or 'contexts,'"[11] but in this case, the temporal and spatial parameters are characteristics of one context, not just two separate contexts. For Deer and Dal Vera, it is up to the actor to demonstrate the dramatic action, but according to Burke, any part of the scene can do so, including the sets themselves. In other words, the sets themselves can motivate the actor's movement, and this is a characteristic of the production of *Aida: The Broadway Musical* we wish to highlight.

On Scene

In this chapter, we detail how students used pentad work in a production of Elton John's *Aida*. Doing so not only allowed students to understand how, where, when, and why they should move on stage, but also how the set itself should move in every scene. Understanding how the sets themselves could move in every scene improved resource allocation between music and theater departments. Resources are constantly an issue in the college/university setting. The struggle of Fine and Performing Arts at many schools often runs up against a lack of resources, both tangible and virtual: money itself as well as administrative support and "how is this project going to bring visibility to our institution." At the same time, however, each department is competing for production space. With as many as four or five programs "in production," university theater spaces are in constant demand for rehearsal time, staging, technical support, and performances. In order to accommodate the rehearsal schedules of theater, dance, and music theater, a repertory schedule was devised. With the musical "in rep" with the theater production, this presented challenges for set design. In our production of Elton John's *Aida*, we opted for an entire fabric set, with fabric curtains flying in and out to indicate and give shape to scene changes. While using fabric as our musical set facilitated easy changes to the built set for the theater production, it also created new ways of communicating *Aida*'s story and the messages we wanted to convey in our production.

These considerations made set design a much more important part of student's preparation for this production. The sets themselves dictated the interpretation of their character's motives and, even more importantly, how each scene could or could not be staged. We have detailed the staging instruction from other acting textbooks in order to draw some contrasts between actor-directed staging and those limitations, especially in these new circumstances. Deer and Dal Vera write, "Designers and directors work to create a visual world that expresses their

Figure 2.1. *Aida* pre-production. Photo credit: Kimberly Beasley

Figure 2.2. Aida and Mereb. Photo Credit: Kimberly Beasley

interpretation of the text. Those visual clues can tell you about the point of view of your production. Designs for a musical often inform the audience about the world of the show more powerfully than anything else. Consider these elements carefully and use them to your advantage."[12] While Deer and Dal Vera tell the acting student to "consider these elements and use them to your advantage," they do not begin to examine how acting students should do this. How is an acting student supposed to incorporate that into their *interpretations* without any guidance on how to do that? How is an acting student supposed to incorporate that into their staging without any guidance on how to do that? We contend that having students describe the scene-act ratio in Burke's dramatistic pentad actually does help students "consider" and "use" the set design elements in their interpretations and staging in ways that multiply the "points of view" of any production.

In addition, Deer and Dal Vera ignore any outside factors other than the actor's own understanding of the production for those considerations. In reality, production decisions made by collegiate directors often do not have anything to do with the "artistic vision" or the "points of view," since many of those decisions are made on outside forces, such as resource allocation, for example. In our case, the imposed limitations of collegiate production, such as having two productions "in rep" with both needing moving sets; specifically how the production scene itself dictated the use of fabric screens for our show and moveable set pieces for the theater show that was simultaneously sharing our one collegiate theater space.

For Deer and Dal Vera, interacting with the set comes later in the rehearsal process, rather than as a motivation:

> Imagine you've been hired to play Curly in a regional production of Oklahoma! You've researched the original production thoroughly and made clear decisions about how to move, sing, and act in the role. On the first day of rehearsal you watch the design presentations where you discover that Laurey wears overalls and no shoes. The prop master offers to teach you how to hand roll cigarettes, and the set for Laurey's farmyard includes a rusting hulk of an old thresher. This is a radically different visual world than you imagined. But, it is the one that your production will live in. Think of the ways you will need to adjust your interpretation to harmonize with this production approach.[13]

Deer and Dal Vera's acting student has "researched the originally production thoroughly and made clear decisions," but they do not help the acting student make any decisions based on that research. Should the acting student merely copy the performances of other productions or work against them? Certainly, there are occasions for both, but Deer and Dal Vera do not help the acting student decide. Would this be based on the circumstances of the time and place of the production, or on the purpose of the production, or on the actors able to play the parts? We simply do not know. Also, while they write, "think of the ways you will need to adjust your interpretation to harmonize with this production approach," they do not provide any guidance to the student actor on how to do that, only to "think of the ways." For students describing the scene in Burke's dramatistic pentad, however, they have a way to harmonize these approaches, and we will attempt to demonstrate how that "harmonization" is detailed in the next few pages.

Since *Aida* relies heavily on dance and choreography, there are only four scenes in the production that are not choreographed. For Deer and Del Vera, the use of a fabric set would constitute this dilemma for student actors: they must adjust their interpretation to accommodate the fabric set. But what if the fabric set were to mimic the movement of the actors from scene to scene? Debra Hawhee writes, "When we talk about bodies, that is, we talk about sensation, touch, texture, affect, materiality, performativity, movement, gesture, habits, entertainment, biology, physiology, rhythm, and performance, for starters."[14] In our case, the fabric set created tactile interactions for the actors, as well as textures, materiality, performativity, and movement. Most importantly, the continuous movement of the fabric demonstrated the fluid interactions among time and space that the story of *Aida* narrates. The fabric screens reinforced the ethereal atmosphere and masked the nuances of the time travel which is seen, but not explicitly stated. The movement of the fabric screens gave the audience another way to participate in the meaning of the performance. Kenneth Burke writes, "In five hours of Wagner, are not at least three of them best salvaged by study? Releasing from the attempt to vibrate *avec*, one watches what he does with the horns?"[15] In this instance, it is not the horns that draw the audience's attention, but our use of the fabric screens to tell our story. By putting the set itself in motion, we were able to find a better ways to involve the audience, and also to accommodate the finite resources of our institution.

Making a Scene

Where and when did the act occur? Where and when did the act occur? It depends on who the where and when is actually for. Until now, we've only been considering the time and place for the characters, but what about the production itself? Deer and Del Vera write, "Beyond creating an aesthetically pleasing frame for the story, design elements offer information about how to build a characterization. Pay attention when designers do their presentations at the beginning of rehearsals. If you're working on a scene on your own, research designs from past productions."[16] Once again, however, it is not clear what the student actor should do with those past production designs. Should they copy them or work against them, and under what circumstances or conditions? What method would they use to decide? The first scene we would like to analyze is the production history of Elton John's *Aida* itself.

In Deer and Dal Vera's advice to "research the production," what will students learn about the production history of *Aida*? If we start researching this production history, what will we find? More importantly, what kinds of descriptions of the act, scene, agent, agency, and purpose will we find? In his article, "On Exoticism, Western Art Music, and the Words We Use," Ralph Locke writes the following:

> In the blockbuster musical entitled Elton John and Tim Rice's *Aida* (2000), Radames, when first meeting the Nubian slave Aida, breaks into song about distant lands. Radames imagines that visiting these distant lands would delight his senses and expand his field of action. Although hailed as Egypt's triumphant military commander, Radames resents that he is not free to question imperial policies, nor even to marry someone of his own choosing. In the 'half-discovered places' of his fantasy, 'there'd be no ties of time and space to bind me,' he explains further to Aida.[17]

In this description, we see how Locke is describing the effect that the distant lands have on the actions of Radames, or as Burke would describe, the effect the scene has on the agent. This *scene-agent* ratio, then, has the greatest effect on the act or on how actors and students would describe what is happening in Aida. This effect on the act is seen in Locke's next description:

> These 'half-discovered places' remain nameless and unformed. Aida asks Radames if he means her distant homeland Nubia, and he can only answer (this question and answer are spoken) 'Yes, in a way.' But singing of those vague Elsewheres has released stifled feelings. Like the captive Aida yet very differently from her, he suffers from the oppressiveness of imperial Egypt. Though his complaints are those of a person of privilege, he is hemmed in, constrained in his actions. Indeed, his life is at risk if he does not follow the dictates of his family, his government, and the religious authorities.[18]

In this description, Locke alters the scene-agent ratio just a bit. For Aida, Nubia is home and Nubia affects how Aida will act throughout the production. For Radames, Nubia is not home but is "not-Egypt." In the previous description, Radames's "visit" to Nubia affects his own motivations, but in this particular description, Radames is affected by the "not-Egypt," or the negative.

The scene-agent ratio is not the only ratio that Locke describes. He writes, "Overt representation—reflecting something outside the notes, in however faithful or distorted a manner—is a central feature of certain important Western classical music, notably opera, oratorio, and symphonic poem. Representation is central also to how music often, or even mainly functions in film, Broadway musical, and pop song."[19] In this description, Locke is moving from the scene-agent ratio, the effect that Nubia has on Radames, to the scene-agency ratio, or how the scene effects the genre. What is reflected "outside the notes" seems equivalent to Burke's dramatistic pentad, and that makes it a useful "extrinsic" tool to enable actors and directors to examine those extrinsic "representations" themselves. Here, the genre of film, Broadway musical, and pop song is affected by the kind of scene.

For Locke, the scenes can be real or imaginary, and this helps us understand the difference between Broadway's *Aida* and its attempt to represent a hedonistic Egypt, and our Jacksonville University *Aida*, with our attempt to "represent" as little as possible. Locke writes, "In my *Musical Exoticism* book, nearly all the works that I explored are ones that belong to the more or less overtly representational Western art-music genres mentioned above. They also have something more specific in common. What sets them apart from other works in the same genres is that they set out to reflect an identifiable—whether real or imaginary—place, people, or culture that the composer understands as being significantly different from home. These works construct an Elsewhere."[20] In our Jacksonville University version of Aida, there is no overt representation, since our sets are the same for Egypt and the same for Nubia. There is not "Egypt" or "Nubia," only an imaginary Egypt and an imaginary Nubia. Because both "Egypt" and "Nubia" are imaginary, the only "distant lands" are those of the imagination. The scene(ery) makes it easier for Radames to go against the wishes of his family, since there are literally no "chains" (or anything else for that matter) to keep him there.

Like Deer and Del Vera, Locke himself suggests what can be done, but offers little "method" to do so, especially for the student actor. Locke writes, "Whatever the process, the creator of an exotic musical work (or the creative team in, say, a stage work) achieves a vision, or a reflection, of a distant and different realm. He or she confides those visions to the page. Skillful, sensitive performers then convey the markings on the page—and the implications behind them—to generations of receptive listeners."[21] But if the performer is just conveying the "markings on the page" and those "implications," then the performer is not conveying the time and place of the character. More importantly, the character is not conveying the time and place of the actor portraying the character. Because both Egypt and Nubia are imaginary, the only distant lands are those of the imagination. More importantly, by using Burke's pentad, students were actually able to describe that particular process. These visions were not handed down to the students to achieve, but we were able to come up with them together throughout the dramatistic pentad process.

Now that we have considered the time and place of the production itself, what about the time and place for the actors? What if we have been only thinking about how the actor inhabits the life of the character, the magical "as if"? What if the character needs to consider the time and place of the actor? This is what we mean by Stanislavski's "Given Circumstances" as a trained incapacity. The focus is always on how the actor can inhabit the life of the character. This has prevented actors from thinking about how their character would inhabit their acting, specifically the *actor's* "Given Circumstances." Burke famously wrote in the *Rhetoric of Motives*, "But once we have a mature set of such abstract fixities, we can turn the matter around; and thus, whereas the philosophic expressions were later translations of earlier narrative ones, we may look upon narrative expressions as translations of philosophical ones."[22] What Burke means here is that Stanislavski's philosophical expression, the "as if" of the actor, is a translation of the narrative expression, the character's time and place. For Burke, the actor's time and place becomes a translation for the "as if" of the character. With that in mind, then, we will set off on how this can be accomplished utilizing the scene-agent pentad.

Act: Staging a performance of Elton John's *Aida* at a private, four-year college of fine arts
Scene: Jacksonville University, on the east bank of the St. Johns River, formerly owned by Anna Kingsley, former slave and plantation owner.
Agent: Students who are shocked at the results of the recent election.

In other words, the actors in *Aida* at Jacksonville University are different characters than the characters in *Aida* on Broadway, since *Aida* did not run on Broadway during the Trump administration. The actors in *Aida* at Jacksonville University are also different characters than the characters in *Aida*, even during the same circumstances as the Trump administration, since they are not at Jacksonville University, "on the east bank of the St. Johns River, formerly owned by Anna Kingsley, former slave and plantation owner." Burke writes, "The matter is obscured when we are dealing with scene in the sense of the relationships prevailing among the various dramatis personae. For the characters, by being in interaction, could be treated as scenic conditions or 'environment of one another'; and any act could be treated as part of the context that modifies (hence, to a degree motivates) the subsequent acts."[23] So, if we start experimenting with how characters in action, or "interaction," can be treated as scenic conditions, we might end up with something like this:

Act: Learning my role as Aida, a woman of color
Scene: 2018, Donald Trump's America, where people of color are not allowed to come into the country.
Agent: A woman of color

In this experiment, the scene has modified, and hence did in fact motivate, the actions of the character played by the agent in this particular case. Burke comments on how this is possible, "The principles of dramatic consistency would lead one to expect such cases of overlap among the terms; but while being aware of them we should firmly fix in our minds such cases as afford a clear differentiation.

Our terms lending themselves to both merger and division, we are here trying to divide two of them while recognizing their possibilities of merger."[24] For the actor playing Aida, her description of her scene was able to be divided from the character's "Given Circumstances," yet we can see how her description of her scene was able to "merge" together with her description of agency.

Again, the "Given Circumstances" can often limit rather than expand a student-actor's staging choices. While Deer and Dal Vera encourage actors to "research the original production," they do not give any direction on what student actors should do with this research. Should they copy it, or should they reject it? What will they find when they research the production history of *Aida*? According to Barry Singer in *Ever After: The Last Years of Musical Theater and Beyond*, "*Elaborate Lives* had no masks. A rock and roll retelling of opera's Aida story, it did have a multiracial cast of twenty-eight relative unknowns, a la, *Rent*, including a *Rent* alumna, Sherie Scott, as the pharaoh's daughter Amneris, and Heather Headley—Broadway's original Nala in *The Lion King*—as Aida, the Nubian slave whom Radames, Amneris's betrothed, loves and ultimately martyrs himself alongside."[25] For Deer and Dal Vera, this description might suggest with the use of the "multi-racial cast," that the staging should be emulated. If we are only considering the character's "Given Circumstance," then this staging would be "accurate," and that seems to be the "argument" of the set designers. However, if the character considers the actor's "Given Circumstance," through Burke's "scene ratio," then researching the original Broadway production of *Aida* gives us specific direction on how the sets should (not) be constructed: "*Aida* onstage was pure kitsch, intentionally punctured by anachronism that allowed for a runway fashion show, vogueing, and Ninja fighters in Pharaonic Egypt. The results were crude and frequently tasteless. But the show was fun for tourists, teens, and Elton John fans. Which was all that Disney could have asked for."[26]

As an academic director, Kimberly wanted a (much) different experience for the students altogether, and Burke's dramatism helped the students become involved in that different experience. Burke writes, "From a motivational point of view, there is implicit in the quality of a scene the quality of the action that is to take place within it. This would be another way of saying that the act will be consistent with the scene."[27] If the "scene" is "Egypt," then Singer's description of the Broadway set design is consistent with that interpretation. However, if we "turn the matter around," describing the scene as "Jacksonville University, a former slave plantation owned by Anna Kingsley," then the design perspective would be to reject the "kitsch" and "tastelessness" of the Broadway production as severely tone-deaf to the (slave) history of the place where our production occurred. The design team, therefore wanted to completely eliminate any kitsch or hyperbole involving Egyptian stereotypes, and we focused on how our theme of change could be "written into" the set. Burke writes the following:

Thus, when the curtain rises to disclose a given stage-set, this stage-set contains, simultaneously, implicitly, all that the narrative is to draw out a sequence, explicitly. Or if you will, the stage-set contains the action ambiguously (as regards the norms of action)—and in the course of the play's development this ambiguity is converted into a corresponding articulacy. The proportion would be: scene is to act as implicit is to explicit. One could not deduce the details of the action from the details of the setting, but one could deduce the details of the action from the quality of the setting.[28]

Burke's phrase, "the curtain rises," has more implications than may at first appear here; however, for right now, if Burke is correct, that when "the curtain rises… the stage-set contains the action ambiguously," then it would also be correct that if the curtain revealed *no stage set*, the curtains themselves would contain the action *explicitly*, rather than implicitly. The movement of the fabric curtains was an explicit articulation of the movement in space—Aida's movement from Nubia to Egypt, Ramades's ability to change his fate—and the movement in time—the ability of characters to go from the present day museum to ancient Egypt and back again. But because we incorporated the scene of where the production takes place, a university on land which was operated by slaveholders, the fabric curtains also articulated the awareness of our community's troubled participation in that history, as well.

This participation is precluded by adhering to Stanislavski's "Given Circumstances," for Deer and Dal Vera write, "Design elements not only entertain and support the story, but also help us to know something more about the characters' world and their experience."[29] By rejecting the kitsch and ostentatiousness of Broadway's Egypt, our curtains helped us know "something" about the actor's world and their experiences at Jacksonville University. That "something" focused our and the audience's attention on the moving, changing curtains as the only set pieces. The curtains also had the effect of directing the actors themselves. Deer and Dal Vera write the following:

> Earlier, we talked about the time pressure in *Brigadoon*. There is a necessary visual element in the script that tangibly expresses the approaching end of their day: fog. As Tommy fights to decide whether to stay in *Brigadoon* or return to his modern life, he knows his time is almost up because the stage begins filling with a low, rolling fog, and he must make a decision immediately. The actor in that role knows this will fuel his performance and he must react to it.[30]

In our production, there is also a "necessary visual element in the words that tangibly expresses the approaching shift in time": the fabric curtains. As Ramades "fights to decide whether to stay in [Egypt] or return to his modern life, he knows his time is almost up because the stage" sets change with the configuration of the fabric curtains to form the museum. For Deer and Del Vera, "That fog also adds an element of real danger for the actors in the chase scene from the same show. Running around scenery, leaping off rocks, throwing each other around in choreographed stage fights all becomes exponentially more complex with wet fog onstage,"[31] and curtains themselves created a similar effect, as actors interacted with the curtains by tying them off or pulling them up. This certainly was more complex for the actors, yet, in contrast to *Brigadoon*'s fog, the movement of our curtains was welcome to the *characters* as they signaled change and their own freedom of movement.

In the original Broadway production of *Aida*, the set designers seem to also utilize Stanislavski's relationship to the set: "The show would also have a pioneering laser-powered set that disdained conventional cables and pulleys in favor of theme-park technology devised by Disney's legendary Imagineering unit; the central element—a vast protean pyramid that deployed dizzyingly before finally entombing Radames and Aida forever."[32] In our production, there were no pyramids, taking the representations of Egypt out of our production. With no Egypt, there were no ties that would bind Ramades or Aida. With no Egypt, there also were no stereotypical racial representations based on the "Given Circumstances" of the characters. The racial stereotyping in *Aida* is one of the many problems with staging this production, and these problems have been well documented. Any student-actor "researching the production" will come across these critiques, perhaps most notably, Christal N. Temple's critique in "Broadway's *Aida*: Deconstructing the Spectacle of an Aggressive Popular Eurocentricism." Temple writes the following:

> In the opera-turned musical *Aida*, which ran for 1852 performances on Broadway—a fifty-four month run, ranging from March 23, 2000 to September 5, 2004, earning over 12 million in profits—the Egyptians are cast as white, and the Nubians are cast as predominately Black. Broadway and American media have sung the praises of the 'multicultural' cast of the show, only to shock Black consumers of the arts into realizing that the show is just another attack on foundations of Afrocentric enterprise, whose foundations of African anteriority with ancient Kennet at its foundation, defy the racial misrepresentations of the dichotomized white/Black Nubian staging.[33]

The results of Stanislavski's "Given Circumstances," when expertly followed, are a trained incapacity, and in this case, exacerbate the problems of an already problematic musical. In the absence of any other "perspective by incongruity" than "Given Circumstances," the directors actually multiplied racist representations of the set design with casting decisions. That was not even the end of the destructive nature of *Aida*'s "Given Circumstances," however. The music itself is based on racial stereotypes, as Temple writes, "By the time Broadway finished with its racialist Euro-American interpretation of Verdi's *Aida*, it was a cultural catastrophe because it was an already manipulated version of ancient Egypt now juxtaposed with an even more deliberate and aesthetically racist hierarchy. In Broadway's *Aida* the Egyptian conquerors are white 'rock and roll' singers while the Nubian 'slaves' are gospel and soul-singing Black characters."[34]

For our production, we wanted a completely different outcome, but in order to achieve this outcome, we needed a different perspective, a "perspective of incongruity," a description of the scene not from the "as if" of the character, but from the "as if" of the actor herself. Since Jacksonville University is not Broadway, we were not looking to entertain the tourist, but to educate both the student actors and the audience members of our historically African-American community. In order to do this, we needed to understand how that version of ancient Egypt and those racist hierarchies had been manipulated. Temple writes, "We, in studying Egyptology, are trying to take back what European history has stolen, completely falsified; to eras the new false identities it placed on the Afrikan Egyptian people."[35] What we needed was to research the false identities it placed on the Nubian people. We needed to turn to the Nubian archives.

The Archival Scene

While the Broadway production decided to feature a pyramid as its permanent scenic element, there are actually no pyramids in the script of *Aida*. Deer and Dal Vera write, "There are times where the script requires a scenic element. Tony and Maria must have a fire escape in *West Side Story* for their version of Romeo and Juliet's balcony scene. Huck and Jim spend about a third of their time in *Big River* on a raft."[36] While the Broadway production, with its focus on "Given Circumstance," utilized a pyramid, our production, with our focus on the scene of the actors themselves, did not. The scenic element that the script of *Aida* actually requires is a museum. Not just any museum, however, a museum of African art and its enclosed sarcophaguses. Since the action in *Aida* begins and ends in a museum of African artifacts, one can determine the kind of museum, or the kind of story the museum tells, based on the set design and casting of what happens in between the museum sets. Since the Broadway production emphasized racial stereotypes in its set design and casting, we can determine that the museum visited by the characters at the beginning and at the end was a Eurocentric telling of the Nubian story. However, what if the story we tell is a "taking back of what European history had stolen"? Would that not mean that the museum scene is itself different?

While the Oriental Institute at the University of Chicago is not necessarily an archive of civic action, when the Nubian collection is put "in motion," its artifacts can serve a civic purpose. In their article, "A Rhetorical Stance on the Archives of

Civic Action," Thomas P. Miller and Melody Bowden write, "A rhetorical stance on these issues can provide us with a historical context for assessing the technological and cultural changes that are transforming the public sphere and the literacies of citizenship. This critical understanding of our historical situation can help us to use archival research to achieve the civic potential that opens up as rhetoric expands its purview beyond the teaching of academic discourse."[37] As such, these archives are archives of civic action, and as archives of civic action, we can examine many of its features. First, we will examine how rhetoric in general and dramatism in particular can help us understand archives and their changing nature, and then we will discuss our research in the Nubian wing of the Oriental Institute at the University of Chicago. Finally, we will discuss how the durable nature of the archive can be altered when it is portrayed by using fabric curtains.

First, rhetoric in general and dramatism in particular can help us conceive of the archive as more than a repository of official, Eurocentric, narratives. Miller and Bowden write, "To move beyond the conservativism of the civic humanist tradition, our sense of civic must acknowledge [Jacqueline Jones] Royster's point that differences enrich a tradition by enabling it to imagine alternatives."[38] This is one of the reasons why we chose the Oriental Institute at the University of Chicago as a site for our research. Here, this Eurocentric narrative is made visible and the Nubian exhibits purport to serve as a countersite or counternarrative to those Eurocentric narratives.

According to the signage in the Nubian wing of the Oriental Institute, "Created for religious and state purposes, these portrayals accentuate Nubians as 'other' than Egyptians," the signage reads. This description illuminates the casting decisions of the Broadway production of *Aida,* so since our scene was different, we wanted to cast our production in a way consistent with these findings in the Oriental Institute. In Tarez Graban's "Decolonising the Transnational Archive," she writes the following: "Examining archives somewhat apart from postcolonial membership or belonging, allows rhetorical historians to recognize the multiple locations and dispersions of African women's liminalities, and to discover the range of their political positioning beyond that of insider or outsider."[39] This became important when casting the role of Aida, but also in how her character would be staged, as well, and we will get to that pentad momentarily. For now, we want to emphasize that rhetorical theory can help us understand the changeable narratives of the Nubian people. We also want to consider how Burke's dramatism in particular can help us understand the drama within the archives themselves.

So far in this chapter, we have considered the "scene of the characters" and the resulting Broadway production contrasted with the "scene of the actors" and the resulting production at Jacksonville University, a former plantation owned by

Anna Kingsley. Since the research for this particular production was conducted at the Oriental Institute at the University of Chicago, we would like to consider the "scene of the archive" and how these particular considerations informed our set design and staging. In their article, "Drama in the Archives: Rereading Methods, Rewriting History," Cheryl Glenn and Jessica Enoch write, "Within the archive (the scene), the researcher (agent) engages (agency) in a variety of recovery and recuperative practices (acts) directed toward a specific end (purpose). And the familiar ratio between those key pentadic terms (scene: act, scene: agent, agent: agency, and so on) provides purchase for an even closer examination."[40] In other words, if the scene is not Egypt or Jacksonville, Florida, but is instead the archives from where the research of the production could come from, then it is these archives which need to be described. Furthermore, when we begin with this scene, then we work towards understanding the act itself. For Burke, the act-scene ratio began the work of the dramatistic pentad. For Glenn and Enoch, the scene-act ratio concludes the work of the dramatistic pentad. The archive in this case is the Oriental Institute at the University of Chicago. This specific museum displays more Nubian artifacts than any other museum in the world. The Nubian wing was created by University of Chicago professor James Henry Breasted. According to Jeffery Abt in *American Egyptologist: The Life of James Henry Breasted and the Creation of His Oriental Institute*, "Breasted was not the first American to explore ancient Egypt. As America's first formally trained Egyptologist, Breasted stood apart from his contemporaries by virtue of his ability to read and translate hieroglyphics."[41] What is interesting to note here is that what separated Breasted from others was his focus on the language use of the Nubian and Egyptian people. What gave him a new perspective was an attenuation to the way that language itself revealed new understandings of their history and culture. This is significant for our application of Burke and dramatism to musical theater since according to Burke, "words move, they shimmer." While Breasted's explorations predate Burke's critical works, we see how Breasted's attenuation to the actual language of Nubia and Egypt could lead to a more contextually driven focus on Nubian culture than had been attempted before. Similarly, Burke's attention to the scene of language, the where and when the act occurred, also leads writers, actors, and agents into more socially conscious performances and dramatistic interpretations. Abt also writes, "Further, in his focus on systematically studying and recording hieroglyphic inscriptions for scholarly purposes, he separated himself from peers concentrating on excavations that were sponsored by individuals or museums mostly interested in developing collections."[42] In contrast to other researchers, Breasted realized the potential for scholarly investigation, rather than mere collecting or hording Nubian and Egyptian artifacts. For our purposes, we also acknowledge the importance of a scholarly attention to music theater production, and we believe that a study of rhetoric in general and Burke's dramatism in particular opens up new adventures for students and directors, in opposition with collegiate performances merely meant to be "crowd pleasers," or "money makers" for universities. To push these notions into performance practice, let's try to think this concept through, utilizing Burke's pentad:

Scene:	a decolonized archive of Nubian images
Agent:	a director set on decolonizing a production of a colonized Elton John's *Aida*
Agency:	conveying the archives of the Nubian exhibition to the student actors
Purpose:	get student actors beyond Stanislovsky's Given Circumstances
ACT:	creation of a heritage tour of the Nubian people at Jacksonville University, the place that needs a heritage tour

The location of Jacksonville University is in Duval County, Florida, and as such, the Duval county school board has jurisdiction over the content of the curriculum. In a recent 10th grade history book written for the Duval County schools, Joyce Appleby writes, "Free African Americans occupied ambiguous position in Southern society. In cities like Charleston and New Orleans, some were successful enough to become slaveholders themselves."[43] What we started to understand was that we were not staging a production of Elton John's *Aida*, we were creating a heritage tour of a misrepresented people in a location of another misrepresented people, such as the myth of the "entrepreneurs" who owned slaves. This narrative of slaveholding success is part of the official narrative of Anna Kingsley and her ownership of the plantation where Jacksonville University currently resides. Fortunately, heritage tourism, a conscious alternative to whitewashing over a region's racist past, is becoming a more prevalent method to introduce and maintain community relations. In their article, "Memories of Freedom and White Resilience: Place, Tourism, and Urban Slavery," Kristan Poirot and Shevaun E. Watson write, "As a quintessentially rhetorical process, 'learning' is not a neutral act and the narratives that people come to accept—narratives that are shaped by the practice of historical tourism—come to define the vexed relationships among city, region, and slavery."[44] What are some of these narratives that our own community has come to accept? Should these narratives be accepted? What are the narratives of the Arlington community, and specifically the property on which Jacksonville University resides? Should those narratives be accepted or should those narratives be critiqued? If they should be critiqued, then should they be highlighted to others, in a kind of "heritage tour"?

Jacksonville University recently installed two plaques near the university entrance detailing the complicated past of the land it now occupies. For our purposes here, we will describe these plaques as "durable" narratives. Jason Farman writes, "Those with economic wealth and political clout tend to be the ones who are able to place durable inscriptions throughout a city. They can afford the statue of a particular war hero or politician, linking the life of this figure to the place where the statue is located."[45]

Based on accounts from Daniel Schafer's *Anna Madgigine Jai Kingsley: African Princess, Florida Slave, Plantation Slaveowner*, the plaques "durable" accounts detail the property's history of slavery:

> From 1847 until sometime before 1860, Jacksonville University campus was the site of the Chesterfield farm of Anna Madgigine Jai Kingsley, former slave and widow of white plantation owner Zephaniah Kingsley. This farm was the center of a rural free African American community unlike any other in northeast Florida. In an area stretching from the Arlington River on the south to Reddy's Point on the north, lived more than seventy free black Americans in fifteen households of white, black, and mixed-race adults and children. Only in the towns of St. Augustine and Pensacola, both once colonial capitals under Spanish governance, could free black communities be found with numbers comparable to those in this Duval County enclave.

While it is true that the land which Jacksonville University occupies was once the center of a free African-American community prior to the Civil War, it is also true that Anna Kingsley owned 15 slaves to maintain the property on which these free African Americans lived and worked. Has Anna Kingsley's narrative contributed to Joyce Appleby's description in the tenth grade Duval County history book of "successful" African Americans who owned slaves? According to Schafer, the reason that they could own slaves in the first place was that many of them had rights to property, and since Anna Kingsley owned the property that Jacksonville University would later occupy, she was allowed to own human beings on that same property. The plaques at the entrance also include the following qualified justification for discrimination after the end of the Civil War:

> The Civil War brought an end to slavery and the large plantations that relied on slave labor. In the succeeding decades up until the Civil Rights movement of the 1960's, the community would adopt the segregated social practices of the South. But at one time this location on the eastern shore of the St. Johns River was a unique place where white, black, and mixed-race families lived and worked in harmony.

While Joyce Appleby's description of slavery in the 10th grade Duval County history textbook ignores the violence, rape, beating, and murder of slavery's past, this phrase, "the community would adopt the segregated social practices of the South" also conceals the violence, rape, beating, and lynching of African American's on the very soil our students and faculty walk as they go to class, to sporting events, and even to the theater.

Poirot and Watson write, "Fully imbricated in the discursive and material transformation of the locale into a tourist destination then, these memories direct attention to tourism's relationship to contemporary practices of public remembering."[46] By staging our production of *Aida* from the perspective of the scene itself, our production of *Aida* was more similar to a heritage tour of our institutional memory than the Manhattan tourist attraction of the Broadway production.

The second plaque at the entrance to Jacksonville University describes the life and times of Anna Kingsley herself, and as a part of the public remembering in our university's place, constituted some correlations to Aida's story, as well. The second plaque reads:

> In 1806, Anna Madgigine, Jai, a 13-year old girl of royal lineage in Senegal, West Africa was sold into slavery and brought to the port of Havana, Cuba. There she was purchased by a 38-year old Zephaniah Kingsley, a wealthy white plantation owner, ship owner and captain, and slave trader. Kingsley took Anna as his wife.
>
> Kingsley took Anna to his Laurel Grove plantation located near present-day Orange Park where she managed his household and assisted with the management of his plantation. On March 4, 1811, Kingsley formally emancipated Anna and their three young children, George, Martha, and Mary. Within a year after gaining her freedom, Anna established her own homestead across the St. Johns River in what is now Mandarin and became the owner of twelve slaves.

So, if you remember our *Aida* pentad from a bit ago, it went something like this:

Act:	Learning my role as Aida, a woman of color
Scene:	2018, Donald Trump's America, where people of color are not allowed to come into the country.
Agent:	A woman of color

However, once we introduce the previous durable narrative of Anna Kingsley into our production, Aida's pentad went something like this:

Act:	Learning my role as Aida, kidnapped and taken into slavery by a wealthy slaveowner
Scene:	Jacksonville University, former plantation owned by slaveholders Zephaniah and Anna Kingsley, Anna a former African princess turned slave, turned leader of her people.
Agent:	A woman playing an African princess on the location of property owned by an African princess turned slave, turned leader of her people.

Tarez Graben writes that "African women premiers occupy ironic outgroups, implied in the discourse but not discursively dominant, and thus becoming historicized neither in the pace of the national nor in the space of the foreigner, but in a third space that operates in tension with dominant discourses."[47] Clearly, this can be seen in the descriptions of Anna Kingsley inscribed on plaques just inside the entrance to Jacksonville University, "In 1847, Anna purchased a 22-acre farm located on the St. Johns River between the homes of her daughters, now owned by Jacksonville University. Her farm, known as Chesterfield, was tended by her 15 slaves." In this inscription, Anna is not a nationalized figure, nor is she a foreigner; according to the dominant discourses, she purchased a farm [that happened to be?] "tended by 15 slaves." For the actors portraying Aida, describing the emotions of having been an African princess was only the first step. Later in the musical, the actors portraying Aida must account with the fact that Aida allows her own servant to give his life for her, allows her own maid to give up her life for Aida's. While the durable narrative of Anna Kingsley lives on just outside the doors of our theater, the durable narrative of Anna Kingsley's slaves is nowhere to be found. Furthermore, the plaque's durable narrative describes Anna's "courage" in fighting off those who would "sell her and her own slaves" into slavery:

> Anna's courage and resourcefulness is evident in 1813 during the Patriot Rebellion. To prevent herself, her children and her slaves from being seized and sold back into slavery by marauding Patriot raiders, she arranged with a Spanish gunboat captain to provide safe passage to Ft. San Nicolas on the south bank of the St. Johns River. She then set fire to her homestead and Laurel Grove to prevent their use by the Patriots. In 1814 Anna, Zephaniah, and their children sailed to their new home on Ft. Georgia Island. There a fourth child, John Maxwell would be born.

Anna is to be admired for keeping her own slaves protected from being enslaved by someone else. This durable narrative, just outside the doors of our university theater, is one of the most significant descriptions of our actors' scenes. For the actors portraying Aida, their pentad descriptions of their own scene and how they themselves would move from "African princesses to slave to respected slave owners" demonstrated the limitations of Stanislavski's "Given Circumstances," but also the limitations of the durable narratives in these same places at very different times. But in order to remember these specific places in Jacksonville's slave history differently than the official durable narratives, we had to put these public memories in motion.

Archives in Motion

We have already mentioned that like Huck's raft in *Big River*, the museum is the only required set piece in *Aida*, and like the fog in *Brigadoon*, the museum represents the change from the present to the past, then again at the end from the past back to the present. In this sense, the museum or archive is in motion, that is to say, the museum or archive is what moves the audience from the present to the past and from the past back into the present. Carolyn Steedman describes this phenomenon in archival methodology in the following way: Certainly, the ways of reading that you are forced into in an archive have something to do with the dislocations of time the epistolary stands in for"[48], and while Kimberly has utilized archival material in many of her shows, bringing back copies of some of these images and having these students in this production of *Aida* read these documents from the Oriental Institute had the specific effect of helping them appreciate that sense of time travel which Steedman describes and the changing museum scenes in *Aida* require. Jeffery Abt records Breasted's own descriptions of this phenomenon during his own 1906 expedition:

> On 24 February, after five weeks, the recording at Abu Simbel [Nubia] as completed. Of the labors there Breasted wrote, "None of our party will ever lose the impressions gained…under the shadow of the marvelous sun-temple. In storm and sunshine, by moonlight and in the golden dawn, in twilight and in midnight darkness, the vast colossi of Ramses had looked out across the river, with the same impassive gaze and the same inscrutable smile…What are the privations of travel, and prolonged separation from family and friends if they allow the creation of records preserving for another thousand years, such matchless wonder![49]

In order to demonstrate this dislocation of time, we needed to put the archives in motion. In the Broadway production, the presence of the pyramid constituted a "durable" inscription, the official narrative by the powerful will not change. If we want to demonstrate the changing nature of an archive, then how can that be portrayed on stage as a set piece? The official stage directions from *Aida*'s script provide some insight into its authorial intent:

> In the Egyptian Wing of a major museum, we find a group of contemporary museumgoers admiring artifacts of a time long ago. The crowd is gathered around the most mysterious of the objects; an ancient burial chamber. *Aida* opens in the present day, and then, as if a dream, dissolves back to ancient times and ancient lands for the telling of the story proper.[50]

If we apply Robert Falls's description to our particular production of Aida, then, our opening set piece would look something like the office stone architecture of the Oriental Institute. In so doing, we would be intensifying the traditional wisdom of the permanence of the archive, as Jeremy Tirrell writes, "The notion of an archive is predicated on a form of stability, wherein stored things remain static. Retrieved memories are verified through comparison to an objective standard of what actually happened."[51] As we have been detailing throughout this chapter, this was not the vision we wanted or needed to have for our descriptions of our times and places, Burke's scene-act ratios. The director's notes for *Aida* seem to also be in line with our own objectives, but on closer examination, we can identify some of the places "where ambiguities necessarily arise," as Burke writes. After the curtain rises on the museum:

> The episodes illuminated thereafter may take place in very specific locales—a banquet room, the banks of the Nile, a map room, a prison cell—or in places of the mind, of the heart; abstract, private environments shared only by a character and an audience. The scenes dissolve freely one to the other, moving the story forward with the fluidity, and inevitability, of a dream – until we are "awakened" into the hard light of the present day at the curtain. Any production of *Aida* will depend, for its emotional impact, on this sense of being drawn back ceaselessly into the past, of the conscious and subconscious, of duty's weight on desire, of passion's play on power.

While Fall's use of the word "dissolve" describes the importance of the set on the desired impact on the audience, our use of the voile as it morphs from one position to another, works as an intensifier of that impact. What was originally seen as a limitation now intensified duty's weight on the desire, it intensified passion's play on power, as Fall describes. Rather than intensifying the power of a stable archive, the fabric curtains dissolve that permanence itself. Tirrell describes this process, "Memory cannot be a process of fixed storage and retrieval; it is always a new assemblage in a present moment."[52] To design the dissolving museum scenes, we utilized the voile drapery as a sort of scrim, and we adjusted the opaqueness depending on how much backlight we used. We opted for sidelights, which along with the fog machine, set up the transition from the present to the past in an ethereal, otherworldly way.

To start the show, Amneris is pre-set center stage with extras milling around upstage of the scrim as if they are browsing through a museum. The movements are pantomimed except for the actors playing Radames and Aida, who are just a man and a woman we do not yet know, while we realize Amneris has "come to life." The juxtaposition of modern-day people engaging with a singing statue in a museum is enough to suspend reality, while sixteen bars of music are enough time to pull the drapery aside, revealing Amneris as she begins to sing "Every story, tale or memoir, every saga or romance…" Once we transition fully into bright light and the curtains are drawn into sails, we are transported to the ship that has captured Aida and the story commences. However, in this brief introduction, we have met the players in the love triangle that will take us on our Nubian journey.

As at the start of the show, the story also ends in the museum. This time we know it is Radames and Aida. In order to transition from the tomb scene back to the museum, Kimberly created the following directions for the stagehands to move the curtains:

Scene	Cue	Voile/Curtains
Scene 10: TOMB	End of Elaborate Lives Reprise	Midstage in most of the way
	Guards exit	Midstage closed
Epilogue	m.41	Black upstage out Upstage voile in Untie upstage voile Fly upstage up and back in
	Reign of peace…	Midstage out
	End of music	Grand in

Figure 2.3. Amneris in the museum. Photo credit: Andrew Brantley Carroll

At the point the midstage is taken out, actors are in place and the voile has returned to top of show positioning, flown out then back in to allow it to drape just perfectly on the floor of the stage. By returning the curtains to their original top of show positioning, we were able to intensify Steedman's "dislocations of time" that occurs when reading in an archive. In other words, we were able to uncover and present the drama in the archives. As Cheryl Glenn and Jessica Enoch write, "Any drama in the archives must account for both the means and purpose the researcher employs to achieve an end. Archival records may be, as Connors writes, an inert duty mass of past records, but they are real sources of data, inert until they are animated by the researcher himself or herself, who is another, equally 'real' sources of data."[53] By animating the durable inscription of the Oriental Institute and portraying it on set with moving curtains, our production began to reject the "official" narratives of the durable archive, both in Fall's museum and the official durable narratives of the Afrikan experience on our campus. Farman writes, "In contrast [to durable inscriptions], graffiti functions similarly to tell a story or life of a place but tends to be done by those without the power or political clout to create durable inscriptions. These inscriptions often serve to stand in opposition to the legal and 'authorized' ways of storytelling about a place."[54] By taking on characteristics of an "ephemeral" narrative, our production engaged in the "memory work" of creating a "new assemblage" in our university and our country's own "present moment."

Utilizing the pentad in conjunction with the archival materials from the Oriental Institute introduces the student actor to rhetorical analysis combined with primary sources research methods. According to Glenn and Enoch, "The drama in the archives is an ongoing one—much to our delight. Each new generation of rhetoric and composition scholars invigorates the archival drama by producing a version of history that in turn, prompts new questions and concerns about the historiographic process and product."[55] Not only do students learn new methodologies, however. One of the more important findings of Glenn and Enoch's research is the how "A concerted attention to the act of choosing archival documents and locations (scenes) can enrich our sense of the kind of texts that can contribute to our historical understandings as well as the places where these texts might be found,"[56] and that certainly was the case with utilizing the archives of the Oriental Institute. When students began their table work, they had no idea that they would be working beyond their character's "Given Circumstances" to include the creation of their own historiography through the archival research from the Oriental Institute. By putting these archives in motion, as well, the students began to feel the importance of understanding their own place in history. They were not part of a production; they were part of the historical record of their character, the members of James Breasted's expeditions, even former residents of the Arlington community itself, such as Anna Kingsley and her slaves. This happens because as Enoch finds, "A greater consciousness of the agents in the archive can prompt us to initiate better networks among scholars and to collaborate with archivists as a means to broaden our historiographic vision and deepen our knowledge of what an archive is and can be."[57] Kimberly began these pentad with herself as the agent, but as the pentad grew, the students portraying Aida and Amneris as agents began to find their place in the history of Jacksonville University as a "distant land" itself.

What is especially understood, near the close of this chapter, is the continued interplay between the scene and the agent, this drama in the archives. While it is often difficult to pin down where one ratio ends and the other begins, Enoch describes the importance of this metaphor in this way:

> "For us this metaphor has been most powerful in its quiet reminder that the ratios of the pentad shift and overlap; their tensions inevitably weaken and collapse before rising again in a different iteration. Despite our attempts to keep the ratios separate, such categories always overlap and sometimes leak. Such leakage reminds us that any categories or ratios that we have set out continue to be sites of theoretical struggle."[58]

The scene-agent ratio is one of the most complicated ratios, and maybe that's why Burke wrote about its power and potential so often. We hope you will enjoy the specific scene work for *Aida* before we move onto the Agent ratio in the next chapter.

Director's Notes

Why This Show

Aida, the Musical, provided the students with what they thought was a historical time period in which to explore "exotic" places and "exotic" characters. I myself have always loved the exoticism of Egypt, pyramids, and Cleopatra, so before utilizing the pentad in our table work, I had no preconceived notions of how we would tell this story. I had no experience with this musical prior to directing it. I knew of some of the songs because they were written by Elton John and I had taught them in the voice studio. I was also familiar with the Verdi opera, *Aida*, having sung "Ritorna Vincitor" (Return, victor!) on a recital a couple of times as well as seeing the production at the Metropolitan Opera. While I was familiar with Kenneth Burke's "trained incapacity," my obsession with Egypt and the story of Aida had become just that, and it would not be until we had completed our pentad work with the Oriental Institute archives that I would understand how our use of the fabric curtains would become a "perspective by incongruity," leading to our all "earning our increment."

Variables

Unlike *Little Women*, *Aida, the Musical*, is definitely a "strong female lead" show, Aida appearing in almost every scene. I had the privilege of working with two fantastic Aida's for this production, each one bringing a unique vocal, and acting presence to the show. Double casting is a challenge, but operating under a casting policy that requires students to have opportunities as a lead in a show before they graduate sometimes demands you take advantage of it, especially in the case of ethnic shows, or leading men. If you have two talented students that can fill those roles, by all means double cast! It can actually be a good experience for the students as they work together and make choices that are unique and different for the same character. Having two different actors who brought their own scene-act ratios to the table made for some lively table work, to say the least.

What added an interesting twist was that due to scheduling issues with other productions in the season, we had decided to run the straight play and the musical in repertory. However, our shop at JU is not big enough to house work on two sets. While this show was not the recipient of any awards or nominations, I was very proud of how we utilized our university's resources by performing this musical in rep with the play. As discussed, we decided to go with a soft set, buying 150 yards of neutral colored voile that we draped from the overhead lines. Avoiding Broadway kitsch, we couldn't and did not build a pyramid on stage. The curtains of voile hung from the ceiling, draped and arranged in various positions, along with intricate lighting design and the use of fog, intensified the ethereal, otherworldly aesthetic, as we have previously discussed.

Table Work

I utilized theme work, objectives, and beats as a foundation for this show. However, my pentad work became part of the table work with the students, not just something I used as a director in my own subtext of my notes. We began by utilizing the archival pictures and research I had done in the Nubian Gallery at the Oriental Institute, and then started planning pentad plan charts for each scene. With double casting of Aida and Amneris in place, as well as letting the covers for each role weigh in, we had plenty of ideas thrown about the room and individual reactions to each aspect of the pentad for each scene, factored along with their objective work. This is where objective and beat work can really become vibrant. As an actor decides that their objective is to attain whatever thing, and they decide how they will do it, any part of the pentad can play an antagonist or protagonist to that desire. Does the scene hinder or help? How does the set hinder or help? Does the act of another actor on stage aid you or stop you? How do you feel about being hindered or helped—by the scene, by the set, by the act, by the agent? Does the purpose of that scene's event leave you ahead or behind? When it was revealed to the cast that their set would be a series of curtains that morphed into different arrangements, this brought another level of deliberation to how the set might motivate the scene. Once deciding that the *scene* of the scene was going to be our theme and relayed this to the actors, they could explore how that affected their objective, their act, and how they wanted to achieve it—but they could also choose other aspects of the pentad in addition to the scene-act ratio.

The Pentad as a Theme

At the point of directing this show, my work with pentad was getting more deliberate. Working with the variable of the historical time period, and one that needed to be conveyed with fabric, provided me with the idea to use the scene as the theme for this production, and we collaboratively wove the scene ratio into our theme for the show: "The story of *Aida* teaches us that while love is not always an easy choice and often requires sacrifice, it is forever—transcending time and place."

In *Aida*, the scene of the museum bookends the show, much like the three women bookend *Street Scene*—which we will discuss in the next chapter. Both *Aida* and *Street Scene* are suitable for this compositional technique in that they both relay a time period in history. The word "history" is from the Greek word "historia" meaning "finding out." The significance of starting and ending a show the same way is that the visual and aural repetition contains the action of what we just saw and heard, just like the cover of a book. It commands a focus on the story as told—nothing open ended and no remaining questions as you leave the theater. We can watch and listen to that time period come alive through these characters and this story, relaxing in the fact that all we are expected to discover will be revealed to us in a single evening.

As the curtain rises on *Aida*, all but Amneris are in street clothing, wandering behind the voile curtains draping and hanging 25 feet from the ceiling, pantomiming looking at statues and relics. Amneris is dressed in full Egyptian costume and headdress, motionless center stage. A fog machine offstage supplies billows of white mist that adds to our imagination and what we will find out. The only stage direction to the actors is not to cross in front of Amneris; otherwise, the stage is theirs. Amneris remains center stage as she sings the Prologue, and as the museum goers disperse, we are immediately transported to Egypt and the River Nile on the lyrics "This is the story."

Many times as actors, we don't feel we have a choice about the music. It is a character we can only react to—it cannot react to us. In that sense, we can relate to the music the way we relate to that actor that doesn't give us much to work with, but perhaps it actually can. Remember that for Burke, literature worked with our "psychology of information," while music works with our "psychology of form." However, working within a pentad system of scene analysis, music is that sixth element that overarches the other five. We can choose to work with it or against it. As Ostwald states in *Acting for Singers*, it isn't whether an acting choice is right or wrong, but rather whether or not it is effective or ineffective. In considering the style of the music in this opening and ending museum scene, we have a theme in a major key that is unadorned and simple. But if you think about being in a museum, objects are displayed in a way so as not to detract from their significance. They stand alone in cases or on pedestals, lit with just the right amount of light. Some museums are noisy, but most, like the Oriental Institute at the University of Chicago, where I went to view installations of ancient Egyptian culture in research for this show, are quiet and contemplative. In this case, I chose to work with the music as a protagonist, letting everything else in the pentad compliment this character:

- Act—storytelling
- Scene—museum
- Agent—Amneris
- Agency—time travel
- Purpose—love is a story worth telling

Since the movement of the curtains tells the story of Aida through time travel, too much motion by the actors on the stage in this scene would detract from the movement of curtains. While the scene is in motion, the agents retain a stillness emoted in the music, and our sense of "finding out" is strengthened by this parallel. Since the first scene of the musical begins in the museum, it was this pentad which became our "perspective by incongruity," helping us learn how to interpret the entire show, helping us learn how to "earn our increment."

The notes that directors give about scene changes and set changes can often be sterile and for the sake of avoiding traffic jams. However, the Scene being the pentad theme allowed actors to react to those set and scene changes in character, moving in conjunction with everything else that is moving. Some notes I gave during rehearsals:

Top of Show/ Museum	ALL	Actors, the fabric set around you is very grand and spacious—you have to seem as large as your surroundings with your stage presence.
Scene 2	ALL	Actors, please move this scene more stage right. We are implying a small space with the light we are using.

Top of Show/ Museum	ALL	Actors, the fabric set around you is very grand and spacious—you have to seem as large as your surroundings with your stage presence.
Scene 3	Nehebka	Strike basin as the scene changes on the text "The Future." Let the scene change start, and then you are part of it.

Slow Moving Act I, Fast Moving Act II

The entirety of Act I is the introduction of each of the major players in very different, unique settings. My focus as a director on each of those introductions allowed for a simple, central placement of the primary character, in which the additional characters react to the scene around them, the curtains moving and morphing into different shapes, forming translucent boundaries, knowing the primary actor was going to stay stationary at center stage amidst that motion. We meet Aida and Radames followed by Zoser, Mereb, Amneris, and Pharaoh. As we work through the locations in Act I, we go from the museum to the boat, Radames's quarters to the docks, inside the palace to Amneris's baths, the dining hall to the slave camp, the river to the marketplace. Secondarily to the theme of scene for the show, establishing the AGENTS, each main character as they are introduced, as scene leaders meant staging them in the center, establishing more of a scene-agent ratio. Other actors recognize that parameter and move accordingly around the leader, utilizing the rest of the stage.

- Ship—Aida
- Ship's quarters—Radames
- The Docks—Zoser
- Hallway—Mereb
- Baths—Amneris
- Banquet—Pharaoh

Act II on the other hand, develops the relationships and the stories behind each main character. If anything, the Act becomes the secondary leader to the theme of scene in Act II, a strong example of the scene-act ratio. In Act II, at the point where all of characters are introduced and these places are revisited, there is a focus on other aspects of the pentad because we know these characters and have seen these locations before. What happens in each of these locations, or the act, becomes much more central for the cast as opposed to their surroundings. New locales in Act II include the prison scene and the judgment hall/tomb scene, befitting of the plot turning actions of planning to escape and the failure of that plan. The acts in these scenes placed the actors' center stage, using very little movement, and only their reaction to their plans and their surroundings—fear, darkness, and the feeling of insignificance, made palpable with the use of a single area of downlight amidst a dark stage.

SCENE	CUE	NOTES	VOILE
Scene 9: judgement hall	Judgement music begins	Black out	Black upstage in Stage left drapes, ties, and lifts
	m. 11 of music	Lights in	
Prison	The Daughter of Isis has spoken	Gradual change to prison gobo	
Scene 10: tomb	End of elaborate lives reprise	Lose upstage Shaft of light center in front of midstage	Midstage in most of the way
	Guards exit		Close midstage
	End of Enchantment reprise	Fade to black 2 bars of music	
Epilogue	m. 41	Tomb light returns	Upstage black out Upstage voile in like top of show
	Reign of peace...		Midstage open
	End of music	Fade to black	Grand in

Scene by Scene

The Baths

We first met Amneris in the museum as a member of the archive. That we are introduced to her as a member of the story in her baths with her ladies in waiting is integral to our understanding of how we should understand her as a narrator.

- Act: getting ready
- Scene: the baths

- Agent: Amneris
- Agency: lots of servants
- Purpose: appearance

My actress who played Amneris saw her objective as "maintaining control." How better to imply that than needing so many people around you that you can easily control. As we progress through the show, we gradually see the effect of Aida and Radames' love for each other penetrate her consciousness, and she becomes increasingly aware that that is something she cannot control. So she turns to her position over her servants and sings "My Strongest Suit" to reaffirm that control. As she orders them to "bring me all my finest" she uses Agency (her servants) as having the greatest effect on the Act. This scene was of course choreographed as a dance number, Amneris maintaining center stage almost exclusively throughout. This position of her on the stage reinforces Agent, although it is easy to see how through movement and placement on the stage, any element of the pentad can be highlighted.

Amneris's Bedroom

This scene is engaging when staged to display the suffocation that Radames is feeling from Amneris's emotions. The pentad for this scene was potentially complicated and had several potential options.

- Act—Amneris seduces Radames
- Scene—Amneris's bedroom
- Agent—Amneris
- Agency—Using Aida to prepare her
- Purpose—reign in Radames/send a message to Aida/convince herself she still has it

Aida and Radames have just had a moment during the song "Enchantment Passing Through." There is definitely a connection and Radames goes so far as to say that he feels chained by the engagement to Amneris. After the scene change to the bedroom, Aida brushes Amneris's hair while she reprises "My Strongest Suit," revealing that she understands the shallowness of her persona. The two are center stage as Radames enters from stage right. This immediately places Aida in the middle between Amneris and Radames. To add to the tension, I had Aida exit to retrieve the glass of wine, from stage right where she had entered. She has to pass Radames in order to leave, allowing them to make eye contact away from Amneris.

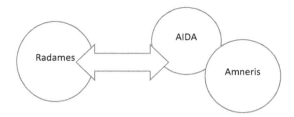

Once Aida returns, Radames is now the one stuck in the middle, between the two women. Amneris exits upstage left behind the voile, getting ready for Radames to come to bed with her. We can see her through the curtain as well as hear her as she repeatedly calls to him during his conversation with Aida downstage. The voile was especially effective here as we could still see Amneris through the fabric. Although upstage and partially concealed, the audience can't help but maintain their focus on her, reinforcing every element of the pentad.

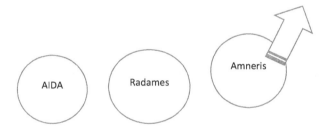

Once Amneris does appear, she now takes the middle spot between Radames and Aida. This is a significant moment, since for me this was the "representative anecdote" for the musical itself. In her discussion of metonymic agency, Graben writes, "The act of coming alongside the other encourages reflection on the possibilities of historicizing women's performances apart from postcolonial metaphors, so as to be more inclusive of their narratives without trying to make them cohere."[59]

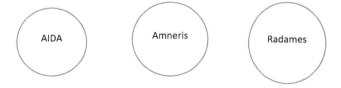

This is the first time that Amneris "comes along the side of" Aida, and as we know, it won't be the last. Since Aida is not Aida's story, but Amneris's story about Aida, our staging of Amneris "along side of" Aida allows her to tell Aida's story in all its complexity. While this staging allows each character to spend several lines of the scene in the middle, it not only visualizes the love triangle that dominates this story, but it also establishes Amneris as a reliable narrator to Aida's story. Graben writes the following:

> West African and Sub-Saharan women in the premier role have historically occupied a liminal position between insider and outsider. This occupation, in turn, creates a dualistic tension between what several comparative scholars have acknowledged as the emic—the ability to study African women's rhetorical practices from within their own social group—and the etic—the need to trust a dominant rhetorical observer from outside their social group.[60]

By positioning Amneris between an emic observer from her own social group, Radames, and between an etic observer from outside her social group, the audience feels the need to trust her rhetorical veracity in the telling of Aida's story.

The Prison

In Scene 2 of Act 2, we have just exited the scene and song "Step Too Far" where the three main characters are in a state of questioning where they stand currently and where they are headed in this love triangle. Using nothing but gobos in down-light patterns, each character steps into the pool of light to sing. The scene quickly changes to the prison.

- Act—plan an escape
- Scene—prison
- Agent—Amonasro
- Agency—Aida
- Purpose—freedom

Amonasro is center stage in a pool of dim light. Aida and Mereb enter with a guard upstage left and run to Amonasro, joining him in the pool of light. The conversation with him establishes the escape plan as well as Amonasro's disapproval of Aida's affection for Radames. The scene changes as Amonasro and Mereb are darkened in order to exit, leaving Aida in the only pool of light. We return to a state of time that is holding still, much like this act begins. I chose to choreograph this number using some of the Nubian slaves as dancers, evoking with their movements what Aida is expressing

Although we are in a sort of median place in terms of Scene, keeping Aida center stage while the dancers surround her reinforces the feeling of entrapment for Aida, playing directly against the purpose of the previous scene. The dancers are moving freely while Aida is stationary. We used a traditional starscape for the back-drop for this scene as well as several others throughout the show anytime we were suspended in time and space. Neutral locations, a sort of non-focus on Scene allow for optimal focus on Agent and other elements of the pentad. You may wonder how Act, Scene, Agent, Agency, and Purpose play in to all these elaborate technical elements. What if these technical elements could possibly inspire great acting? That the actors are given only a pool of light 4 feet in circumference in which to work means that the development and enactment of the pentad is forced to happen in a small space, all the more revealing the necessity of options for the actor in which to choose to work. The embodiment of those choices is expressed in the voice and in gesture, movement about the stage being limited by the scene created.

The Tomb

Following the Judgment Hall scene where Amneris petitions her father to allow the prisoners to die together, Radames and Aida are left to their fate. This was an exercise in moving parts to transition from the hall to the tomb. The upstage black comes in allowing the upstage voile behind it to fly. Using the midstage traveler, I created a passageway between the upstage and midstage blacks. In this case, the actors could choose an Act–Scene ratio for motivation—that this is the end of their lives as they know it, or the Scene-Purpose—that they are sacrificing this life together for perhaps a meeting in the afterworld.

- Act—death
- Scene—tomb
- Agent—Amneris
- Agency—buried alive
- Purpose—punishment/sacrifice

Once "Elaborate Lives (Reprise)" is finished, the midstage comes in almost to center, concealing Aida and Radames. Two guards enter from either side and lead Aida and Radames through the opening created by the midstage traveler. We very obviously get the sense that we are coming from a larger space into a smaller space. Once the guards exit, the midstage closes all the way. The only light is a down pool—familiar from the earlier prison scene, but more upstage. As "Enchantment Passing Through (Reprise)" is sung, the concealed upstage voile is flown in preparation for our return to the museum. When Aida expresses her fear in the darkness of the tomb, Radames comforts her, assuring her they will meet again, that he will search for her.

Figure 2.4. Aida and Radames. Photo Credit: Kimberly Beasley

Return to the Museum

As an example of Burke's "conventional form," we again visit the museum. Burke writes that conventional form establishes the kind of expectations "which an audience brings to the theatre as an established institution,"[61] and the museum, as that established institution, signals the ending of the drama. The tomb scene has just concluded a blackout on Aida and Radames after watching them slowly accept their fate, standing closely facing each other in a pool of downlight that confines them to no more than 4 feet of circumference. A swift exit by Aida and Radames in the dark finds Amneris in the same blackout spot before the light slowly comes back up and we are again in the museum. The midstage traveler, pulled in for the tomb scene, gradually is withdrawn to reveal the voile and the museumgoers.

Amneris's liminality, her in-betweenness, once established in the bedroom scene, has now come full circle. Graben writes that the liminality given to African women premiers "requires that rhetorical historians measure women's influence, not by reconstructing their performances into coherent memory events, but by

Figure 2.5. Aida Dancer. Photo Credit: Andrew Brantley Carroll

tracing the diffusion of their ideas and identifications across boundaries and differences. As a result, women leaders in these regions have effectively become a discursive third agent."[62] As before, Amneris acts as this third agent, as we recognize Aida and Radames among the museum visitors. Again, Amneris remains center stage and allows Aida and Radames to find her and thus each other, the "diffusion" of their "ideas and identifications across boundaries and difference." This happens just before a final blackout, with the mist of fog still lingering in the air.

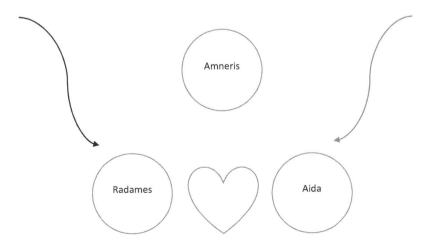

Notes

1 Kenneth Burke, *A Grammar of Motives* (Berkeley: University of California Press, 1945), 129.

2 Linda Brodkey, "Modernism and the Scene(s) of Writing," *College English* 49, no. 4 (1987): 400.

3 Ibid., 401.

4 Cynthia Sheard, "Kairos and Kenneth Burke's Psychology of Political and Social Communication," *College English* 55, no. 3 (1993): 306.

5 Ibid.

6 Ibid.

7 Ibid.

8 David Ostwald, *Acting for Singers* (Oxford: Oxford University Press, 2005), 28.

9 Ibid.

10 Joe Deer and Rocco Dal Vera, *Acting in Musical Theatre: A Comprehensive Course* (New York: Routledge, 2008), 247–248.

11 Cynthia Sheard, "Kairos and Kenneth Burke's Psychology of Political and Social Communication," *College English* 55, no. 3 (1993): 306.

12 Joe Deer and Rocco Dal Vera, *Acting in Musical Theatre: A Comprehensive Course* (New York: Routledge, 2008), 128–129.

13 Ibid., 129.

14 Debra Hawhee, *Moving Bodies: Kenneth Burke at the Edges of Language* (Columbia: University of South Carolina Press, 2009), 5.

15 Kenneth Burke, "Musical Chronicle," *Dial* 86 (June 1929): 537.

16 Joe Deer and Rocco Dal Vera, *Acting in Musical Theatre: A Comprehensive Course* (New York: Routledge, 2008), 128.

17 Ralph Locke, "On Exoticism: Western Art Music and the Words We Use," *Archiv fur Musickwissenshaft* 69 (2012): 222.

18 Ibid.

19 Ibid., 322–323.

20 Ibid., 323.

21 Ibid.

22 Kenneth Burke, *A Rhetoric of Motives* (Berkeley: University of California Press, 1950), 14.

23 Ibid., 7.

24 Ibid.

25 Barry Singer, *Ever After: The Last Years of Musical Theater and Beyond* (New York: Applause Books, 2004), 160.

26 Ibid., 198.

27 Kenneth Burke, *A Grammar of Motives* (Berkeley: University of California Press, 1945), 6.

28 Ibid., 6–7.

29 Joe Deer and Rocco Dal Vera, *Acting in Musical Theatre: A Comprehensive Course* (New York: Routledge, 2008), 128.

30 Ibid.

31 Ibid.

32 Barry Singer, *Ever After: The Last Years of Musical Theater and Beyond* (New York: Applause Books, 2004), 160.

33 Christal Temple, "Broadway's Aida: Deconstructing the Spectacle of an Aggressive Popular Eurocentricism," *Africalogical Perspectives: Historical and Contemporary Analysis of Race and Africa Studies* 2, no. 2 (2005): 45.

34 Ibid., 47–48.

35 Ibid., 50.

36 Joe Deer and Rocco Dal Vera, *Acting in Musical Theatre: A Comprehensive Course* (New York: Routledge, 2008), 128.

37 Thomas P. Miller and Melody Bowden, "A Rhetorical Stance on the Archives of Civic Action," *College English* 61, no. 5 (1999): 594.

38 Ibid., 597.

39 Tarez Samra Graban, "Decolonizing the Transnational Archive: Re/Writing Rhetorical Histories of How African American Women (Can) Govern," *African Journal of Rhetoric* 9 (2007): 82–83.

40 Cheryl Glenn and Jessica Enoch, "Drama in the Archives: Rereading Methods, Rewriting History," *College Composition and Communication* 61, no. 2 (2009): 322.

41 Jeffery Abt, *American Egyptologist: The Life of James Breasted and the Creation of His Oriental Institute* (Chicago: University of Chicago Press), 129.

42 Ibid., 129–130.

43 Joyce Appleby, *United States History and Geography: Florida Edition* (New York: McGraw-Hill Publishers, 2013), 54.

44 Kristan Poirot and Shevaun E. Watson, "Memories of Freedom and White Resilience: Place, Tourism, and Urban Slavery," *Rhetoric Society Quarterly* 45, no. 2 (2015): 92.

45 Jason Farman, "Site-Specificity, Pervasive Computing, and the Reading Interface," in *The Mobile Story*, ed. Jason Farman (New York: Routledge, 2014), 6.

46 Kristan Poirot and Shevaun E. Watson, "Memories of Freedom and White Resilience: Place, Tourism, and Urban Slavery," *Rhetoric Society Quarterly* 45, no. 2 (2015): 92.

47 Tarez Samra Graban, "Decolonizing the Transnational Archive: Re/Writing Rhetorical Histories of How African American Women (Can) Govern," *African Journal of Rhetoric* 9 (2007): 83.

48 Carolyn Steedman, "Archival Methods," in *Research Methods for English Studies*, ed. Gabriel Griffin (Edinburgh: University of Edinburgh Press, 2013), 26.

49 Jeffery Abt, *American Egyptologist: The Life of James Breasted and the Creation of His Oriental Institute* (Chicago: University of Chicago Press), 139.

50 Aida script,

51 Jeremy Tirrell, "Latourian Memoria," in *Thinking Along with Bruno Latour in Rhetoric and Composition*, ed. Paul Lynch and Nathaniel Rivers (Carbondale: Southern Illinois University Press, 2015), 174.

52 Ibid.

53 Cheryl Glenn and Jessica Enoch, "Drama in the Archives: Rereading Methods, Rewriting History," *College Composition and Communication* 61, no. 2 (2009): 323.

54 Jason Farman, "Site-Specificity, Pervasive Computing, and the Reading Interface," in *The Mobile Story*, ed. Jason Farman (New York: Routledge, 2014), 7.

55 Cheryl Glenn and Jessica Enoch, "Drama in the Archives: Rereading Methods, Rewriting History," *College Composition and Communication* 61, no. 2 (2009): 340.

56 Ibid.

57 Ibid.

58 Ibid.

59 Tarez Samra Graban, "Decolonizing the Transnational Archive: Re/Writing Rhetorical Histories of How African American Women (Can) Govern," *African Journal of Rhetoric* 9 (2007): 101.
60 Ibid., 84.
61 Kenneth Burke, *Counter-Statement* (Berkeley: University of California Press, 1937), 55.
62 Tarez Samra Graban, "Decolonizing the Transnational Archive: Re/Writing Rhetorical Histories of How African American Women (Can) Govern," *African Journal of Rhetoric* 9 (2007): 85.

Bibliography

Abt, Jeffery. *American Egyptologist: The Life of James Henry Breasted and the Creation of His Oriental Institute*. Chicago: University of Chicago Press, 2011.

Appleby, Joyce. *United States History and Geography: Florida Edition*. New York: McGraw-Hill, 2013.

Bitzer, Lloyd F. "The Rhetorical Situation." *Philosophy and Rhetoric* 1, no. 1 (1968): 1–14.

Brodkey, Linda. "Modernism and the Scene(s) of Writing." *College English* 49, no.4 (1987): 396–418.

Burke, Kenneth. *Counter-Statement*. Berkeley: University of California Press, 1937.

_____. *A Grammar of Motives*. Berkeley: University of California Press, 1945.

_____. "Musical Chronicle." *Dial* 86 (June 1929): 538–539.

_____. *A Rhetoric of Motives*. Berkeley: University of California Press, 1950.

Deer, Joe and Rocco Dal Vera. *Acting in Musical Theatre: A Comprehensive Course*. New York: Routledge, 2008.

Farman, Jason. "Site-Specitivity, Pervasive Computing, and the Reading Interface." In *The Mobile Story*, edited by Jason Farman, 3–16. New York: Routledge, 2014.

Glenn, Cheryl and Jessica Enoch. "Drama in the Archives: Rereading Methods, Rewriting History." *College Composition and Communication* 61, no. 2 (2009): 321–342.

Graban, Tarez Samra. "Decolonizing the Transnational Archive: Re/Writing Rhetorical Histories of How African Women (Can) Govern." *African Journal of Rhetoric* 9 (2017): 82–118.

Hawhee, Debra. *Moving Bodies: Kenneth Burke at the Edges of Language*. Columbia: University of South Carolina Press, 2009.

John, Elton and Tim Rice. *Aida: The Broadway Musical*. New York: Music Theatre International, 2000.

Locke, Ralph P. "On Exoticism: Western Art Music, and the Words We Use." *Archiv für Musickwissenschaft* 69 (2012): 318–328.

Miller Thomas P. and Melody Bowden. "A Rhetorical Stance on the Archives of Civic Action." *College English* 61, no. 5 (1999): 591–598.

Ostwald, David. *Acting for Singers: Creating Believable Singing Characters*. Oxford: Oxford University Press, 2005.

Poirot, Kristan and Shevaun Watson. "Memories of Freedom and White Resilience: Place, Tourism, and Urban Slavery." *Rhetoric Society Quarterly* 45, no. 2 (2015): 91–116.

Schafer, Daniel. *Anna Madgigine Jai Kingsley: African Princess, Florida Slave, Plantation Owner.* Gainesville: University Press of Florida, 2003.

Sheard, Cynthia. "Kairos and Kenneth Burke's Psychology of Political and Social Communication." *College English* 55, no. 3 (1993): 291–310.

Singer, Barry. *Ever After: The Last Years of Musical Theater and Beyond.* New York: Applause Books, 2004.

Steedman, Carolyn. "Archival Methods." In *Research Methods for English Studies,* edited by Gabriel Griffin, 18–31. Edinburgh: Edinburgh University Press, 2013.

Temple, Christel. "Broadway's Aida: Deconstructing the Spectacle of an Aggressive Popular Eurocentricism." *Africalogical Perspectives: Historical and Contemporary Analysis of Race and Africana Studies* 2, no. 2 (2005): 44–59.

Tirrell, Jeremy. "Latourian Memoria." In *Thinking with Bruno Latour in Rhetoric and Composition,* edited by Paul Lynch and Nathaniel Rivers, 165–184. Carbondale: Southern Illinois University Press, 2015.

Vatz, Richard E. "The Myth of the Rhetorical Situation." *Philosophy and Rhetoric* 6, no. 3 (1973): 154–161.

CHAPTER THREE

Agents in Motion: Dramatism in Kurt Weill's *Street Scene*

In the third chapter, we begin by helping student writers understand the growing roles they play in the college writing classroom. We then utilize the dramatism of Kenneth Burke to help student actors understand the growing roles they play in interpreting the language of their characters through the agent-scene ratio. We conclude the chapter with demonstrating how agents in motion can empower for the student actors in language and motion. We consider this chapter analogous to Burke's description of Agent, and through a description of the performance practice of Kurt Weil's *Street Scene*, students used pentad work to examine how linguistic differences between cultures informed how they characterized and responded to differing immigrant groups. In this example, students can use pentad in order to not only determine how, where, when, and why they should move on stage, but also how the immigrants themselves moved in and around New York City's Lower East Side. For the musical theater director, utilizing Burke's dramatistic pentad for teaching the history of immigration achieved specific learning goals. This chapter concludes with exercises in focusing on the Scene-Agent ratio for self-directed staging.

Writing Agents

It might sound simple to say that collegiate writers play larger roles in their own writing than in high school or first year writing, but this is increasingly the case

Figure 3.1 *Street Scene*: "Three women." Photo Credit: Sara Eckman

in the collegiate writing classroom. While estimates conclude that as many as 5 million United States students take the AP Language text and 10 million are enrolled in mandatory first-year writing courses in 2018, what this means for student writers is that they previously have not had much choice in how they compose a paper over the last five to seven years. If you are a student, think about the last time you were assigned a paper? What did you do first? Look at the assignment sheet? Study the rubric used to assess the paper? If you did that, then the assignment sheet or rubric has more authority in how you are composing that paper than you do. As you move forward in your college career, you will be expected to invent your own topics for your writing or invent the style or design of the paper. You might even be even more in control of where that writing goes. For example, maybe you have the choice to create a website instead of a paper or perhaps you are presenting your work in a poster session at a conference. If that is the case, you are utilizing the rhetorical canon of *delivery*, or where your writing is performed.

For many of you, these rubrics emphasize the features of your writing, whether you have them or not, or how effective they actually are. For example, this rubric below scores the presence of a thesis statement as any score above "0," with the highest score belonging to the "best" thesis statement. This is an emphasis on the "intrinsic" characteristics of your writing, and this is common in Advanced Placement scoring and state-mandated assessments of your writing in first-year writing courses. However, if we change the emphasis from the "intrinsic" characteristics of a text, like the presence and quality of a thesis statement, to the "extrinsic" features of a text, then we change the entire writing situation. We focused in the last chapter on the "Scene" and the next "extrinsic" feature we will consider here in this chapter is the role of the Agent.

Perhaps an example will be helpful here. In the 2008 edition of the Bedford St. Martin's *Handbook of Composition*, Andrea Lunsford utilizes a student paper as an example of the "ideal" student persuasive essay. The assignment is written by Heather Ricker, a student in Andrea Lunsford's first year writing class in the fall of 2001. The assignment tells us that she begins this paper based on her own experiences with violent video games, yet there is no mention of her experiences in the entire paper. In fact, we have no idea how she actually feels, or even if she ever played a video game in the first place. If we notice the top of the paper, we see her name, her professor's name (Andrea Lunsford), the course (a first-year writing course), and the date (the fall of 2001).

Instead of judging Heather's use of specific features of writing like thesis statements and counterarguments, what if we simply describe who she was when she wrote this paper? Based simply on her thesis statement, one description might be "A student who hates video games." However, we know that it is right around Thanksgiving and from the last chapter we know that she might be away from home and could be heading back home after September 11, 2001. In this case, we could describe her differently, perhaps something like "A student who is looking for internal certainty in an uncertain world." If we describe her this way, her choice of thesis sentence "Parents should be responsible," makes sense, but we have to go outside the text in order to do this. Changing our emphasis from those intrinsic writing characteristics, like thesis statements, to thinking about what kind of person would write this particular paper, increases the authority you have in your own writing process. Writing teachers should understand the consequences of highlighting rubrics at the expense of their students own creative processes. Levi Bryant writes about this difference in terms of "brightness" and "darkness."[1] By making rubrics "darker," we can make student writing "brighter." As a student moving into higher level writing classes, you'll be expected to utilize your own experiences and emerging expertise in the development of ideas and in the completion of projects.

If we take the example even farther, it has important consequences for our Agent ratio. In the 2008 edition of the *Bedford St. Martin's Handbook*, Andrea Lunsford writes in her introduction, "The *St. Martin's Handbook* remains a collaborative effort in the best and richest sense of the word."[2] Lunsford then addresses no fewer than eighty-six compositionists who have helped in the construction of the Handbook which bears her name. "Judy Voss and Wendy Polhemus-Anibel, the Handbook's multitalented copyeditors, edited and reorganized the text efficiently and sensibly," Lunsford wrote.[3] In other words, in a grammar handbook that we would say Lunsford wrote, she was not ultimately responsible for the grammar in her grammar handbook. We take some pains to point this out only for the sake of the importance of how even more attention is given to student writers as AGENTS, since they are usually held accountable for all facets of the writing process, from the copyediting to the research to the way the paper is printed and delivered to their instructors. In the *Bedford St. Martin's Handbook*, Andrea Lunsford goes to great lengths to demonstrate that she is not responsible for all of these facets of the writing process, yet student writers are held accountable for all of them. Who wrote the Bedford St. Martin's Handbook? Who is the agent responsible? According to Lunsford, there are many co-agents that are responsible for its creation. Who wrote "Violent Video Games: Buyer Beware," the student essay written by Heather Ricker? According to Lunsford, there is only one agent responsible for the writing of that paper, yet Burke continues to move us outward, to help us understand that "it is more complicated than that."

Agent Ratios

While the concept of identifying "who" committed the act might appear simple, Burke challenges us to consider how complicated it could be in describing that particular agent. For example, is the agent acting alone or with others? Is the agent acting with other objects? Is the agent acting consistently with their circumstances in time and space or inconsistently? How do we describe the agent? Do we describe the agent favorably or unfavorably? By describing an agent favorably, does that suggest that we empathize with that agent or are we describing that agent favorably because of other circumstances? If so, which ones? In our writing example of Heather Ricker, if we describe her as "a student writer trying to get a good grade," is that a more or less favorable description than "a student writer following directions"? Does one demonstrate a more empathetic attitude towards

Heather than the other? Perhaps we are describing her unfavorably, although we understand she doesn't have much choice other than to "follow directions." Burke wrote that "Our term Agent, for instance is a general heading that might, in a given case require further subdivision, as an agent might have his act modified (hence partly motivated) by friends (co-agents) or (enemies) counteragents."[4] In our writing example above, then, a writer teacher could be working as a "friend" or an "enemy" by modifying the writer's act. How would we distinguish the difference? Perhaps we might say that a writer teacher who modifies the student writer's act with the writer's purpose in mind might be considered a "friend," but the writing teacher who modifies the student writer's act contrary to the writer's purpose might be considered an "enemy." Take this example from the *Bedford St. Martin's Handbook*, the student writer Emily Lesk. Lunsford uses Emily's process of narrowing her thesis as an example of how a student can "narrow your topic to focus on a more workable idea."[5] Lunsford records Emily's attempts to narrow her topic:

First focus attempt:	"American advertising and national identity" Hmm…I may be onto something. How about portrayals of women and how they affect U.S. identity? Go back to the idea of choosing a large company that might be linked to American identity: McDonald's? Coca-Cola? Wal-Mart?
Second focus attempt:	"Advertising icons that shape American identity" Yes, but how many icons are there? LOTS—and I just named a few. Should I go with a company—and symbol—that have been around a long time? Better choose one.
Narrowed topic:	"The Coca-Cola logo and American identity."[6]

In this example that Lunsford provides, we see this student begin by asking about "portrayals of women and how they affect U.S. identity," but ultimately settles on a more "focused" topic, that of "Coca-Cola is a cultural icon that shapes American identity."[7] While Lunsford praises Emily for the successful narrowing of her thesis, we can see how her final thesis statement is the least like her, but also how in this instance, Lunsford is changing the writer's act away from her purpose of the portrayals of women in U.S. advertising. Paul Heilker wrote of how thesis/support writing seems to do this more often than not. In his text, *The Essay: Theory and Pedagogy for an Active Form*, he wrote the following:

> To what extent does our teaching of the thesis/support form lead students into an unconscious buttressing of the societal pyramid that has rich, young, able-bodied, highly educated, scientific, white, Christian, business-minded, materialistic, type-A males at the top and everyone else somewhere below them, trying to assimilate those values and become 'empowered'?[8]

For Emily Lesk, her initial curiosity in how "portrayals of women affect U.S. identity" was replaced by a justification of the importance of corporations in our society. When we work against the purpose of a student writer to modify their writing acts, we are working less as a "co-agent" and more like a "counteragent," according to Burke. In fact, when our actions are motivated in any direction, we are utilizing the Agent ratio, "Again, under Agent one could place any personal properties that are assigned a motivational value such as ideas, the will, fear, malice, intuition, the creative imagination."[9] Whether we are using fear or the creative imagination with our students, we are acting as co-agents or counteragents in the development of their writing acts.

Rubrics and Act-Agent Ratios

While writing teachers might not be so explicit in their motivations as to actually tell students that they are working with the students' purposes or against them, any feedback given to students, whether in the form of comments, rubric designations, or grades is an Act-Agent description. In Mike Rose's *Lives on the Boundary*, he told the story of James, a student who came to the UCLA tutoring center for help. James is having trouble avoiding summary in his writing, and he defends his work, "I'm not a C-," he explained.[10] His teacher had given him that grade, and that is how James has internalized who he is, a "C-." This can be especially true in the use of rubrics, and even more so when the rubrics used to describe the characteristics of student writing also label and describe the students as well: labels such as "novice" or "expert." When rubrics utilize such descriptions, they describe the Act-Agent ratio as having the greatest effect on that act, despite a student's Scene, Agency, or even Purpose. For example, James Berlin's 1987 work on composition pedagogies altered composition teachers to the impact that our pedagogies as an Agency have on the outcome of student writing.[11] Yet despite this type of scholarship that rhetoric and composition has offered to the discussion of student writing, the success or failure of student writing is laid squarely on the shoulders of students, despite the conditions the student was writing under, despite sometimes contradictory assignments and pedagogies they must justify, and despite contending purposes between students and teachers.

This is especially troubling in light of recent scholarship on the use of acculturationist rubrics in writing assessment. Valerie Balester has written, "The problem with uncritical uses of rubrics is that they oversimplify and standardize writing, thus failing a significant segment of our student population, namely, students of color or students who first language is not always Edited American English."[12]

When rubrics describe students of color or students whose first language is not EAE as "novices" on the basis of their acculturation to Edited American English, then this description takes on new meaning. Balester described the effects of one such rubric from St. Mary's College:

> At the "novice" level, severity and quantity of error come together to create incomprehensibility: 'Contains many and serious errors of punctuation, spelling, and or capitalization; errors severely interfere with meaning." The "novice" writer's paper is also inappropriate in that it "lacks and awareness of a particular appropriate audience for the assignment; tone and point of view are somewhat inappropriate or inconsistent" (St. Mary's College, 2009). In other words, we have a rhetorical effect caused by an accumulation of errors.[13]

For this accommodationist rubric, the act "lacks awareness of the appropriate audience," and this act was committed by "a novice" *by means of* "many and serious errors of punctuation." By describing this writer as a "novice," one must ask how confident this writer will be in taking risks in their writing, using their own home language, or even writing to challenge the language of hierarchy or of the academic institutions which exacerbate this obedience. Contrast this description of a "novice" writer with Mike Rose's description in *Lives on the Boundary*: "A traveler in a foreign land best learns names of people and places, how to express ideas, ways to carry on a conversation by moving around in the culture, participating as fully as he can, making mistakes, saying things half right, blushing, then being encouraged by a friendly native speaker to try again."[14] For Rose, the act is described as "making mistakes, saying things half right," but the description of the agent is as a "traveler," not a novice. Because the agent is described differently, then the agency is as well, "moving around in the culture, participating as fully as he can," and there's even room for scene and purpose in Rose's descriptions, as well. "What he must not do is hold back from the teeming flow of life, must not sit in his hotel room and drill himself on all possible gaffes before entering the streets. He'd never leave the room."[15] This is exactly the scene of the writer from the acculturationist rubric example. By describing this writer who makes mistakes of Edited American English as a "novice," they will never want to leave the room, never explore what linguistic adventures are available to them.

The acculturationist rubric is not the only target of Balester's critique, however, and in this case, Rose's description of the "friendly native speaker" who encourages our traveler to try again is the "accommodationist." Balester wrote on how the accomodationist rubric is better than the acculturationist, but still imposes a kind of cultural imperialism on student writers through those descriptions, as well:

In the accommodationist rubrics, the notion of sophistication is tied to voice. Voice is an especially important element in the Texas Education Agency rubric. The required voice must not only be appropriate,' but it also must be playful, inventive, creative, and original. And how might a writer achieve a high score? In part by creating an 'authentic' voice and in part by 'correctly applying the conventions of English language." In the language of the rubric there is no recognition that the voice may be tied to multilingualism. Since the essay must be 'readable,' it must conform to the 'conventions of the English language.' The very fact that these conventions need no definition makes it clear: they are the norms of Edited American English, of course. To make this even clearer to graders and teachers, voice is defined in terms of connecting with the reader—the representative of the educational system, naturally.[16]

For Balester, accommodationist rubrics are those that apply "code-shifting" as the *means by which* the agent performs the act. However, as she argues here, the arbiter of these code shifts and their successful "connection to the reader," is always the "representative of the educational system," not a speaker of the writer's original language. For the student writer attempting to utilize her language as a way of communicating her most important meanings, this attempt might garner acceptability as "original," "creative," and "authentic," but will only do so as long as the conventions of the English language are "correctly applied." Balester contrasts the accommodationist view with the multicultural view, one in which the conventions of the English language are not applied at all. "As Cangarajah (2006b) observes in his case study of a multilingual writer: "the author is not only being creative in shuttling between communities, he is also choosing the terms in which he wants to represent himself" (p. 600). Appropriate language is judged based on the whole rhetorical situation, the identity of the writer included."[17] For Cangarajah and for Balester in this instance, the act of "choosing the terms in which he wants to represent himself" is performed by an agent who is allowed to reject the conventions of Edited English in favor of the language of his own culture, which acts as a "means by which" an agent is allowed to choose the terms in which he wants to represent himself. In this case, the writing instructor is acting as a friend, as opposed to a counteragent, the writing teacher who insists on requiring the non-native speaker of Edited English to conform to a different language variety. Balester described how writing teachers who not just allow, but encourage students of color or non-native speakers of English to use their own linguistic varieties can actually become co-agents:

Also promising is the rubric used at St. Marys University of Minnesota, which relies on both consistency and appropriateness and subsumes them under style. There is a sense that the writing is manipulating grammar for rhetorical purposes rather than to simply conform to an expected standard. The reader is pleased because the writer is achieving his or her rhetorical purpose.[18]

In this case, the writing teacher encourages students to utilize their own languages and is a co-conspirator in the upheaval of Edited American English. Here the act of "pleasing the reader" is performed by the "writer achieving his or her rhetorical purpose," and the means by which this is accomplished is the "manipulation of grammar for rhetorical purposes rather than to simply conform to an expected standard." In order for this means by which to perform this act, however, the student must know that the writing teacher views the writer's purpose more important than the conformity to an expected standard. This is how writing teachers can act as co-agents in helping students accomplish their purposes, not the goals of an instructor or institution.

Stage Agents

If the history of writing instruction is any standard, it is in the world of theater that the Act-Agent ratio is even more solidified. As the writing instructor puts all responsibility for the invention, research, arrangement, style, and delivery of a student's paper, the theater director puts all the responsibility for inventing a character, the research, the characterization, and the final delivery of a student's character role upon the student herself. Summarizing the characterization method of Stanislavski, Ostwald writes, "In order to behave as if you are your character, you need to describe her reality clearly and in detail."[19] The act here is to clarify the character and the agent is the actor. The means by which this act is accomplished is through "the Given Circumstances," but notice how inseparable the agent and the agency are in Ostwald's description:

> To develop your description, you draw on the information the composer and librettist embody in the score. Because the creators of the piece supply it, this information is commonly called your Given Circumstances. Answering the following six questions as your character and in the first person will enable you to extract the essence of those circumstances from a wealth of material in a score: When are the events taking place? In history? In her own life? Where is my character? In the world? In her surroundings? Who is my character—including her relationships to the other characters? What does my character want? (Your character's want distills the need that drives her to do what she does). For the entire piece? (This is called your character's super-objective). For each scene or stanza? (These are called your character's objectives). Why does she want it? For the entire piece? For each scene or stanza? What has just happened— literally, what has just occurred that causes her to sing? When you are developing the Given Circumstances for your character in a song or lied, you may have to use your imagination to augment the information in the score—particularly to describe your character's want, why, and what, since often they are not well defined.[20]

There are many cognitive skills which Ostwald requires of actors in this passage. The first is that the actor (the agent) is responsible for hermeneutic practices of reading and interpreting the libretto and the score. This is similar to the directions of many college English professors who on one hand tell students to "find the meaning in the passage for themselves," while on the other hand already have a preferred interpretation of the literary passage in mind. So, there's this first hurdle the student actor must clear, literary interpretation. The second skill which Ostwald requires is then in determining the character's desires, so now the student actor is not only responsible for clear hermeneutic practices, but now is responsible for clear gestalt practices. While it is difficult enough to identify who the character is, it is now up to the student actor to determine the character's wants based on those characteristics. If the student actor can clear this second hurdle, then the third skill which Ostwald requires is then "using your imagination" to fill in what is left. This is how we feel the agent-agency ratio has been tied too closely together in this method: while Ostwald requires three cognitive skills for the actor student in this description, the only one that he provides the "means by which" to accomplish is the "Given Circumstances." There is no guidance on how student actors are supposed to "use their imaginations" in order to fill in these gaps.

Of course, we are using Ostwald's description in order to demonstrate the ability of Burke's dramatistic pentad as a "means by which" students can interpret the text and "use their imaginations," since Ostwald's direction to "describe her reality clear and in detail" will not be able to help student actors accomplish this. Ostwald's goal seems consistent with how James Berlin described "positivistic" epistemologies, "Truth is prior to language, is clearly and distinctly available to the person who views it in the proper spirit, and is ultimately communicable in clear and distinct terms. Disagreement has always to do with faulty observation, faulty language, or both, and never is due to the problematic and contingent nature of truth."[21] For Berlin, one of the important ways in which truth is discovered is through an investigation of how truth is complicated, perhaps even unknowable. This is in sharp contrast to Ostwald's directive to students to discover and communicate the truth of their characters easily and without difficulty. In other words, a character's truth might be difficult to communicate by a student actor not because the student actor has not "done their work," but because the truth of that character is itself difficult to discover and perhaps even more difficult to communicate. Berlin described the limitations of this method when it comes to the writing classroom, but they seem to also apply to the classroom of the theater, as well. Ostwald's advice to "be creative" rings hallow for students who have not had much practice in being able to "be creative" in their classrooms:

For now, it should be noted that this rhetoric makes the patterns of arrangement and superficial correctness the main ends of writing instruction. Invention, the focus of Aristotelian rhetoric, need not be taught since the business of the writer is to record careful observations or the reports of fellow observers (in the research paper, for example). In the world of current-traditional rhetoric, all truths are regarded as certain, readily available to the correct method of investigation.[22]

For Ostwald, the directive to "be creative" is the final insult to many students, who despite their best efforts, look at their teachers or directors with puzzled looks. In order to "be creative," students must be allowed to not be clear, or to deliver their message in "clear terms." Perhaps an example may be of interest here. When James was growing up, he used to think the water in the streams of his family's hometown in Minnesota was the clearest water he had ever seen. But later, after visiting the pools of water in Mexico, he came to realize an important lesson about clarity. In Mexico, one could see all the way to the bottom of a pool some seventy-feet deep. What he learned was that the water in Minnesota was not necessarily clear, but it was shallow. There was a difference between being clear and being shallow. When students are given instructions to "be clear," what they often do is to become unnecessarily "shallow," in their writing, and in their characterization of dramatic actions on stage. James Berlin wrote, "The dismay that students display about writing, I am convinced, at least occasionally result from teachers unconsciously offering contradictory advice about composing—guidance grounded in assumptions that simply do not square with each other."[23] What does not square with one another in this instance is Ostwald's goal of a "being creative" that conflicts with his method of doing so, that of a "clear presentation of character." At this point, the student actor may throw up her hands in frustration since the "Given Circumstances" do not allow for any kind of creative license. Once a student actor has exhausted the "Given Circumstances," there is no material to "be creative" with. Burke wrote of the importance of this larger "scope" of the act-agent ratio:

> To this writer, at least, the act-agent ratio more strongly suggests a temporal or sequential relationship than a purely positional or geometric one. The agent is an author of his acts, which are descended from him, being good progeny if he is good, or bad progeny if he is bad, wise progeny if he is wise, silly if he is silly. And conversely, his acts can make him or remake him in accordance with their nature. They would be his product and or he would be theirs.[24]

For Burke, there is a kind of fluidity to the act-agent ratio. An act can be both created by an agent and an act can also create the agent. This is in contrast to how Ostwald describes how student actors should describe their characters. For Ostwald, agents have always committed the act, never the other way around. Burke's dramatism allows for student actors to be able to see how the acts of their characters can change their own interpretation of their characters as they are happening. This is that "temporal or sequential" relationship that Burke describes rather than "a purely positional or geometric one." For Ostwald, it is required of the student actor that they understand the characters' actions, never how the character's actions might necessitate a temporary suspension of analysis, since the character is in the act of becoming, based on the character's actions.

But we are also interested in pointing out how the act-agent ratio here also holds student actors accountable for bringing interpretations that do not account for other pentadic ratios, such as scene, agency, and or purpose. For Ostwald, the student actor is responsible for creating this character, despite the fact that the characters are created not by agents, not by the student actors which inhabit them, but also by the scenes themselves. By describing the kind of character that would commit the act, we describe the Act-Agent ratio. However, Kenneth Burke connected the Agent to the Scene in important ways and believed this Scene-Agent ratio to be one of the most important ratios in the dramatic sequence.

> Both act and agent require scenes that contain them. Hence the scene act and scene agent ratios are in the fullest sense positive or positional. But the relation between act and agent is not quite the same. The agent does not contain the act, though its results might be said to preexist virtually within him. And the act does not synecdochically share in the agent, thought certain ways of acting may be said to induce corresponding moods or traits of character.[25]

For Burke, the scene-agent ratio means that while both act and agent share the scene, act and agent do not seem to work independently from the scene. An act-agent ratio must account for the presence of the scene, yet the act ratio cannot account for the independence of the scene in its relationship with agent. In our example of Florida's red tide, the scene of "the protected coastal waters for fish and wildlife" contains both the act of "red tide corrupting the waters of the eastern Gulf of Mexico" and the agent "corporations who pollute the waters of the Gulf of Mexico." This agent, "corporations who pollute the waters of the Gulf of Mexico" does not contain the act of "red tide corrupting the waters of the Gulf of Mexico." It is the scene of "the protected coastal waters for fish and wildlife" that contains both the act and the agent. In our example of the student writer, we could also say that the scene contains both the act and the agent. The scene of "a first-year writing class right after September 11, 2001" contains both the act, "an attempt to follow directions" and a description of the agent, "an insecure first year students." In this case, the agent most certainly doesn't "contain" the act, but it is true that the results existed and had a dramatic effect on the act of wanting to "get a good grade" in an uncertain world with an uncertain future.

If the scene contains both the act and the agent simultaneously, then we could analyze the act-agent relationship in a unique way through making the scene the "brightest" ratio. This is why Burke's scene-agent ratio is so important, for it is through this "sideways glance" that we can understand the agential temporality of which Burke describes. In the last chapter, we focused on the act-scene ratio by putting the scene in motion. In this chapter, we are able to focus on the act-agent ratio because the scene is as immovable as possible, and for that, we wish to test Burke's theory through a production of Kurt Weill's *Street Scene.*

Agents in Kurt Weill's *Street Scene*

If Ostwald's descriptions of character analysis seem static compared to Burke's, then Deer and Dal Vera's are almost frigid. According to Deer and Dal Vera:

> What is a character? As much as we like to think of characters as having human qualities, it is important to remember a character is an it, not a "who." Characters are invented by writers and don't exist independently of the writer or, later, of the actors who embody them on the stage. Characters are limited in the scope of their actions to what the author wanted or needed them to do in order to make his point.[26]

For Deer and Dal Vera, characters are like the example of our student writers at the beginning of this chapter. These student writers are understood as "its" rather than "who's." By making assessment procedures "darker," we demonstrated how we can increase the brightness of the student writer. For Deer and Dal Vera, they seem to apply the same criterion to characters in a musical. In being able to describe these character's as who's, rather than "it's," student actors can increase the brightness of the characters and directors can help student actors increase the brightness of their characterizations of these agents on the stage. While we have been describing how Burke's dramatism is able to increase the agency of the student writer, we hope to demonstrate in our examination of *Street Scene,* how Burke's dramatism is able to increase the agency of the agent, both characters that are agents and the actors portraying those agents on the stage. The ramifications of Deer and Dal Vera's position are striking when the characters on the stage are minorities or people of color. This is why we believe a performance of *Street Scene* or other musicals which depict racial diversity cannot afford to insist on the characters as an "it," but must work around this trained incapacity inherent in adhering to Stanislavski's "Given Circumstances."

Student actors who follow Deer and Dal Vera's advice to "research the production history" of a given musical will discover the complex amalgamation of writers and musicians who contributed to Weill's libretto and score. In his program notes for *Street Scene: An American Opera*, Kurt Weill stated that "in discussing the problem of lyrics for a show in which the music had to grow out of the characters, we decided that the lyrics should attempt to lift the everyday language of the people into a simple, unsophisticated poetry. We chose Langston Hughes for the job."[27] Hughes, a Harlem Renaissance poet, was often criticized for his sometimes-unattractive depiction of black life in America. Doris Abrahamson wrote, "The need to be accepted or recognized was doubtless part of what motivated Garland Anderson, Frank Wilson, Wallace Thurman, Hall Johnson, Langston Hughes and Huges Allison—six black writers whose plays reached Broadway in the twenties and thirties."[28] Deer and Dal Vera's direction to ignore the "who" of the character and to focus on the "it" of a character, then, works against the very work of the writers themselves. The Pulitzer Prize winning play by Elmer Rice depicting tenement life in New York City provided the ideal setting for these conflicts. The collaboration of the German Jew Kurt Weill, Pulitzer Prize playwright Elmer Rice, and "poet of the people" Langston Hughes produces a musical work that presents a collage of musical languages and political issues. According to Abrahamson:

> Inevitably a different audience required a different treatment of subject matter, and black playwrights with an eye on Broadway had to treat their themes in such a way as not to rock the American boat. Black plays of the twenties did not even pretend to have social themes. When the plays of thirties do make such a claim, they are not truly controversial, for the Broadway influence tempers and dilutes whatever message may exist.[29]

Rather than working against the "who" of these characters, it was Kenneth Burke as a young critic who stepped outside the "intrinsic" criticism of his time, to utilize the "scene" ratio inherent in the interactions of dramatic characters:

> Kenneth Burke, writing for the *Saturday Review of Literature*, observed that, in contrast to the gentle lulling *Green Pastures*, Hall Johnson's play brought out the power side of the Negro. "In *Run Little Children*, one sees a Negro genius," he wrote…"an attractive positive ability exemplified with a conviction, a liquidness, a sense of esthetic blossoming, and a gift of spontaneous organization." Of the three, all distinguished critics, only Kenneth Burke had something new to say: he showed a sensibility verging on prophecy.[30]

This description from Abrahamson tells us much about the differences between Burke's criticism and the criticism present during this time. For Burke, he was able to detect the emerging need of diversity and inclusion, not just in language or in literature, but in society or in life.

Who Agents

In researching the characters in *Street Scene*, students will learn much about the history of immigration in the United States. They will learn that in 1910, 15% of the U.S. population was foreign born. First generation immigrants were considered "white"—even distinguished from the Chinese attempting to immigrate. As these immigrants settled in New York City and their numbers began to demand policy changes, the Johnson-Reed Act of 1924 focused on creating legal discriminations for Eastern European Jews and Italians. All immigrants were required to take a mental fitness test upon entering the country. Rhetoric and violence from groups like the Ku Klux Klan condemned the Jews as "mongrel hordes" threatening "Anglo-Saxon civilization." Signs that said "No Jews or Dogs Allowed" hung in shop windows. Ivy league schools made effort to keep them out. Eleven Italian immigrants were lynched in New Orleans in 1891 and later second-generation Italian Americans are targeted as the source of organized crime in America. Blue-collar work, especially in the garment industry, remained Italian while Jews found clerical and managerial sales jobs. It is this time period that precedes and is the background for the conception, creation, and production of *Street Scene* in 1945–1947. The Lower East Side of New York City had become crowded with 160,000 people living across blocks of the area in 325-square foot apartments called tenements, sometimes families of 10 sharing one space.[31] The set of *Street Scene* is one of these tenement houses, and the heteroglossia of language within just one is one of the most unique features of the staging of this musical, for we are not staging just characters, but we are staging languages. As Kurt Weill retells his meeting with Elmer Rice in his preface in the original production program, "In discussing the problem of lyrics for a show in which the music had to grow out of the characters we decided that the lyrics should attempt to lift the everyday language of the people into a simple, unsophisticated poetry." As such, Burke dramatism is uniquely positioned to feature the languages in motion within any given scene. In his article, "Dell Hymes, Kenneth Burke, and the Birth of Sociolinguistics," Jay Jordan wrote, "Burke advises Hymes to 'think of language more on the rhetoric-poetic side than on the phonetic-philologic side,' thus opening analysis to 'social norms (with their corresponding modes of action).'"[32] When the Johnson-Reed Act of 1924 cracked down on immigration, this decreased the population by about 60,000. Although Jews began to leave the neighborhood in the late 1800s even as Italians moved in, at the end of the holocaust, Jewish immigrants again arrived and settled on the lower east side with its establishments of synagogues and shops. As a German Jew, Kurt Weill had defected in 1935 and eventually made it to the United States. Weill recruited Elmer Rice, who won the Pulitzer Prize for the play in 1929 and eventually Langston Hughes, the Harlem Renaissance poet known for his real and honest depiction of black life in America. Perhaps more than any other playwright at the time, Weill realized the power of languages that were in motion for the material of the drama in the musical. Burke's positive reviews of African-American playwrights in the 1930's and his subsequent theories of language in motion, or more importantly language as "symbolic action," makes Burke's dramatism an essential stance to understand the linguistic complexities of a musical like *Street Scene*.

Languages in Motion

Langston not only got to write for black life in *Street Scene*, he also got to write for Jewish, Italian, and German immigrant life. Weill's own experience with ethnic discrimination imbued him with a sort of empathy that equalized the troubles of all people: black, white, Jewish, and Italian. The music that accompanies the Langston lyrics is varied; at one moment blues, at another operatic; sometimes swing, then a musical theater ballad. The dichotomy between the music and the formality or lack thereof of the lyrics is often striking. We offer a list of the musical numbers here, with their corresponding dialects:

Ain't it Awful, the Heat? – Blues. A German, Italian, and an American sing about the heat using words like "Ain't," "damn," and "gonna."

I Got a Marble and a Star – Blues. "I got a halo and a hat But my halo I don't wear. I'm gonna save that halo until I get up there."

Get a Load of That – Patter. "Ain't she got no shame? A woman ought to know her place and act like decent women do."

When a Woman has a Baby – Swing, musical theater. "Of course I'm just a beginner, that's why I'm in this state. I guess I'll be much calmer when we get to number eight."

Somehow I Never Could Believe – Opera. "Somehow I never could believe that life was meant to be all dull and gray. Somehow I always will believe there'll be a brighter day."

Ice Cream Sextet – Opera, chorus. "First time I come to da America, First thing I see is da ice cream cone."

Let Things Be Like They Always Was – Opera. "Let things be like they always was, that's good enough for me."

<u>Wrapped in a Ribbon and Tied in a Bow</u> – Swing, musical theater. "To our street has come good news and glory, wrapped in a ribbon and tied in a bow."

<u>Lonely House</u> – Blues. "Lonely house. Lonely me. Funny with so many neighbors how lonely it can be."

<u>Wouldn't You Like to Be on Broadway?</u> – Swing, dance number. "Wouldn't you like to see your name up in the bright lights, in the white lights that gleam and glow? Wouldn't you like to be the leading lady in my heart, but also in some Broadway show?"

<u>What Good Would the Moon Be?</u> – Musical Theater ballad. "What good would the moon be unless the right one comes along? What good would dreams come true be if love wasn't in those dreams?"

<u>Moon-Faced, Starry-Eyed</u> – Jitterbug, dance number. "Moon-faced, starry-eyed, peaches and cream with nuts on the side. I never knew there was anyone living like you."

<u>Remember That I Care</u> – Opera. "In the dooryard fronting an old farmhouse near the whitewash'd palings stands the lilac bush tall growing with heart-shaped leaves of green. A sprig with its flower we break and the lilac bush is ours. Nothing can take it away. And when you see the lilac bush bright in the morning air, remember, always remember."

<u>Catch Me if You Can</u> – Children's song, folk. "Fat, fat the water rat, fifty bullets in his nat. One, two, three, for superman come and catch me if you can."

<u>There'll be Trouble</u> – Opera. "Why don't you look after your own home and let other people look after theirs?"

<u>A Boy Like You</u> – Musical Theater ballad. "To know I have somebody wonderful, to know I have a boy like you."

<u>We'll Go Away Together</u> – Musical Theater ballad. "We'll go away together, just we two, just you and I, we'll build a house to shelter us beneath a happier sky."

<u>The Woman Who Lived Up There</u> – Chorus. "The summer's bright in warm and golden weather and all the children in the streets laugh as they run. But love and death have gone away together to find their morning in the sun."

<u>Lullaby</u> – Folk, music theater. "Hush baby hush. Your Daddy is a lush. Shut your eyelids tight. He's plastered every night."

<u>I Loved Her Too</u> – Opera. "I'd been drinkin' Rose, see what I mean? There always was something inside of me right here like a wall. Seems like I never could break through. But I swear to God, Rose, that I loved her, too."

<u>Don't Forget the Lilac Bush</u> – Opera. "Remember that I care."[33]

Hughes's reference to the Walt Whitman's poem, "When Lilacs Last in the Dooryard Bloom'd," written upon the assassination of Abraham Lincoln, is about death—the death of a President, the death of slavery. "Remember that I care" at the end of Act I foreshadowed this final duet of the opera with another reference to the Whitman poem. With the added layer of its musical interpretation, Weill gives the poem additional meaning and importance. Rose is singing to Sam, saying goodbye to her dead mother, the imprisonment of her father, her relationship to Sam, inequality, and the Lower East Side itself. Arnold Rampersad writes in Volume II of the *Life of Langston Hughes*,

> That two highly successful white artists with scores of veteran white lyricists at their command, had asked a black writer to join their work on a drama dealing almost exclusively with white people was so remarkable as to be virtually without parallel in recent decades. Ten years later, a sense of wonder still lingered in Langston's recollection of their choice. "That I, an American Negro, should be chosen to write the lyrics of *Street Scene* did not seem odd or strange to Kurt Weill and Elmer Rice," he wrote. "They wanted someone who understood the problems of the common people…They wanted someone who wrote simply…I did not need to ask them why they thought of me for the task. I knew."[34]

With these three men committed to the production, *Street Scene* and its depiction of immigrant life on the Lower East Side would prove to push the envelope even further than previous productions. Gershwin's *Porgy and Bess* had only just preceded *Street Scene* the previous decade and was one of Weill's favorite productions. Weill actually tried to get the director of Porgy and Bess, Rouben Mamoulian, to direct *Street Scene*. He ensured him that

> …the love story between the gentile heroine, Rose Maurrant, and a Jew, Sam Kaplan, would be 'made more important and more passionate' than in the original play; that Rice's left-leaning political slant would be considerably softened; that Sam 'instead of being always the beaten Jew, will be the young poet trying to adjust himself to the world and the hateful surroundings he is living in'; and that because of the event in Europe anti-Semitic sentiments expressed by some of the neighbors would be eliminated.[35]

Mamoulian turned down the job for higher paying gigs in Hollywood, but after the success of *Porgy and Bess*, he would have been perfect for it. Regardless, *Porgy and Bess* and its depiction of black life amidst a soaring, operatic score cast with operatic black singers had opened the door for *Street Scene* in that Weill hired Metropolitan Opera singers as well, not Broadway musical theater singers, to depict the roles of Jewish and Italian immigrants. However, because it was titled *Street Scene: An American Opera*, it needed to open on Broadway. The Metropolitan

Opera was international in the productions it hosted, but Broadway was very New York City and, again, this was "an American Opera."

The term "American Opera" itself had many ways of connecting and dividing the musical scene when *Street Scene* premiered, and in this way functions as a "god term." According to Cynthia Sheard, "When invoked by individual members of a culture or society, they draw those individuals, whatever their differences, into a cohesive group—a community. God-terms serve as the grounds for identification between strangers as well, whether their goal is to assimilate into a local community (like some social organization or university) or a global community (like the United Nations)."[36] Because *Street Scene* was marketed as the first "American Opera," its characters "serve as the grounds for identification" between disparate members of a community. For student actors, however, the term "American Opera" bridges the gap between the characters as "its" and "who's," according to Deer and Dal Vera. Deer and Dal Vera offer four means of expression in order to "tell you all you need to know" about the character's life and world: characters tell us about themselves, characters tell us about each other, authors tell us about characters, and that the characters actions tell us about them."[37] It is this final category that is important for our purposes here, since we are interested in the Act-Agent ratio:

> A character's actions speak loudly about what is important to him. This can be the trickiest way of finding out about a character because so much of the action we ascribe to characters in performance is decided in rehearsal between actor and director. But scripts do tell us important pieces of stage business, such as when Julie is riding the carousel for the first time in *Carousel.* When Billy Bigelow waves to her, Hammerstein tells us, "It means so much to her that she nearly falls off!" This is a good indication of her feelings and her state of mind.[38]

For Deer and Dal Vera, the actions described here are not the actors' interpretations of those actions, but only what the author tells actors what those actions may mean. In other words, in order to interpret what a character's actions may tell us, we have to look for what the author tells us those actions mean. This is limiting for the student actors in their characterization of diverse characters, and it is limiting in their ability to stage the symbolic actions of those "who" characters. For Burke, "Ultimate terms also enable us to adjust to the changes that occur beyond our control and to initiate changes ourselves by converting a current system of orientations into another or by translating existing orientations into new norms. Hence the search for god-terms is preliminary to successful social as well as symbolic action."[39] Utilizing *Street Scene* as "an American Opera," means that this "god term" brings the "who" of their characters to the surface at the expense of the "its."

Agents in Motion

Street Scene as a depiction of the social values of the 1930s, specifically where the country stood on issues of immigration and citizenry, demands the listener to meet the characters at the point of their purpose or motivation. Why are they complaining about the heat? Why don't they just leave? Why does Mrs. Maurrant need the companionship of the milkman? Why does Frank kill her? Why does Rose want to leave the tenement? Why does Sam need to stay? These are all motivations that need to find their place in the staging of this musical. For students using Deer and Dal Vera's text, they will find this advice: "There are many schools of thought about what to do when staging a song. One says that you should not stage it at all. People in that camp believe that simply playing your objective will be enough to create organic movement, and that anything extra will come off as phony or artificial. Others say that you need to plan every movement and gesture thoroughly to express your ideas about the journey of the song."[40] For *Street Scene*, the first and last scenes take place with the same characters talking about the same things, almost as if nothing has happened and no time has passed. Student actors portraying their characters as "its" might be able to stage these characters using either of these two poles of purposed staging. However, student actors portraying their characters as "whos" will not be able to stage their characters using either of these two poles. Deer and Dal Vera write that they believe a middle ground between these two poles is best. "Our opinion is that whatever your choice about movement and staging, it should be conscious choice and should be appropriate for the song, the style and the circumstance. And no matter how heightened the theatrical reality of your song, it needs to appear to be a spontaneous experience for the character in the context of your production."[41] When they write that staging should "appear to be spontaneous experience," they seem to be describing a kind of dramatic neo-Aristotelianism here, for Aristotle wrote in the *Rhetoric* that "we can now see that a writer must disguise his art and give the impression of speaking naturally and not artificially."[42] Deer and Dal Vera offer no guidelines or suggestions on how to make a student actor's "artificiality" appear natural, however. What they do suggest, is that this artificial naturalness comes not by any particular method, but by mere practice. "Mature performers with years of experience learn to stage songs on their feet, as they are performing them, and develop instincts about when to move and when to stay still and let the power of their voice and the song carry the moment. But their instincts were developed over years of studying, experimenting and watching the work of others whom they respect."[43] With this we would agree that it is the embodied motives which can create the characters that actors wish to embody, the difference between when a character is an "it" and when that character becomes a "who." For Deer and Dal Vera, however, there is no way to impart this to inexperienced actors; "Chances are that you are not at that place yet. So, this is the beginning of your development of those instincts," they write.[44] What is unfortunate for them, but fortunate for those that study Burke's dramatism, is that this embodiment of motives can actually be understood by those beginning these instincts. Let's examine the first scene of *Street Scene* to understand how we are "bodies that learn language." First Scene: "Ain't It Awful the Heat":

ACT:	introduction of characters
SCENE:	lots of different nationalities in one place
AGENT:	a grumpy Jewish immigrant
AGENCY:	the stifling, always present heat
PURPOSE:	to unify – they all have the same frustration

While the rehearsal syllabus incorporates character analysis, background research and dramaturgy, music analysis, and acting applications like objectives and sub-text, incorporating over fifty dramatistic pentad in our production of Kurt Weil's *Street Scene* allowed the students to not only use them to motivate their blocking on stage, but also to understand how immigrants of differing nationalities moved about the tenement house and around the Lower East Side. Burke writes of this perspective in *Permanence and Change*, "Imagine beginning your course of study precisely by depriving yourself of this familiarity, attempting to understand motives and purposes by avoiding as much as possible the clues handed you ready made in the texture of the language itself. In this you will have deliberately discarded available data in the interest of a fresh point of view, the heuristic or perspective value of a planned incongruity."[45] In the pentad that students completed on the first song, "Ain't It Awful the Heat?" students identified that the agent was Kaplan, the Jewish defector. This immediately identifies Jewish immigration as the latest group of immigrants, and Kaplan as a member of that "out-group." The pentad that the actor who portrayed Kaplan looked like this:

ACT:	introduction of Sam Kaplan
SCENE:	where the women are
AGENT:	a successful Jewish immigrant
AGENCY:	reading
PURPOSE:	youth and generational change—hope for the future.

In this case, the scene had the greatest effect on the act, since "where the women are" described a gendered space that also connected to the purpose ratio: hope for the future. This motivated the staging for Abraham Kaplan, his father, through the following directions: "Try to get the women's attention more. Talk to Olson even more. Always have your paper and be trying to read it when you are in that window." By utilizing the paper as a kind of agency, Abraham Kaplan is able to create a kind of "consubstantiality" between his son and with the ladies of the tenement. Olson wrote about the importance of consubstantiality among differing hierarchies:

> Burke maintains that societies are held together by a principle of hierarchy that accounts for differences between human beings and the resulting divisions between us. Hierarchies are like ideologies when these are legitimized and enforced by contract like constitutions; hierarchies are structured and sanctioned by ideologies, and both operate as stabilizers within a society. Such control is always rather tenuous, however, for hierarchies are susceptible to challenges from both within and without, and this can lead, as Brummet explains, to the need for guilt or blame, or scapegoating.[46]

In *Street Scene*, Kaplan is most susceptible to these challenges, and it is in the second act that Kaplan is assigned the blame for the tension with the neighbors. The actor who portrayed Kaplan wrote this pentad for this scene in Act II:

ACT:	tension with the neighbors
SCENE:	where Rose doesn't want to be
AGENT:	a Jewish immigrant
AGENCY:	antagonism, anti-Semitism
PURPOSE:	inspire Rose to leave

In this instance, it is a description of the Agent that is still the same, and the Agency of anti-Semitism seems to have the greatest effect on the act. If the purpose of assigning blame to Kaplan is to "inspire Rose to leave," then Kaplan acts as a scapegoat in helping her leave the tenement. Olson wrote, "Burke continuously emphasizes that *we are bodies that learn language.* Put differently, our symbolic capacities allow us to identify, interpret, and make sense of that which is first gleaned from somatic experience."[47]

The stage directions based on this pentad resulted in the following note: "Rose, don't cross directly to Sam on your 'I've heard' line. Take that downstage right, then turn to him on 'Oh, if we could do it, Sam!' Use your last line to actually walk to him and take his hands. Olson described this experience in this particular way:

> For Burke, the senses function, as 'recording instruments that turn certain events into a certain kind of sign, and we find our way through life on the basis of these signs.' As such, he reaffirms his fundamental concern with human physiology while dialectically connecting it to language, the communicative embodied self and other and, accordingly, identification and division.[48]

The phrase "if we could do it," is not merely an event, it is a sign embodied in the "taking his hands." The character of Frank Murrant works in the same way. We took the actor's pentad and were able to create agent-motivated staging from the actor's descriptions of his "who" character. With Frank's character, we were able to work with the scene/agent ratio in some interesting ways. Burke wrote on how the scene/agent ratio helped us understand Weill's message on tenement life. "The logic of the scene agent ratio has often served as an embarrassment to the naturalistic novelist. He may choose to indict some scene (such as bad working conditions under capitalism) by showing that it has a brutalizing effect upon the people who are indigenous to this scene."[49] Frank Murrant pentad:

ACT:	introduction of Frank Maurrant
SCENE:	where his "castle" is
AGENT:	a man afraid, afraid of tyranny
AGENCY:	man of the house
PURPOSE:	pessimism and antagonism

In this pentad, the students discussed how the scene, "where his castle is," had the greatest effect on how they described the act of "the introduction of Frank Maurrant." Burke warned against the scene having too great a scope in the creation of characters who are "contained" in their scenes. "But the scene-agent ratio, if strictly observed here, would require that the brutalizing situation contain brutalized characters as its dialectical counterpart. And thereby, in his humanitarian zeal to save mankind, the novelist portrays characters which, in being as brutal as their scene, are not worth saving."[50] Later in Act II, Frank kills his wife Anna, and this is the pentad which students developed from this act:

ACT:	murder of Mrs. Maurrant
SCENE:	The tenement where everyone of every nationality is
AGENT:	the king of his castle
AGENCY:	Frank's fear of losing his castle
PURPOSE:	to complete Rose's drama

In this pentad, the students discussed how the purpose of "to complete Rose's drama" had the greatest effect on the act of "the murder of Mrs. Maurrant." Based on this understanding, then, the staging directions from this pentad were: "Rose, be more pleading in your kneeling in front of Frank. I also want you to stay down on your knees until he leaves the stage. Shirley, help her up, then leave to go inside so Rose is alone to head up the stairs." We also see how the description of agent, "the king of his castle" limited his ability to see beyond that castle and the actions of his consequence. Burke describes this limitation on the role of the scene-agent ratio.

"We could phrase this dilemma in another way: our novelist points up his thesis by too narrow a conception of scene as the motive-force behind his characters; and this restricting of the scene calls in turn for a corresponding restriction upon personality, or role."[51] While Burke never wrote a musical review of *Street Scene*, his description of the restriction upon personality or role seemed to bear itself out in our own descriptions of Frank Maurrant's scenes and their corresponding effect on how we described the act. Olsen wrote, "Like tragedy, comedy is ameliorative; it sets conditions right again."[52] Because Frank Maurrant's actions, "let things be as they always was," did not set everything right again, it is up to comedy to do that, and the following scene, "Lullaby," does just that: "Hush baby hush. Your Daddy is a lush. Shut your eyelids tight. He's plastered every night," they sing. The actors who portrayed the nurses who sing in this scene created the following pentad:

ACT:	Walking the baby
SCENE:	Where the women are
AGENT:	witnesses to the crimes
AGENCY:	comedic lightness
PURPOSE:	set everything right again, return to the heat

The description of the purpose from the students had the greatest effect on the act, and when we created the pentad for the last scene, a reprise of "Ain't It Awful the Heat," this is the pentad that the students created:

ACT:	Life goes on
SCENE:	lots of different people
AGENT:	Kaplan, the Jewish immigrant
AGENCY:	the heat
PURPOSE:	return to normal

As the students discussed which ratio had the greatest effect on the act of "Life goes on," they decided that their description of the agent, "Kaplan, a Jewish immigrant," had the greatest effect on the act of "Life goes on." That the issue of immigration is still front and center, almost as if nothing has happened and no time has passed, demonstrates the viability and importance of Kurt Weill's *Street Scene* in the cultural history of theater history. *Street Scene's* depiction of tenement life through a black lyricist, a first-generation German Jewish composer, and a second-generation German Jewish playwright shows the collaboration how music and lyrics in motion is the driving agent in a scene that searches for equality and tolerance. In this third chapter, we detailed how utilizing Burke's dramatistic pentad for teaching the history of immigration achieved specific learning goals. In this production of Kurt Weil's *Street Scene*, students used pentad work in order to not only determine how, where, when, and why they should move on stage, but also how the immigrants themselves moved in and around New York City's Lower East Side.

Director's Notes

Why This Show

Street Scene was chosen as a diversion from the musical lineup, featuring some of our talented opera singers in a mainstage production. This was the year I had a baritone who could play Frank and a dramatic soprano who could play Anna, so I did not pass up on this show. My previous experience with this show was in undergraduate school at the University of Colorado. In tech class at the time, my assignment was light board operator and the show was *Street Scene*. I never forgot this show, and as soon as I had the opportunity to do it as a director, I did. This was my "trained incapacity," though, as the director, and what I was looking for was a way to see around that trained incapacity. Burke's pentad was able to give me that "perspective by incongruity" that I needed.

While ticket sales might be one of the most important goals on a music or theater department level, the director of collegiate musical theater is not completely free to make decisions based on entertainment and ticket sales alone. In her role as dramaturg, the director's most important task is incorporating production research into rehearsal practice. Many schools have casting policies, required by NASM or NAST. We are obligated as teachers to provide students with opportunities, ensuring them at least one leading role by the time they graduate as fulfillment of the program's objectives. To this end, we often pre-cast, choosing shows we know we can cast, possibly compromising our own artistic aspirations in order to accommodate our student population. In collegiate musical theater, the director is both dramaturg and professor, so directors must engage the performers as actors and students. To this end, it is vital that the preparation for their roles is also congruent with teaching and learning objectives as part of the student's education. Stacy Wolf writes the following:

> Most universities do produce one musical a season, and these tend to be sure-fire money makers and crowd pleasers. The yearly musical often requires the most labor and money—sometimes more than the rest of the season combined. It is also usually the production that brings in the most revenue. How often, though, is the musical seen as part of the intellectual project of the department. How often do these productions garner the same study and attention as plays by Shakespeare, Ibsen, or Hansberry? And during rehearsals for these productions, how much research do actors actually do? How does a dramaturg function on a musical?[53]

In answer to Wolf's questions, the Director-Professor and the actor-students have worked together to understand the story, the design, and the music of the production. With the help of Burke's dramatistic pentad, this chapter has examined how directors can demonstrate how students are achieving institutionally mandated learning goals, such as "developing knowledge and understanding of diverse perspectives, global awareness, or other cultures" in conjunction with the institutionally mandated learning objective of "developing creative capacities (inventing, designing, writing, performing in art, music, or drama)." As the successful demonstration of institutionally mandated learning objectives is vital for the collegiate director's progress toward tenure and promotion, this chapter has tried to synthesize how the learning process itself is the catalyst for maintaining equilibrium with all the other components of collegiate production.

The pentad also gave us the opportunity to study Kurt Weill, Langston Hughes, and Elmer Rice—literature, music, and history all at the same time, as Wolf questions: "How often, though, is the musical seen as part of the intellectual project of the department. How often do these productions gather the same study and attention as plays by Shakespeare, Ibsen, or Hansberry? And during rehearsals for these productions, how much research do actors actually do? How does a dramaturg function on a musical?[54] Because we were able to step outside of the disciplinary structures of theater and literature, Burke's pentad was a way to bridge the gap between "literature and life."

Variables

The variable in this show is the fact that there is one set. Two stories of painted brick with only 24 hours to work with provide a new kind of challenge for the theater director. From my Director's notes for the show:

> Our story encompasses a 24-hour time period on one block of New York City: black, white, Italian, Jew, Russian, German, poor, working class, children, adults, love, loss, violence, and addiction. After touring the Tenement Museum on New York's Lower East Side, I learned that in one tenement building there were living together 111 people in just 22 apartments. In our production we have attempted to keep the tenement building realistic and gritty, the only ray of hope being the lilac bush off to the side of stage right in reference to the Walt Whitman poem quoted by Elmer Rice in the original play, "When Lilacs Last in the Dooryard Bloom'd," itself an elegy to Abraham Lincoln written within weeks of his assassination in 1865. If this lilac can survive amidst this squalor, then so can Rose and Sam—or do they?

The Broadway version of the *Street Scene* set was actually somewhat glamorous. The brickwork was ornate, the steps wide, the front door imposing. In reality, tenements on the Lower East Side were walk-ups with narrow front doors, rickety stairs, and noisy businesses on the lower levels. The scene of the Lower East Side in 1945–1947, when Kurt Weill and Langston Hughes were writing the production, had become crowded with 160,000 people living in 325-square foot apartments, sometimes families of 10 sharing one space. Although Jews began to leave the neighborhood in the late 1800s even as Italians moved in, at the end of the holocaust, Jewish immigrants again arrived and settled on the Lower East Side with its establishments of synagogues and shops.

As Kurt Weill chose Langston Hughes as the lyricist in order to "lift the everyday language of the people into a simple, unsophisticated poetry," so does the set for *Street Scene* need to provide Rose the impetus to make the choices she makes throughout the show. I kept my set as gritty and unfinished as possible, with scaffolding obviously offstage right, no apparent roof above, the lonely, struggling lilac bush a token of the struggle every family is facing to survive. Weill's composing blossoming despite a backdrop of oppression and torture in Hitler's Germany, the lyrics of Hughes, a Harlem Renaissance poet, persevering in spite of his unattractive depiction of that heritage—the confluence of these elements inspires this story of Rose rejecting her surroundings in the hope of finding a better life.

The Pentad as a Theme

With an immovable set unchanged for a three-hour show, the pentad theme for this show definitely involved "Scene." The scene is fixed for this production, so the story becomes how the agents interact with this permanent fixture for three hours. The "who" interacting in a permanent and fixed "where" is what becomes interesting and challenging for the director.

I could make treat the agent individually, making each character on the stage their own agent. This is a big show, so that is a lot going on! However, as I analyzed the construction of this show, it became clear to me what agent would be the focus. Weill opting to bookend the show with the same song, "Ain't It Awful, the Heat." This number introduces us to the three women—Olga, Greta, and Emma. And although we think of the story of *Street Scene* as Rose and Sam and Anna and Frank, the three women are a consistent commentary on the actions of the other characters throughout the show. That Weill ends the show with the same song sung by the three women back on the front steps gossiping and talking about the weather, seemed to me a clue I needed to follow. My pentad theme was the three women, treating them collectively as the "Agent." A secondary, supplementary scene, "where the women are," became an easy focal point for all the other reaction on stage. No matter when or where they appeared on stage, all other action was reaction to them.

Table Work

As I like to do with every show, we started with theme work. Theme work brings your cast together around the common goal of telling the story of the show and what they want that to look like. Our theme for *Street Scene*, once complete, looked like this:

> *Street Scene* teaches us to believe in a brighter day, allowing us to emerge from the night of our past into the light of our future.

In order to arrive at that theme, we looked at key words, emotional themes, prejudice, and race, main characters, secondary leads, and ensemble scenes.

- Rose embodies conflict but can and does escape
- Life goes on
- Love, hate, family, loneliness, fear, defenses
- A "day in the life" setting, snapshot, static
- Appearances: black, white, European
- Prejudice and bias about race and ethnicity
- Song title key words: heat, star, get, baby, believe, ice cream, always, wrapped, lonely, house, Broadway, moon, starry, care, catch, trouble, boy, away, there, lullaby, loved, forget.
- Songs that are questions:
  o Ain't it Awful, the Heat?
  o Wouldn't You Like to Be on Broadway?
  o What Good Would the Moon Be?
- Song titles that depict emotions: life and death, hope, containment/trapped, rejecting/forgetting, hoping/wishing/questioning
- Rejecting circumstances, we are not a victim of our circumstances
- Aspiring for something better, reaching for the stars, hoping for something better

After completing these theme charts, we began to work on character "abstracts." Our character abstracts provided many contrasts for us to work with:

Character	Color	Fabric	Animal	Drink
Anna	Red	Chiffon	Hummingbird	Hot tea
Frank	Black	Sandpiper	Bear	Bourbon
Rose	Yellow	Silk	Robin	Champagne
Emma	Brown	Burlap	Vulture	Old fashioned
George	Gray	Cotton	Goldfish	Whiskey
Mae	Purple	Floral	Butterfly	Berry martini
Vincent	Dark red	Leather	Weasel	Whiskey
Olga	Yellow	Wool	Bear	Margarita
Carl	White	Cotton	Lion	Soda
Kaplan	Purple	Wool	Dying elk	Vodka
Shirley	Brown	Burlap	Mother bear	Coffee
Sam	Blue	Fleece	Turtle	Milk
Greta	Green	Jacquard	German shepherd	Wine
Lippo	Yellow	Satin	Bulldog	Peach martini
Jennie	White	Cotton	Dove	Lemonade
Daniel	White	Cotton	Family dog	Milk
Henry	Sky blue	Cotton blend	Owl	Lemonade
Steve	Baby blue	Polyester	Ostrich	Mike's hard lemonade
Easter	Gray	Faux suede	Vulture	Scotch rocks
Dick	Green	Tweed	Bear	Whiskey

Even imagining having the drink in their hand that their character chose inspired actors to walk and talk a certain way! Their choices of fabric informed their costume design. While thinking about the choice of fabric, we also completed super objectives. Some of these were heavy, weighty, and emotional:

> I, Anna, want validation
> I, Frank, want to be powerful
> I, Rose, want to escape my family

> I, Emma, want to expose my neighbors for who they really are
> I, George, want to drink in peace
> I, Mae, want to be accepted for who I am
> I, Vincent, want Rose to pay attention to me
> I, Carl, want to blend in
> I, Olga, want to keep my past a secret
> I, Greta, want companionship
> I, Lippo, want to stay positive despite my surroundings
> I, Abraham, want to be heard
> I, Shirley, want everyone to mind their own business
> I, Sam, want to not feel lonely anymore
> I, Daniel, want to be the best husband and father
> I, Jennie, want to make my mother happy
> I, Laura, want to shield my family from hypocrisy
> I, Henry, want to live in peace
> I, Steve, want to escape my present
> ·I, Dick, want to find a family
> I, Furniture Mover, want to provide for my cats

Finally, the different family units of the Kaplans, the Jones's, the Maurrants, the Olsens, the Fiorentinos, and the Hildebrands all had back stories as to how and why they came to the United States. We talked about the year of the play, 1929, and the year of the musical, 1946. A lot was going on in the European countries these families came from. The stock market crashed on October 24, 1929, and the 1940s was dominated by World War II. Kurt Weill himself had defected from Germany in 1933, and, along with many others, immigrated to the United States. We discussed Ellis Island, first generation immigration and second-generation immigration. We talked about anti-Semitism and anti-capitalism, tenement living and the Alien Registration Act. All of these motives informed the acting in this show and were critical to the process.

Scene by Scene

Ain't It Awful, the Heat

This show opens and closes with the same musical number. Additionally, the drama that occurs between that bookends is unbelievable given the way that Weill unceremoniously introduces us to these characters and then leaves us saying goodbye at the end. It is almost like no time has passed, no one has died. The pentad for these scenes is exactly the same:

Act – sitting outside on the porch steps

Scene – tenement on the lower east side

Agent – the three women

Agency – the heat

Purpose – to unify, support

The underscoring commences and the women begin to chat in a rhythmic, non-pitched notation. Mrs. Fiorentino says "Good ev'ning" to Mrs. Jones and they begin to commiserate with each other about the heat. Eventually the women begin to sing melodic phrases.

Mrs. Fiorentino:

SO I JUST TAKE OFF MY CORSET AND LET MYSELF SPREAD.

Mrs. Jones:

I THINK I'LL TAKE A NICE HOT BATH BEFORE I GO TO BED.

Mrs. Fiorentino:

THE TROUBLE WITH A BATH IS THAT WHEN YOU GET DONE,

YOU'RE JUST ABOUT AS HOT AGAIN AS WHEN YOU BEGUN.

Both:

AIN'T IT AWFUL THE HEAT, AIN'T IT AWFUL. DON'T KNOW WHAT I'M GONNA DO.

Mrs. Olsen joins the gathering, completing the Agent, our collective of the three women together—something to analyze throughout this show, the moments when all three women are on the stage and the moments when they are not, whether that is only one of them present or two of the three. While this is not for discussion in this particular scene-by-scene breakdown, it is an encouragement of sorts to any directors and actors that encounter this show.

Once Mrs. Olsen expresses her feelings about the heat, the song proceeds with the introduction of each of several of the main tenants of the tenement, additional establishment of the Scene of our pentad. By situating the three women center stage on the big staircase, all the other characters gradually appear and orient themselves around them. The focus for the other actors on the three women as the Agent of the Scene maintains a continuity of action and reaction, everyone moving with and around a "stationary" target. The songs concludes with everyone singing "Ain't it awful the heat, ain't it awful."

"Lonely House"

We will use the antagonism of absence rather than presence of the Agent in directing this scene. Sam's response to his surroundings after a page of dialog with most of the members of the tenement is a striking contrast to our Scene-Agent ratio. By the time we get to the song, he is the only one on stage, "agentless" as it were. It is their absence that is the inspiration for this number.

Because of all the preceding dialog, subtext is important in analyzing this scene. As in other shows, I had the actors rehearse the scene only in subtext, but the inspiration of the pentad on the subtext is evident whether reciting the actual lines or not.

Sankey, the milkman, has just entered the scene as the celebration of Jenny's graduation is winding down. Anna is dancing with Lippo, but Sankey and Anna have been having an affair. The scene is full of conflict for the actors, especially Sam.

The pentad for this number looked like this:

- Act: Sam is left alone
- Scene: the tenement
- Agent: absence of the three women
- Agency: loneliness
- Purpose: Development of Sam—we haven't seen much of him.

In this pentad, the Agency has the greatest effect on the Act. For example, when Frank says to Anna after discovering her dancing with Lippo, "Well, what I'm tellin' you is, you oughta be lookin' after your kids, 'stead of doin' so much dancin'," and Anna replies with "Why, it's the first time I've danced in I don't know when," her subtext of *"Don't take this moment away"* speaks directly to her own loneliness and the Agency of loneliness that inspires the entire set up to the song "Lonely House."

Another element of this pentad is the Purpose, the development of Sam. You could personify this purpose for Sam as him wanting to assert his presence and role as a member of this tenement "family" or simply play director and state it as above: the Purpose of this scene in the show is to develop Sam for the audience—we really have not seen much of him in the show so far. Sam comes on stage with Willie who is crying because he was having a fight with his bully buddy, Joe Connelly. We realize something about Sam and Purpose immediately upon his entrance.

(Willie enters, sobbing, accompanied by Sam)

Mrs.	M: Willie, what's the matter?
Sam:	He was having a fight, so I thought I'd better— *This little brat*—[Sam is maybe feeling that Willie needs some attention because he isn't getting much, or possibly using this opportunity to make his presence known, that he can handle something important like breaking up a fight.]
Mrs. M:	Oh, Willie, have you been fighting again? *I care about your safety.* [This subtext is in direct response to Sam's in that she needs to prove that she cares about Willie even if Frank is a horrible father. Reaction by Anna can be in response to Sam, Willie, or Frank with this subtext. Emphasize the "I" or insert an "I *also* care" in voice inflection. If empathizing with Sam in feeling lonely, she may even physically acknowledge Sam with touch as she retrieves Willie from his care, a sort of "thank you" that validates Sam.]

Mrs. Maurrant exits the stage once Frank decides he's "goin' around to Callahan's for a drink" and Mrs. Fiorentino appears at the window. Mrs. Jones and Lippo have remained in the scene during all the other action. Once Anna takes Willie inside, Sam stays on stage, but I start to isolate him, requiring other actors to go to him to involve him in any way with the ensuing conversation. We start to see in spite of Sam's efforts to interact, he struggles to fully take part.

Mrs. F:	Did he say something? *Anything happen?*
Mrs. J:	No, not till after Sankey was gone. Then he wanted to know who he was an' what he was doin' there. "He's the milk collector," she said.
Mrs. F:	It's just awful! *This is going to end up bad.*
Mrs. J:	Oh, an' then Willie comes home. *That brat.*
Lippo:	Da boy tella 'eem 'is mamma ees a whore, and Weelie leek 'im!
Mrs. J:	Well, an' what else is she? *She is a whore.*
Sam:	Stop it! Stop it! Can't you let her alone? Have you no hearts? Why do you tear her to pieces like a pack of wolves? It's cruel. *Got to get away from these people.*
	(He rushes off right) [We don't know where Sam goes exactly, but it is not into the tenement. Stage right in the Scene of this pentad and this show is where Henry the janitor "lives." It is opposite the street lamp, it is dark, it is where the stairs go down into the basement level of the tenement. A director or actor can deduce what they would like from there, but the moment before for Sam could possibly have been trying to find Henry. He obviously is not around and Sam returns to the stage – alone.]

It is now, finally in the absence of the Agent on stage, that the character of Sam is realized in his singing of "Lonely House."

(Sam comes on slowly at right, looks at the house desperately)
AT NIGHT WHEN EVERYTHING IS QUIET
THIS OLD HOUSE SEEMS TO BREATHE A SIGH.
SOMETIMES I HEAR A NEIGHBOR SNORING.
SOMETIMES I HEAR A BABY CRY.
SOMETIMES I HEAR A STAIRCASE CREAKING.
SOMETIMES A DISTANT TELEPHONE.
THEN THE QUIET SETTLES DOWN AGAIN---
THE HOUSE AND I ARE ALL ALONE.
LONELY HOUSE, LONELY ME!
FUNNY—WITH SO MANY NEIGHBORS,
HOW LONELY IT CAN BE!
[Sam could be thinking directly back at Mrs. Jones's comment to Lippo:
Lippo: Da boy tella 'eem 'is mamma ees a whore, and Weelie leek 'im!
Mrs. J: Well, an' what else is she?]
OH, LONELY STREET!
LONELY TOWN!
FUNNY—YOU CAN BE SO LONELY WITH ALL THESE FOLKS
    AROUND.

The Introduction of Rose

We don't even meet Rose until over halfway through the first act. We have met every other family and character living in the tenement. We understand everyone's feelings about the tenement and about each other. We have fallen in love with Henry, we dislike Frank, we worry for Anna, and we feel for Sam. We don't meet Rose coming out the front door onto the steps. We meet her coming home from work accompanied by her boss, Mr. Easter. The pentad for this scene looked like this:

- Act: Rose's attempted seduction
- Scene: the tenement—where she doesn't want to be
- Agent: the three women
- Agency: a married man, Mr. Easter
- Purpose: Introduction of Rose

In this pentad, the Scene of the tenement echoes our earlier play on opposites with Agent—the absence of the Agent in the singing of "Lonely House" in that the tenement is where Rose lives but she does not want to live there. Her antagonism with the Scene throughout the show supplies endless motivations for the actor who plays Rose. The Scene has the greatest effect on the Act of this scene as we get to know Rose for the first time in this show.

Rose's subtext for this scene is interesting and gets at the scene-agent ratio. She doesn't want to be home, but is actually grateful knowing she has company. Two of the collective agents make an appearance in this scene: Mrs. Fiorentino is sitting upstairs in her window watching and Mrs. Olsen returns from an errand.

Rose:	This is where I live, Mr. Easter. *The shit show.* [The voice inflection the actor needs to deliver this line with so much contradiction between what she wants Mr. Easter to hear and what she feels inside is interesting to direct.]
Mrs. F:	(at window) Good evening, Miss Maurrant. *Watch out Rose!*
Rose:	O, good evening, Mrs. Fiorentino. (Mrs. Fiorentino looks at them for a moment, then pulls down the shade and turns out the lights) *Ugh!*
Rose:	Well, good night, Mr. Easter. I've had a lovely time. *Ok, leave now.*

Instead of Mr. Easter letting Rose go, he tries to get fresh with her. Thankfully, another one of the Agents saves the day.

Rose:	Please, don't, Mr. Easter. There's somebody coming. *Stop it, jerk!* (She frees herself as Mrs. Olsen comes up the cellar steps, with a pail filled with wastepaper).
Mrs. O:	Goot evening, Miss Maurrant. *Am I interrupting?*
Rose:	Good evening, Mrs. Olsen. How's the baby? *Thank God!*
Mrs. O:	(Putting the pail on the sidewalk) She vas cryin' all the time. *I'm tired.*
Rose:	Oh, the poor little thing! What a shame! (As Mrs. Olsen goes down the steps again) Good night, Mrs. Olsen. *Please stay out here!*
Mrs. O:	Goot night, Miss Maurrant. *Good luck.*

Mr. Easter finally succeeds at kissing Rose. The song that follows, "Wouldn't You Like to Be on Broadway?", is one of the songs in *Street Scene* in the form of a question. It gets directly at Rose's Super Objective: she desperately wants to escape the tenement. We just met her and she is immediately challenged by the choice between family loyalty and escaping—with somewhat of a promise of it actually working out. Her super objective of wanting to escape her family is something Easter capitalizes on and the effect of the Scene on the Act is why Easter's attempt at seduction gets as far as it does in this song. The underscoring commences as Easter tries to convince Rose she is better than the job in her real estate office.

Rose:	Don't be silly, how could I ever get a job on the stage?
Easter:	East as walking around the block, for a girl that's got all you've got. Just leave it to me. I've got three or four friends in show business. Ever hear of Harry Porkins?

Rose: No.

Easter: Well, he's put on a lot of musicals. He's an old pal of mine, and I'd just say to him: "Harry, here is a little girl I'm interested in," and you'd be all set.

Among other things, Easter reveals to Rose everything she is missing in life, from nice clothes to a nice home to some personal attention and promotion—and all just a few blocks over from the tenement which she hates.

WOULDN'T YOU LIKE TO BE ON BROADWAY

AND WEAR SOME BERGDORF GOODMAN CLOTHES?

RED ALLIGATOR SHOE, A BRIGHT GOLD ANKLET, AND SEVENTEEN DOZEN NYLON HOSE?

HEY KID?

WOULDN'T YOU LIKE SOME PERSONAL PROMOTION

TO A NICHE ON THE GREAT WHITE WAY?

WOULDN'T YOU? HEY KID?

HOW ABOUT IT? HEY KID?

WOULDN'T YOU LIKE TO BE ON BROADWAY?

IT'S JUST A FEW BLOCKS OVER,

I KNOW THE WAY.

HEY, KID? IT'S EASY.

I'LL SHOW YOU THE WAY.

Rose's answer is the song "What Good Would the Moon Be?", again another song that asks a question. Her father confronts her in the middle of it, fueling her desire to escape. By the end of the song, she has answered HER own question, acknowledging that her path will not be laden with primroses, diamonds, or gold:

BUT MAY BE THERE WILL BE

SOMEONE WHO'LL LOVE ME,

SOMEONE WHO'LL LOVE JUST ME

TO HAVE AND TO HOLD

Upon Mr. Buchanan's call for help for his pregnant wife, Rose leaves again to go get the doctor. This pattern continues throughout the show with Rose always needing to be somewhere—other than home. While initially the presence of Mrs. Fiorentino and Mrs. Olsen is irritating, she ends up wanting Mrs. Olsen to hang around a bit longer if it means she has to talk to Mr. Easter. Rather than just auxiliary characters, again the three women are a central element to the show and every scene they appear in, even if momentarily.

"Don't Forget the Lilac Bush"

Sam almost convinces Rose to just leave with him in "We'll go away together," but she wants to think it over. Once her mother is shot by her father, there *really* is nothing keeping her there. Sam still wants to leave with her, but Rose decides to do it by herself. The tenement as home for so many is only one bad memory for Rose, so much so that she doesn't even want Sam to be part of her life going forward.

The pentad for this scene looked like this:

- Act: Frank's arrest
- Scene: the tenement
- Agent: the three women
- Agency: they warned everyone this would happen
- Purpose: establishes Rose's departure

In this pentad, the Agent, our three women, has the greatest effect on the Act. No matter how many people were around, it did not stop what happened from happening. If it only matters whom she's with, not where, then she cannot be with Sam.

OH, SAM, IT'S LOVE THAT I WANT MORE THAN ANYTHING IN THE WORLD.

BUT LOVING AND BELONGING--

THEY'RE NOT THE SAME.

LOOK AT MY FATHER, MY POOR MOTHER.

IF SHE HAD BELONGED TO HERSELF,

IF HE HAD BELONGED TO HIMSELF,

IT NEVER WOULD HAVE HAPPENED.

AND THAT'S WHY, EVEN THOUGH MY HEART BREAKS,

I CAN'T BELONG TO YOU,

OR HAVE YOU BELONG TO ME.

I'M SO FOND OF YOU SAM.

AND NO MATTER WHERE I GO OR WHAT I DO,

I'LL BE THINKING OF YOU.

AND DON'T' FORGET THE LILAC BUSH BRIGHT IN THE MORNING AIR.

REMEMBER, ALWAYS REMEMBER, REMEMBER THAT I CARE.

Rose's last line inspired another part of the table work for our production. Because of the immense resources of the Kurt Weill Foundation, I knew that I would incorporate archival work as part of my research for this production. I had applied for and received the College/University Performance Grant from the Foundation, and after researching in the Kurt Weill Foundation Library and the New York Public Library Performing Arts Library at Lincoln Center, I found the following letter from Kurt Weill to his cast on the opening night of *Street Scene*. We close this chapter by letting Kurt Weill have the last words as I read the same letter to our cast before our first performance in 2013:

New York, January 9th, 1947

Dear Friends,

The show we are giving to-night is to me the fulfillment of an old dream – the dream of a serious, dramatic musical for the Broadway stage which might open up a new field of activity for singers, musicians, writers and composers....I want you to go out to-night in the spirit of fighting an important battle. I have seen you doing it – you have moved me and the audience to tears through the beauty of your singing and the emotional intensity of your acting. And if you put your heart into it again to-night you will win them again – and that is our strongest weapon.

Good luck to you all!

Kurt Weill[55]

Notes

1 Levi Bryant, "Dark Objects," *Larval Subjects Blog* (May 25, 2011), Online.

2 Andrea Lunsford, *St. Martin's Handbook* (New York: Bedford St. Martins, 2008), xvi.

3 Ibid.

4 Kenneth Burke, *A Grammar of Motives* (Berkeley: University of California Press, 1945), xix–xx.

5 Andrea Lunsford, *St. Martin's Handbook* (New York: Bedford St. Martins, 2008), 60.

6 Ibid., 61.

7 Ibid, 62.

8 Paul Heilker, *The Essay: Theory and Pedagogy for an Active Form* (Urbana, IL: National Council of the Teachers of English, 1996), 7.

9 Kenneth Burke, *A Grammar of Motives* (Berkeley: University of California Press, 1945), xx.

10 Mike Rose, *Lives on the Boundary: A Moving Account of the Struggles and Achievements of America's Educationally Underprepared* (New York: Penguin, 1989), 177.

11 James Berlin, "Contemporary Composition: The Major Pedagogical Theories," *College English* 44, no. 8 (1982): 766.

12 Valerie Balester, "How Rubrics Fail," in *Race and Writing Assessment*, ed. Asao Inoue and Mya Poe (New York: Peter Lang, 2015), 63.

13 Ibid. 69.

14 Mike Rose, *Lives on the Boundary: A Moving Account of the Struggles and Achievements of America's Educationally Underprepared* (New York: Penguin, 1989), 142.

15 Ibid.

16 Valerie Balester, "How Rubrics Fail," in *Race and Writing Assessment*, ed. Asao Inoue and Mya Poe (New York: Peter Lang, 2015), 69–70.

17 Ibid, 71.

18 Valerie Balester, "How Rubrics Fail," in *Race and Writing Assessment*, ed. Asao Inoue and Mya Poe (New York: Peter Lang, 2015), 73.

19 David Ostwald, *Acting for Singers: Creating Believable Singing Characters* (Oxford: Oxford University Press, 2005), 29.

20 Ibid., 29–30.

21 James Berlin, *Rhetoric and Reality* (Urbana, IL: National Council of the Teachers of English, 1987), 11.

22 Ibid., 9.

23 James Berlin, "Contemporary Composition: The Major Pedagogical Theories," *College English* 44, no. 8 (1982): 766.

24 Kenneth Burke, *A Grammar of Motives* (Berkeley: University of California Press, 1945), 16.

25 Ibid., 15–16.

26 Joe Deer and Rocco Dal Vera, *Acting in Musical Theatre: A Comprehensive Course* (New York: Routledge, 2008), 135.

27 Kurt Weill, "Program Notes," in *Street Scene: An American Opera* (New York: Kurt Weill Foundation Archives, 1947), Series 50A.

28 Doris Abrahamson, "The Great White Way: Critics and the First Black Playwrights on Broadway," *Educational Theatre Journal* 28, no. 1 (1976): 46.

29 Ibid., 51.

30 Ibid., 52.

31 "Overview," 102 Orchard Street (New York: Lower East Side Tenement Museum), Online.

32 Jay Jordan, "Dell Hymes, Kenneth Burke's 'Identification,' and the Birth of Sociolinguistics," *Rhetoric Review* 24, no. 3 (2005): 270.

33 Kurt Weill, *Street Scene: An American Opera* (New York: Chappell and Company, 1948), iii.

34 Arnold Rampersand, *The Life of Langston Hughes, Vol. II: 1941–1967, I Dream a World* (Oxford: Oxford University Press, 2002), 109.

35 Foster Hirsch, *Kurt Weill—On Stage: From Berlin to Broadway* (New York: Alfred A. Knopf, 2002), 259.

36 Cynthia Sheard, "Kairos and Kenneth Burke's Psychology of Political and Social Communication," *College English* 55, no. 3 (1993): 299.

37 Joe Deer and Rocco Dal Vera, *Acting in Musical Theatre: A Comprehensive Course* (New York: Routledge, 2008), 137–138.

38 Joe Deer and Rocco Dal Vera, *Acting in Musical Theatre: A Comprehensive Course* (New York: Routledge, 2008), 138.

39 Cynthia Sheard, "Kairos and Kenneth Burke's Psychology of Political and Social Communication," *College English* 55, no. 3 (1993): 299.

40 Joe Deer and Rocco Dal Vera, *Acting in Musical Theatre: A Comprehensive Course* (New York: Routledge, 2008), 247.

41 Ibid.

42 Aristotle, "Rhetoric," in *The Rhetorical Tradition: Readings from Classical Times to the Present*, ed. Patricia Bizzell and Bruce Herzberg (New York: Bedford St. Martins, 2001), 238.

43 Joe Deer and Rocco Dal Vera, *Acting in Musical Theatre: A Comprehensive Course* (New York: Routledge, 2008), 247.

44 Ibid.

45 Kenneth Burke, *Permanence and Change* (Berkeley: University of California Press, 1984), 121.

46 Jaclyn Olson, "Our Bodies and the Language We Learn: The Dialectic of Burkean Identification in the 1930's," *Rhetoric Review* 38, no. 3 (2019): 301.

47 Ibid., 262.

48 Ibid.

49 Kenneth Burke, *A Grammar of Motives* (Berkeley: University of California Press, 1945), 9.

50 Ibid.

51 Ibid.

52 Jaclyn Olson, "Our Bodies and the Language We Learn: The Dialectic of Burkean Identification in the 1930's," *Rhetoric Review* 38, no. 3 (2019): 303.

53 Stacy Wolf, "In Defense of Pleasure: Musical Theatre History in the Liberal Arts," *Theatre Topics* 17, no. 1 (2007): 62.

54 Ibid.

55 Kurt Weill, *Letter to Opening Night Cast* (New York: Kurt Weill Foundations Archives, January 9, 1947), Series 50A.

Works Cited

Abramson, Doris. "The Great White Way: Critics and the First Black Playwrights on Broadway." *Educational Theatre Journal* 28, no 1 (1976): 45–55.

Aristotle. "Rhetoric." In *The Rhetorical Tradition: Readings from Classical Times to the Present*, edited by Patricia Bizzell and Bruce Herzberg, 169–240. Boston: Bedford St. Martins, 2001.

Balester, Valerie. "How Rubrics Fail." In *Race and Writing Assessment*, edited by Asao Inoue and Mya Poe, 63–78. New York: Peter Lang, 2012.

Berlin, James. "Contemporary Composition: The Major Pedagogical Theories." *College English* 44, no. 8 (1982): 765–777.

Burke, Kenneth. *A Grammar of Motives*. Berkeley: University of California Press, 1945.

Burke, Kenneth. *Permanence and Change*. Berkeley: University of California Press, 1984.

Bryant, Levi. "Dark Objects." *Larval Subjects Blog*, 25 May 2011. Online. https://larvalsubjects.wordpress.com/about.

Deer, Joe and Rocco Dal Vera. *Acting in Musical Theatre: A Comprehensive Course*. New York: Routledge, 2008.

Hawhee, Debra. *Moving Bodies: Kenneth Burke at the Edges of Language*. Columbia: University of South Carolina Press, 2012.

Heilker, Paul. *The Essay: Theory and Pedagogy for an Active Form*. Urbana, IL: National Council of the Teachers of English, 1996.

Hirsch, Foster. *Kurt Weill – On Stage: From Berlin to Broadway*. New York: Alfred A. Knopf, 2002.

Jordan, Jay, "Dell Hymes, Kenneth Burke's "Identification," and the Birth of Sociolinguistics." *Rhetoric Review* 24, no. 3 (2005): 264–279.

Lunsford, Andrea. *Handbook of Grammar and Composition*. New York: Bedford St. Martins, 2008.

Olson, Jaclyn S. "Our Bodies and the Language We Learn: The Dialectic of Burkean Identification in the 1930's." *Rhetoric Review* 38, no. 3 (2019): 258–270.

Ostwald. David. *Acting for Singers: Creating Believable Singing Characters*. Oxford: Oxford University Press, 2005.

"Overview: 103 Orchard." Retrieved from http://103orchard.tenement.org/stories/103-orchard/?_ga=2.44151908.1993770605.1509209126-1808345435.1508589044#.

Sheard, Cynthia. "Kairos and Kenneth Burke's Psychology of Political and Social Communication." *College English* 55, no. 3 (1993): 291–310.

Rampersad, Arnold. *The Life of Langston Hughes, Volume II: 1941–1967, I Dream a World*. 2nd ed. Oxford University Press, 2002.

Weill, Kurt. *Letter to Opening Night Cast*. New York: Kurt Weill Foundation Archives. January 9, 1947. Series 50A.

_____. *Street Scene: An American Opera*. New York: Chappell and Company, 1948.

Wolf, Stacy. "In Defense of Pleasure: Musical Theatre History in the Liberal Arts." *Theatre Topics* 17, no. 1 (2007): 51–60.

CHAPTER FOUR

Agency in Motion: Dramatism in Stephen Sondheim's *Into the Woods*

In the third chapter, we focused on the agent ratio and its use in writing, in interpretation, and in musical theater staging. In this fourth chapter, we focus on Burke's agency and the agency ratio, or "by what means" has the act been accomplished. This seems like a simple question, but like all the other ratios, it grows more complicated the further we describe these means, for the focus is on the description of those means, not the literal name or object. How we describe "by what means the act occurred" has important consequences on how we view student writers, how actors create believable interpretations, and how directors can motivate agency-directed staging.

Agency Ratios

In an analysis of the dramatistic pentad, Burke continues with agency, or "by what means the act occurred." In our example of the red tide phenomenon in Florida, we might describe the "means by which the act occurred" as "harmful pollutants" or we could describe the "means by which the act occurred" as "mother nature." One description supports a climate crisis interpretation, while the other one does not. In our example of President Kennedy's assassination on November 22, 1963, we could describe the "means by which the act occurred" as a Carcono Infantry

Rifle or we could describe the "means by which the act occurred" as "anti-Kennedy sentiment among a disaffected veteran." One description supports the gun as the cause of the act, while another supports Oswald's motivations for purchasing the rifle in the first place. We will discuss the relationship between a gun and its holder when we discuss materialism later on in this chapter, but how we describe the agency complicates, in productive ways, our journey of understanding the act.

It is not now November 1963, but December of 2019, and the United States House of Representatives is taking a vote on articles of impeachment against President Donald Trump. For only the third time in history, the United States Congress is impeaching a U.S. President. By what means is the U.S. House of Representatives impeaching this President? We could describe the means by which the House is impeaching the President as "the impeachment articles in the U.S. Constitution," or we could describe these means as "political partisan powers." One description supports the House of Representatives holding the Executive branch of government accountable for its actions, while the other description supports the Executive branch holding the Legislative branch accountable for its actions. If you are reading this book in the fall of 2020 for a course, you will already have known the outcome of these proceedings: Will the U.S. Senate convict or acquit? Will President Trump remain in office? Will he win another election? Speaking of the election of 2016, what if we began a pentad of that act? What if we began describing that act as "Donald Trump was elected President of the United States"? What if we also began by describing that act as "The country of Russia engaged in a complicated plan to assist Donald Trump's presidential campaign"? One description of this act ignores Russia's influence, while the other description includes it. As we are analyzing the function of agency in this chapter, "by what means" was the act accomplished, then we could go ahead and describe the agency for both of these acts. If we described the act as "Donald Trump was elected President of the United States," then we might describe the agency as "the will of the people of the United States," or "the electoral college system." However, if we describe the act as "The country of Russian engaged in a complicated plan to assist Donald Trump's presidential campaign," then we might describe the agency as "Russian propaganda through social media," or even "Collaboration between Roger Stone and Wikileaks." One description of the agency implicates the president's campaign in Russian interference in our election, while the other one does not. What will happen? By what means will it happen? How you answer these questions reveals how you interpret the means by which the world works, the means by which history is changed.

As a student, you might be thinking about the next assignment you have for a class. Does this assignment ask you to think about the "means by which" you accomplish that assignment, or does it ignore the many "means by which" you complete your assignments? While we want our students to think about their methods to accomplish tasks outside of the writing classroom, we sometimes spend very little time helping students develop those methods in the writing classroom. All too often, the "means by which" students' writing assignments are completed are simply "the assignment sheet," or the "assignment rubric." We will consider how important these particular objects are in the writing process in a moment, but for now, our focus is on developing the concept of agency in student writing contexts. Burke certainly does not want to clear things up, either. He purposively makes agency one of the murkiest, if not the most inscrutable of the ratios, as he writes, "What looked 'scenic' was actually 'pragmatic,' since the writer's medium is an agency."[1] For Burke, the writer's medium was more than just a "means by which" the act is accomplished. The writer's medium takes in all the "means by which" communication can occur. For example, let's take our example of the student writer completing a writing task. We might describe the act as "Persuading an audience of the writer's position on an important issue." We also might describe the act as "Trying to get a good grade in the class." If we follow through towards agency, we might describe the first agency here as "An Apple computer given as a graduation gift to change the world," but we also might describe the second agency as "Following the exact instructions on the instruction sheet," or "Following the demands of the writing rubric." One description is less scenic and more pragmatic than the other in this scenario. The Apple computer is more pragmatic, but the instruction sheet or the writing rubric is more scenic. Burke described this process, "Once agency has been brought to the fore, other terms readily accommodate themselves to its rule. Scenic materials become means which the organism itself is a confluence of means, each part being at the service of the other parts."[2]

It also might be worth discussing among both students and teachers the misconceptions of these agencies, both "pragmatic" and "scenic." Pragmatic agencies in the writing situation might be described as access to computers or features of word processing, such as voice-to-type capabilities, etc. While we have discussed the trained incapacity that many faculty members seem to have regarding their students "objective conditions" under which students write, there may be the same tendency to believe that all students have access to the same kinds of computers or word processing capabilities as they write. We have also analyzed the difference between the intrinsic characteristics of writing, such as thesis statements and counterarguments, and those extrinsic characteristics, such as curiosity, flexibility, and persistence. If we describe the writing act as "Persuading an audience of the writer's position on an important issue," then the agency might be those intrinsic characteristics of writing, "by means of a thesis statement and counterargument," but if we define the writing act as "trying to get a good grade in the class," then we might start moving from the pragmatic agencies, into those scenic agencies which

Burke describes. These "scenic" agencies are less visible to students themselves, but are perhaps even more powerful. For example, if we describe the act as "trying to get a good grade in the class," then the agency could run the spectrum from these extrinsic characteristics, such as "by means of curiosity, flexibility, and persistence," to "by means of following the exact rubric directions offered by the teacher." In other words, scenic agencies are no less powerful than pragmatic ones, but their differences are important. In order to examine the student writer's scenic agency we need to introduce a rhetorical concept we will be working with throughout this chapter, the concept of materialism, or material agency, into helping us answer the question "by what means" did the act occur?

According to Clay Spinuzzi, the principal of materialism is that "human and non-human agents are treated alike when considering how controversies are settled. This symmetry involves keeping constant the series of competencies, of properties, that human and non-human agents are able to swap by overlapping with one another."[3] What this means is that in order to discover how a student writer's scenic agencies might be affecting the act of writing, we need to list, we need to describe, every human and nonhuman "thing" in that writing situation. Paul Lynch writes, "The best we can do is imagine a project of gathering the various human and non-human disputants together and a project of casuistically stretching old demands to accommodate new ones."[4] So, let's begin our gathering of "things" in the writing situation: student, teacher, classroom, syllabus, other students, assignment sheet, rubric, computer, notebook, pen, pencil, calculator, phone, Google, Google Scholar, or Sparknotes …, okay, that is good for a start. What are the human and the nonhuman actors here, then? For the human actors, we have student, teacher, and other students. For the nonhuman actors, we have syllabus, assignment sheet, rubric, computer, notebook, pen, pencil, calculator, phone, Google, Google Scholar, and Sparknotes. Now, we can see the number of nonhuman actors in this list is much longer than the human actors, right? The rhetoric of scenic agency asks to think about which of these actors, human or nonhuman, has the greatest effect on the act, then? When students write a paper, which has more effect on how they write that paper, their peers or the assignment sheet? What has more effect, the rubric or the student themselves? In order to answer these questions, we can use the rhetorical terminology of Levi Bryant. For Bryant, objects are either "bright," those objects that "strongly manifest themselves and heavily impact other objects," or "dark," objects that "are so completely withdrawn that they [will] produce no local manifestations and [will] not affect any other objects."[5] So, which objects in the writing situation would you describe as "bright"? Your teacher, your instruction sheet, your rubric? Which object would you describe as "dark"? Your classmates? Yourself? Bryant's descriptions of these objects might be discouraging to you, but what is important to note about these descriptions is that once we have them then their brightness or darkness can be manipulated. James has written in another venue about this manipulation, "In this way, the brightness of assessment tools such as rubrics are diminished and made increasingly unobtrusive, while the writing of the student is made brighter through its unfolding traceability." If student writing is therefore associated with "bright" objects, then according to Bryant, those writings will "strongly manifest themselves and heavily impact other objects." If assessment tools such as rubrics become more associated with "dark" objects, then according to Bryant, they will become "so completely withdrawn that they [will] produce no local manifestations and [will] not affect any other objects."[6] In other words, how "bright" are your writing instruction sheets or rubrics? How "bright" is the student writer? If your rubric is "brighter" than the student in the writing situation, then by making the rubric "darker," we can make student writers "brighter."

The parlor: Make a list of the human and nonhuman actors for the last assignment you have had. Discuss those lists with your classmates. Which ones have the greatest effect on the writing act? Why? What do you think about this?

We have been discussing Burke's agency as it relates to the writing situation, but what about agency as it involves the rhetorical situation? For Bitzer, the speaker is the "agency" that steps into a specific rhetorical scene, but for Vatz, the scene is the "agency" that creates a new rhetorical situation. For Bitzer, the agency is pragmatic, but for Vatz, agency is more scenic. In this case, the writing rubric seems to be a result of pragmatic agency, yet Burke differentiates between the pragmatic function of instruments and how they may become scenic, "by means of" rhetorical situation creators:

> Instruments are essentially human since they are the products of human design. And in this respect, the pragmatist feature of agency seems well equipped to retain a personal ingredient in its circumference of motives. But as regards the functioning of agency on the symbolic level, we are advised to be on the lookout for a personal principle of another order, stemming from the fact that the human being in the stage of infancy, formatively experiences a realm of personal utility in the person of the mother.[7]

For Burke, a writing rubric might not necessarily constitute a nonhuman actor, since it is the product of human design. However, earlier in the *Grammar of Motives*, Burke wrote the following qualification:

> As for agency, Aristotle has this 'fifth' cause also in his list; but in accordance with the imperative genius of the purpose-agency (or end-means) ratio, instead of dealing

with agency as a special kind of cause (say, an 'instrumental cause') he introduces it incidentally to his discussion of 'final' cause. Thus after the Peripatetic has said that the desire for health might be the end, or final cause of walking, he goes on to say: 'The same is true of all the means that intervene before the end,' as 'purging, drugs, or instruments' may also be used for the sake of the same end. Thus, through this thinker, whose studies of logic traditionally go under the name of or the Organon (that is, the tool or instrument) omits agency as a fifth kind of cause, he clearly enough takes it into account.[8]

So, by taking into account not just the agency ratio, but the agency-purpose ratio, we are able to determine whether our rubric is a human actor, since for Burke instruments are human agencies, or whether our rubric is a nonhuman actor, since for Burke agencies can be more "purpose"-like than "agency-like. "We have cited enough to show that in Emerson secular agency is a function of divine purpose. Obviously if we narrow the circumference, by dropping the concept of final cause, we get to the true pragmatist stress upon agency as the ancestral term."[9] If the rubric is the instrument for "persuading an audience of a student's belief," then that rubric describes Vatz's rhetorical situation, and is scenic. If the rubric is the "means by which" getting a good grade is concerned, then the rubric is a nonhuman actor, more Bitzer-like in its approach to the rhetorical situation, and is more pragmatic, since its "desire for the end" of writing is operating more toward the purpose end of the agency-purpose ratio.

Scenic Agency

In the same way, we are not often attuned to the students' writing agencies in our reading and responding to their writing, we are often not attuned to the difficulty of implications of dramatic interpretation "by means of" Stanislavski's method. Constantine Stanislavski provided theater students one of the most widely used "by means of" methods, yet Stanislavski's method itself can work as a "trained incapacity," what Burke described as when our success blinds us to seeing a situation in any other way than what we've been conditioned to. According to David Ostwald:

> In order to behave as if you are your character, you need to describe her reality clearly and in detail. To develop your description, you draw on the information the composer and the librettist embody in the score. Because the creators of the piece supply it, this information is commonly called your Given Circumstances.[10]

We have examined how beginning with the information the composer and librettist supply is starting from an intrinsic point of view, so the use of these given circumstances starts from a position of starting to build the actor's character. If we describe the actor's "act" as "building my character interpretation," then the "means by which" the actor builds her character is "Stanislavski's Given Circumstances." Stanislavski's method is one of the most widely held agencies in all of theater production. But because it is one of the most widely held "by means which," it can also therefore be one of the most misleading. Ostwald writes, "Answering the following six questions as your character and in the first person will enable you to extract the essence of those circumstances from the wealth of material in a score: When are the events taking place? Where is my character? Who is my character? What does my character want? Why does she want it? What has just happened?"[11] Despite the fact that Stanislavski's method is one of the most widely used "by means which" actors develop their characters, you might notice a question that is missing from Stanislavski's list. Yes, you guessed it: "What are the means by which…my character uses to get what she wants." Students who faithfully follow Stanislavski's method will be left without examining the "means by which" their character is developed. In the second chapter we examined how Stanislavski's method is described as "the most efficient way to develop your character," and we examined how Burke's dramatism provides a "perspective of incongruity" to evade the "trained incapacity" of Stanislavski's method. In this chapter, we do not need to contrast them, for in Stanislavski, there is no opportunity to examine "the means by which" at all. What is interesting is that in Ostwald's description of Stanislavski's method, he seems to understand that the gap between actor and character is a difficult one to bridge, and he also seems to understand that even after following Stanislavski's method, there will still be gaps between the actor and character:

> The gap between you and your character can be closed by a clear analysis of your character's when where, who, want, and what, to which you apply the Magical *If*. On a more fundamental level, any gap between you and your characters, as well as between you and your audience, is closed by your shared humanity. It is your shared humanity that provides the common universe of feelings that make communication possible.[12]

The kind of "identification" being described here by Ostwald is not the identification that using Burke's dramatistic pentad allows us to get at. Jaclyn Olson described the process by which this happens:

> By attending to Burke's continued wrestling with the materiality of the body, I argue that we can see identification in a new light—not only as the means by which an individual situates herself into a social texture, but also as the ultimate rhetorical human motive, one that must be understood as anchored in the material existence of the "symbol using animal."[13]

The identification that eludes Ostwald in Stanislavski's "Given Circumstance" is the "means by which" actors can situate themselves "into a social texture." Not only that, but our shared humanity is not in our shared "understanding," but our shared [symbol] "using." We are able to "bridge the gaps" between actors and characters because of an understanding of the "means by which" the act occurred, and because we bring those agencies to the forefront, we can see where there is agreement and disagreement as part of our "common humanity."

Since Stanislavski's "Given Circumstances" also forms the basis for any character, scene, or staging analysis, it is not surprising that Deer and Del Vera do not explicitly address the "means by which" the act occurred in their instructions to acting students, either. The only time that Deer and Del Vera seem to discuss agency in their text, *Acting in Musical Theatre: A Comprehensive Course*, is in their discussion of "strategy and tactics" as a subset of acting "beats":

> Since you had a clear sense of what you were fighting against (obstacle), you were *spontaneously* developing how (tactics) to pursue those goals and overcome those obstacles. Strategy is the big how. Tactics are the little hows. Strategy is the big plan and tactics are the *moment-to moment* lunges, feints, jabs, retreats and counterattacks to what is *happening now*. Strategy is the way you plan to win large unit objectives, and tactics are the ways you pursue beat objectives.[14]

For Deer and Del Vera, the "means by which" to pursue goals and "overcome obstacles" are "spontaneously" developed. If we describe the act as "creating believable characters," then according to Deer and Del Vera, we would have to describe the "means by which" as "moment to moment reactions" to our given circumstances. One of the differences between Deer and Del Vera's concept of "the means by which" and Burke's is that by incorporating "the means by which" into the very discussion of the act itself, students can see whether or not these "means by which" are not spontaneous at all, but part of an overall schema consistent with their characters. In fact, through the dramatistic pentad, students might identify that the agency, the "means by which" the act was accomplished might have the most effect on the act itself, rather than just a "moment-to moment" reaction in their overall motivation.

In their examination of agency as a "spontaneous, moment-to-moment" reaction, Deer and Del Vera once again are utilizing the rhetorical concept of *kairos*. In chapter two, we discussed how for Deer and Del Vera, the actor was responsible for providing the *kairos* of a given situation, and yet it seems that now that agency is a spontaneous, moment to moment reaction, the actor is not responsible for providing the *kairos* of a given situation, but is reacting to it. Utilizing Burke's dramatistic pentad allows students to consistently apply *kairos*, "the right occasion," whether it is for understanding the "where and when" an act occurred, or whether it is for understanding "the means by which" the act occurred. For Deer and Del Vera, not only should that spontaneity be "timely," it should also appear "natural." In their description of the many "schools" of staging, Deer and Del Vera wrote the following:

> There are many schools of thought about what to do when staging a song. One says that you shouldn't stage it at all. People in that camp believe that simply playing your objective will be enough to create organic movement, and that anything extra will come off as phony or artificial. Others say that you need to plan every movement and gesture thoroughly to express your ideas about the journey of the song. Our opinion is that whatever your choice about movement and staging, it should be a conscious choice and should be appropriate for the song, the style and the circumstance. And no matter how heightened the theatrical reality of your song, *it needs to appear to be a spontaneous experience for the character in the context of your production.*[15]

For Deer and Del Vera, it does not matter whether or not the staging is spontaneous, but it only matters that it *appear* spontaneous. This may seem like a trivial distinction, but their description actually reveals a rhetorical motive. It was Aristotle who first spoke of appearances in rhetorical situations, "The whole business of rhetoric being concerned with appearances, we must pay attention to the subject of delivery, unworthy as it is, because we cannot do without it."[16] There seems to be a kind of theatrical neo-Aristotelianism running throughout Deer and Del Vera's description of "the means by which" actors can achieve their goals, as well. For them, staging is the result of being "in the moment," and this description is especially significant when we understand its similarities to the description of staging in Ostwald:

> Mature performers with years of experience learn to stage songs on their feet, as they are performing them, and develop instincts about when to move and when to stay still and let the power of their voice and the song carry the moment. But their instincts were developed over years of studying, experimenting and watching the work of others whom they respect. Chances are that you're not at that place yet. So, this is the beginning of your development of those instincts.[17]

For Ostwald, the expert stages by instinct, through osmosis of her experiences and situations. This description is not surprising, however, since in the absence of an analysis of the "means by which," who really knows how staging decisions are made. In other words, Ostwald seems to be saying that it must be instinct, since we are not able to describe that process. But the reason that process cannot be described is not because it does not exist, but because they begin by utilizing Stanislavski's "Given Circumstances." Since Stanislavski's "Given Circumstances" do not allow for a "means by which," then it makes sense that they cannot account for a staging method. We quote these descriptions at length to emphasize a particular point: Stanislavski's "Given Circumstances" are a kind of trained incapacity, keeping Ostwald from being able to describe a staging method. And again, this is ironic since they cannot describe a staging method while utilizing the most often used method of acting available. For both Ostwald, he cannot specifically explain how this happens, because of their trained incapacity from Stanislavski and the absence of any kind of "means by which" analysis of agency.

Speaking of Aristotle, perhaps one of the reasons why it is so easy to contrast character, scene, and staging analysis between Deer and Dal Vera's text and Burke's dramatistic pentad is found in the very definitions of rhetoric themselves. What is unique about Deer and Dal Vera's text is that they actually do pay attention to how rhetoric works in the staging process itself, but how they define rhetoric gives us some clues to why they ultimately differ with Burke's dramatism for character, scene, and staging analysis:

> Rhetoric is both the way a character makes his argument and the argument itself. So far, you've been concentrating on rhythm, poetic and prose structures, and the small sound units of consonants and vowels. You've been encountering the text through each of these as a way of engaging the sensory experience of the words. These various encounters with the text are designed to reveal dimensions and perspectives we might miss otherwise.[18]

For Deer and Dal Vera, rhetoric is the "way a character makes his argument and the argument itself." It seems then, that for Deer and Dal Vera, "argument" is the "means by which" the character, scene, or staging has occurred, making argument itself the agency by which actors move on stage. For example, if we describe the "act" as "Cinderella's staging after attending the ball," then the "means by which" that act is accomplished is "through Cinderella's argument and the argument itself." However, this relies on the assumption that each actor has "an argument to make" in every scene, in every situation. This dramatic neo-Aristotelianism leads to the assumption that there is an argument in every rhetorical act, and that therefore, "everything's an argument." This is where Burke and Deer and Dal Vera depart, since for Burke, argumentation is a characteristic of "old" rhetoric. "If I had to sum up in one word the differences between the old rhetoric and a new, I would reduce it to this: the key term for 'old' rhetoric was persuasion, and its stress was upon deliberate design. The key term for 'new' rhetoric would be identification, which could include an unconscious factor in appeal."[19] Remember that for Burke, dramatism was a "means by which" an actor could locate the places "where ambiguities necessarily arise," which is antithetical to Deer and Dal Vera's approach. Since they describe their "method" as "efficient," they need a method to avoid ambiguity and therefore it makes sense that they turn to argument as that "means by which"

AGENCY IN MOTION | 155

to avoid ambiguity. What is even more telling is how they describe the scholarly approach to theater performance:

> Next, well look at the ways of discovering meaning in the words. It isn't that we need to explore meaning because the sense of the lyric is obscure. Most musicals have librettos that are easy to follow. So, meaning in this case isn't about understanding in an intellectual way. It is about finding an emotionally evocative connection with the text through the argument of the piece.[20]

Nothing could be more antithetical to the study of theater performance, especially at the collegiate level. Not only does a use of Burke's dramatistic pentad in theater performance treat characterization, scene, and staging as a scholarly pursuit, but since "identification" itself is "a mind helping a body think," dramatism will reject simplistic "argumentation" as a "means by which" actors motivate their actions.

In the world of rhetoric and composition, writers have examined the consequences of these sets of assumptions on communication in these similar situations. Assuming that there is an argument to be made in a situation when the writer does not know what argument to make leads the speaker or writer away from an investigation of "means by which" the act occurred and toward a mere justification of any kind of argument to be had. For example, in our case of creating staging for Cinderella after her ball experience in *Into the Woods*, we might say that the "means by which" is "through Cinderella's argument and the argument itself." Deer and Dal Vera write the following:

> Even when a character is completely befuddled and banging around blindly in unreasoning confusion, there is still a logic to her experience. Sometimes, to sort things out, it helps to reduce what she's saying to the simplest level. At its most basic, every sentence has a subject, a verb, and sometimes an object (the thing the subject acts on).[21]

Here, Deer and Dal Vera's advice reduces the options for actors rather than expands upon them. However, if Cinderella does not have an argument to make, then these choices become justifications for her actions, rather than investigations into the dramatic possibilities at our disposal for creative staging. Since Deer and Dal Vera rely on argumentation as "means by which" Cinderella's staging may be justified, it discourages the actor portraying Cinderella to develop alternatives than simply confusion over her decisions. For Deer and Dal Vera, the task of the actor is to make a complex situation simple, but for Burke, it is to make as simple situation complex. Again, Deer and Dal Vera's own definitions of rhetoric seem to prevent them from being able to do this, and the student actors who follow their directions, from examining the ambiguity in ambiguous situations.

Every lyric has a point of view or an argument. You can take this as a given because every character is pursuing an objective. Rhetoric is the name applied to the persuasive devices writers and speakers use to carry their arguments. The way characters use words to push for their ideal outcome is their specific form of rhetoric. Looking at sentence structure is one way to reveal the argument or reasoning pattern. You might have a tendency to think of rhetoric as something rational. Actually, most arguments are a struggle between feeling and reason. Rhetoric is most persuasive when it appeals to the emotions (an explanation for why we have a paucity of reasoned political debate—it doesn't move people).[22]

By continually limiting rhetoric to the arguments that actors make, or the "persuasive devices writers and speakers use to carry arguments," Deer and Dal Vera double down on an Aristotelian rhetoric of logos, ethos, and pathos. Perhaps you have heard or may have studied these characteristics before. Logos is generally described as appeals to reason, ethos is usually described as appeals to the speaker's character, and pathos is generally described as appeals to emotion. Here, Deer and Dal Vera must incorporate appeals to emotion in order for rhetoric to be effective, since they already know that mere argument cannot achieve persuasion alone. However, what they miss is not just naming the incorrect part of these three terms, but by making persuasion the goal of the actor in the first place. For Burke, persuasion is not the goal, but identification, and as identification is "a mind making a body think," then "the means by which" that is accomplished is not any kind of argument that can persuade an audience, but the dramatistic act of identifying the bodily movement that the audience connects with that drama. How do you find the bodily movement that the audience will connect with? In order to do that, we need to make the character, scene, and staging analysis more complex, not less. Burke's pentad provides the opportunity to take a complicated show, such as Stephen Sondheim's *Into the Woods*, and not make it simpler, but to amplify its complexity, to demonstrate what a richly complicated production *Into the Woods* actually is. Jack Vietel wrote, "Because of its multiple plots (four of Grimm's fairy tales and an invented fifth one all woven together by James Lapine and Stephen Sondheim), *Into the Woods* leapfrogs through much of what we think of as traditional structure, seeking inventive solutions, and getting in and out of trouble. Its audacity more than makes up for its occasional murkiness, however, and it is never less than clear thematically. It deals primarily with parents and children and the gulf that accompanies the love between them."[23] Directors whose instinct is to simplify so there is an efficiency to the production process, ignore the complexity inherent in the lyrics and music of a production like *Into the Woods*, and as intellectual leaders in higher learning, Burke's dramatistic pentad allows students to be more complex learners, not less.

Casting Agency

To examine the complexity of *Into the Woods* a bit further, we can learn much from its production history. While textbooks such as Deer and Dal Vera's advise the student actor to "research the original production," they again do not give any direction on what student actors should do with this research. Should they copy it, or should they reject it? What will they find when they research the production history of *Into the Woods*? According to Barry Singer, "With *Into the Woods*, Stephen Sondheim did not so much attempt to awaken audiences as to infiltrate their dreams. A psycho-sexual deconstruction of selected Grimm fairy tales, *Into the Woods*—which preceded *Phantom* on Broadway by two months, opening at the Martin Beck Theater in November 1987—hardly pandered to the lowest common denominator that *Phantom* did."[24] Singer's description of *Into the Woods* as an "attempt to infiltrate their dreams" and not to "awaken audiences" seems important to note, here, and it seems counter to the lyrics of the texts themselves:[25]

So, the student reading this production history of *Into the Woods* will be told that it is not important to get their audiences to think during the performance. Deer and Dal Vera's advice to study the production history of a show, without giving advice on what to do with that production history, therefore, would seem to both reinforce Singer's description and Deer and Dal Vera's advice that "meaning in this case isn't about understanding in an intellectual way. It is about finding an emotionally evocative connection with the text through the argument of the piece.[26] Because Kimberly wanted both the students and the audience to experience *Into the Woods* on an intellectual, not an emotional level, she wanted her production to have the opposite effect that the Broadway production had had, as described in its production histories. Barry Singer supported his description by his assumptions of the audiences for *Into the Woods*, "In the nursery rhyme underpinning of many of its songs, *Into the Woods* could even be viewed as a grab for some Sondheim-lite, the great musical theater iconoclast's tentative, perhaps even unconscious, attempt at reaching a tiny bit larger, ever-so-slightly less discriminating crowd."[27] Singer's description highlights some important questions for the collegiate director: should a collegiate production aim for a more emotional message to reach a "tiny-bit larger, ever-so-slightly less discriminating crowd," or should a collegiate production "awaken audiences" from their slumber? Once again, students reading the production history without a sense of whether their performances should mimic the Broadway productions or work against them will generally try to find "an emotionally evocative connection," rather than being challenged to find "meaning in any intellectual way." In a collegiate performance setting, Kimberly believed that challenging students to find meaning in "many intellectual ways," could lead the students and audiences out of their slumber to be challenged on an intellectual level just as much as an emotional one. But in order to qualify himself, Singer added, "This is not to say that the show's score in any way lacked Sondheim's usual penetrating and sophisticated musical and verbal artistry. Commercially, it simply wasn't the tale of *Sweeney Todd* this time. Or even *Sunday in the Park with George Seurat*."[28] In other words, Singer needs Broadway's version of *Into the Woods* to be a psychological experience, rather than an intellectual one, but in order to justify this particular claim, he has to downplay the "musical and verbal artistry," and contrast *Into the Woods* with even less artistic musical and verbal shows such as *Sweeney Todd* or *Sunday in the Park with George*. Why does he need to do this? Why critique the cast and audience's intellectual challenges in performing *Into the Woods* in the first place? Since Singer contrasts *Into the Woods* with *Sweeney Todd* and *Sunday in the Park with George*, students must identify how those shows would be different, and the most obvious answer is that both of those shows focus on one individual, while *Into the Woods* does not. Singer seems to imply that *Into the Woods* is less accessible than *Sweeney Todd* or *Sunday in the Park with George* because of the heteroglossia in *Into the Woods*. Heteroglossia is probably not a term you are very familiar with, but it has its theoretical roots in Mikhail Bakhtin, a Russian literary critic who studied this phenomenon in the novels of Dostoevsky.[29] In Dostoevsky, Bakhtin found instances of situations in which several characters from differing socio-economic status were in one scene. More importantly, the characters who would be considered from lower socio-economic status ranks had as much authority as those from higher socio-economic status ranks, and Dostoevsky was able to achieve this through dialog. For Bakhtin, dialog is what gives characters of lower socio-economic rank an equal footing with those from higher socio-economic ranks. The same can be seen in Shakespeare, when Lear's fool is given some of the most important lines, or in Charles Dickens, when Stephen Blackpool and Sissy Jupe are given as much equal footing, even more so, in comparison to the "facts, facts, facts" of Thomas Gradgrind. Into the Woods operates on such levels, as well. Sondheim creates sub-characters that are just as important as major characters, and even more importantly, has sub-characters deliver important lines that move the story along, creating the phenomenon known as heteroglossia. For Singer, however, the heteroglossia of *Into the Woods* is a reason for its lack of popularity in contrast with shows that feature major characters throughout. For the acting techniques of Stanislavski demonstrated through the textbooks of those like Deer and Dal Vera, it is the actor's job to take a complicated scene and make it simpler. But for Burke and a dramatistic approach to music theater staging, it can be the actor's opportunity to demonstrate how complicated a scene actually is. More importantly, if student actors just need to "research the performance history" without any method on how to contextualize that history or justify challenging that history, then it becomes even more difficult to contextualize that history or challenge that performance for any reason, let alone the important challenge of creating intellectually challenging experiences for both student actors and audiences alike.

What was unique about *Into the Woods* that students will learn from researching its performance history is that it went through an extensive reading process before production. Singer described this process in detail:

> Written and directed by James Lapine, *Into the Woods* had received its first readings under Andrew Bishop and Ira Weitzman's auspices at Playwright's Horizons in November, 1985, followed in June 1986 by a pair of fully-staged readings at 890 Broadway, the rehearsal studio building that Michael Bennett had created with some of his profits from *A Chorus Line*.[30]

This was one part of the performance history of *Into the Woods* that we wanted to copy. Since the role of the Narrator/Mysterious Man is able to do this on stage—his words directly affect the movements of the characters—in early rehearsals, we took turns reading from the original Grimm fairy tales, just to get into the "Once upon a time" narrative structure of the plot. Once the student actors felt as if they were a narrator every time they delivered their lines, they began to feel as if they themselves were animating their own actions by their lines. Again, this had more of an intellectual, rather than an emotional impact, an aspect which Singer reverts back to in his own production history:

> The show then had premiered at the Old Globe Theater in San Diego in December, thus gaining for itself an out-of-town tryout in the traditional sense. This 50-performance run proved a creative boon, with Sondheim delivering the second act's 11 o'clock number, "No One is Alone," during the last days of rehearsal. "I remember him sitting down at the piano in our rehearsal room and singing this song he'd just written," recalled Ira Weitzman, "and all of us just cried.[31]

If the performance histories of *Into the Woods* support a more emotional interpretation than intellectual one, then in order to create an intellectual experience for the student actors and our audience, we needed to assemble a different performance history. We have already discussed the importance of Jeremy Tirrell's concept of the archives as a "new assemblage for a present moment," and this concept applies once again here in our production of *Into the Woods*, as well. In order to "assemble a new production history for a present moment," we turned to the Dance, Music, Recorded Sound, and Theater Divisions at the New York Public Library for the Performing Arts at Lincoln Center. While many of the archives of *Into the*

Woods are held at the Stephen Sondheim Society archives at Kingston University, London, it is the New York Public Library for the Performing Arts that holds the papers of Tony Straiges, Tony-award winning lighting designer for the Broadway production for *Into the Woods*. In their work, "Learning from the Archives," John Brereton and Cynthia Gannett encourage researchers to read the "narratives of archival construction itself."[32] Therefore, in this collection, Straiges's lighting designs take center stage, and it was this research that encouraged Kimberly to see lighting as a "means by which" the complexity of this story could be amplified.[33] One example of how this was done was through the use of lighting to characterize the Giant. In Singer's history, he wrote the following about the Broadway production's characterization of the Giant:

> Having the benefit of a tryout out of town did not spare *Into the Woods* a fairly brutal preview period on Broadway with premature sniping in the press and frantic rewrites nearly up until opening night. The authors never did quite solve the show's second act Giant problems. *Into the Woods* proved, nevertheless, a delight on many levels, particularly during a first act filled with charming melodies, disarming lyrics and a comedic classic in the song, "Agony." When in the second act things turned willfully darker, Sondheim-exploring the aftermath of "happily ever after"—offered three of his most poignantly heartfelt expressions, "No More," "No One is Alone," and "Children Will Listen," all songs of consolation and hope for fathers and sons, mothers and daughters. *Into the Woods* went on to enjoy what, for a Sondheim musical, constituted a very healthy Broadway run, 764 performances.[34]

For Singer, the "Giant problem," is one that must be minimized, but for the academic director, maybe the "Giant problem" is one that should be amplified. If it is to be amplified, then we wanted to make the Giant problem, "brighter," as Levi Bryant helps us understand materialist agency. Based on research done in the Dance, Music, Recorded Sound, and Theater Division at the New York Public Library for the Performing Arts at Lincoln Center, Kimberly utilized lighting to amplify the Giant's presence, with set directions that included flashing Gobos to indicate the danger that the Giant poses. The flashing gobos also signal the kind of heteroglossia that is possible as well, as when the Giant justifies her actions with theirs. The flashing gobos amplify the Giant's reasons, giving her reasons more weight, not less, and the flashing gobos focus the audience's attention and invite them to ponder, and possibly accept, this reasoning. In this case, Burke's agency ratio of "lighting" becomes the "means by which" we were able to "create an intellectual experience for both student actors and audiences." By making the Giant's reasoning "brighter," our production deemphasized the emotional pain that the Giant has inflicted upon the characters in order to amplify the intellectual complexity of the Giant's motives.

Into the Woulds

In order to make lighting an agency, a "means by which" in *Into the Woods*, we made the decision to have a forest of aspen woods rather than the traditional oaks and pines, and the white of the aspens would allow us to utilize color to portray moods or attitudes. The identification of woods with moral or psychological exploration is not new, most noticeable in Henry David Thoreau's *Walden*: "I went to the woods because I wished to live deliberately, to front only the essential facts of life, and see if I could not learn what it had to teach, and not, when I came to die, discover that I had not lived."[35] For Kimberly, the combination of the white woods was especially personal, since she was from Colorado and spent many days wandering the tall, white aspen "woulds" of her future. To give the perception of height on the stage, a large drop was created with no tops to the woods, just the trunks extending past the height of the proscenium. In addition, two groups of woods were made moveable, sliding on different tracks horizontally across the stage. Characters using this element of the set were also in charge of moving the woods to accomplish their purpose of hiding or misleading. Most often, this was the Witch and the Mysterious Man, two characters with the most to lose, or the most to gain, in the show. They used the woods to hide, to change clothes, to move through the woods, as when the Mysterious Man appears to Jack in Act I, Scene 2.

Other characters also use the woods to eavesdrop and spy. As the Wolf stalks Little Red Riding Hood (LRRH), he deftly uses the woods to approach her in Act I, Scene 2, but the Baker also "appears behind a tree and eavesdrops," assuring the safety of Little Red. The Baker proceeds to observe the song "Hello, Little Girl" from behind the tree. As the song comes to an end and the Wolf and Little Red exit the stage, the Baker appears from behind the tree, but now realizes that he is being spied on by the Witch, who is also watching and eavesdropping on him. When asked about stealing Little Red's cape, the Witch says, "I could if I *would*," which then motivates her movement into the "woods," hiding behind the tree. The word "would" is a pun on "wood," but it also serves as a "means by which" she is motivated to act on stage. Remember that definition of rhetoric which Deer and Dal Vera used? "Rhetoric is both the way a character makes his argument and the argument itself."[36] The phrase "the way a character makes his argument," seems to be some sort of agency, a "means by which." For Deer and Dal Vera in this instance, the word "would" becomes a "means by which" the "Witch" carries out her argument, as they write, "So far you've been concentrating on rhythm, poetic and prose structures, and the small sound units of consonants and vowels. You've been encountering the text through each of these as a way of engaging the sensory experience of the words. These various encounters with the text are designed to reveal dimensions and perspectives we might miss otherwise."[37] However, while these "woulds" do reveal these new "dimensions and perspectives," for the Witch, it really is not an argument at all. In this case, the "woulds" are the "means by which" the "Witch/Which" leaves the argument, ignores the argument, and abdicates her role in the argument. These are sometimes called "rhetorical refusals," when writers or speakers refuse to enter into conversation or any other rhetorical situation. We use the moveable "woods" set pieces for the actors to retreat into the "woulds," those rhetorical refusals which suspend conclusion.

What is important about using the "woods" for "woulds" is how they intensify the intellectual impact of the script. Again, Deer and Dal Vera's character, scene, and staging analysis seem to ignore any kind of intellectual connections the actors or the audiences could make. "It isn't that we need to explore meaning because the sense of the lyric is obscure. Most musicals have librettos that are easy to follow. So, meaning in this case isn't about understanding in an intellectual way. It is about finding an emotionally evocative connection with the text through the argument of the piece."[38] Sondheim's libretto is extremely difficult to follow. Deer and Dal Vera would have us simplify the intellectual interplay of Sondheim's words into emotions, and their "means by which" they hope to accomplish this is through "finding the argument." What is interesting is that for Deer and Dal Vera, argumentation is a "means by which" an emotional connection can be made, not an intellectual one. While we often encourage students heighten the argument by "raising the stakes," Burke's dramatism demonstrates that this additional "trained incapacity," only seems to encourage the actor to argue louder, not differently. It would seem that an "argument" would evoke a more intellectual connection, but this description tells us how argumentation is not an "intellectual means by which," or at least not as much of an intellectual "means by which" as utilizing the "woulds," and those subsequent rhetorical refusals, as motivated staging with the "woods."

Scenic Agency

Just when it seems that Burke's dramatistic pentad should have come to the end of their usefulness, they reveal even further "means by which" to generate character, scene, and staging analysis, and it is his extension of "scenic agency" that we find our examples in theater production, especially music theater production. Burke wrote that "The sixth element, spectacle, he assigns to 'manner,' a kind of modality that we should want to classify under scene, though Aristotle's view of it as accessory would seem to make it rather a kind of scenic agency. It was not until modern naturalism in drama that scene gained its full independence, with the 'property man' giving the environmental placement that was regularly suggested in Elizabethan drama, for instance, by the use of verbal imagery."[39] In this chapter, we will detail how utilizing Burke's dramatistic pentad for props and their movement on stage creates new ways for audiences to think about the role of art. In this production of Stephen Sondheim's *Into the Woods*, students used pentad work not only to determine *how*, where, when, and why they should move, but also how the objects should move on stage in every scene.

We have already introduced the rhetorical theory of Bruno Latour and the principal of materialism in the writing classroom. If you will remember, materialism is that "human and non-human agents are treated alike when considering how controversies are settled. This symmetry involves keeping constant the series of competencies, of properties, that human and non-human agents are able to swap by overlapping with one another."[40] This symmetry means that there are object-using humans (quasi-subjects), and human-using objects (quasi-objects). This symmetry has yet to be explored in musical theater production, and this chapter details how the director encouraged students to use this symmetry to inform their characterizations and their movement as blocking on stage.

While it might seem strange to treat humans, nonhumans, and objects alike, Disney films operate on such a basis. The mice save Cinderella and sing. Candlesticks also talk and sing. In *Into the Woods*, there is a cow-using Jack, who is different from a bean-using Jack. There are Jack-using beans, which are different from the Baker's Wife-using beans. Objects are important in *Into the Woods*:

- The Cow as white as milk
- The Cape as red as blood
- The Hair as yellow as corn
- The Slipper as pure as gold

Students completed pentad on the act of taking the object from the point of view of their character. For example, the Baker's wife completed a pentad with the act being "Taking the slipper":

Not only is pentad done from the perspective of the actors, but also from the perspective of the objects.

- Act—what has happened to the object
- Scene—describe the setting from the point of view of the object
- Agent—describe the person taking the object from the point of view of the object
- Agency—describe the means by which the object is taken from the point of view of the object

- Purpose—describe the reason why the object was taken from the point of view of the object

Then the students completed a pentad from the point of view of the object itself, in order for them to see how their character feels about the person taking their object, and also how the objects themselves feel about being taken. So, for example, the actor portraying the Baker's Wife indicated that in the first pentad from her perspective, the purpose had the greatest effect on the act of taking the slipper. But when she completed the pentad from the perspective of the slipper itself, the Baker's Wife indicated that the Agent had the greatest effect on the Act, "The slipper is used to having one owner, and then goes to 'who the hell are all these people?'" This perspective not only informed her characterization but also her interaction with the slipper itself, how she held it, and how she moved on stage with and without the slipper. Therefore, a pentad from the perspective of the object looks something like this:

- Act—taking the slipper
- Scene—I have tar all over me, and where is my mate?
- Agent—maybe she can help me find my mate or at least get this tar off me.
- Agency—she has really strong hands—I hope she doesn't grab me again.
- Purpose—I'm no good without my mate, so I might as well go ahead and go with this person who seems to really need me.

While dramatistic pentad help actors understand how their character is part of another character's life in that story, materialist symmetry helps actors understand how their character is part of another object's life in that story. In contrast, here is how Deer and Dal Vera describe how student actors should utilize props in their characterization, scene, and staging analysis:

> The physical shape of the playing space can add opportunities and obstacles to your performance. Props can have the same effect. Tevye hauls a milk can around the stage for much of *Fiddler on the Roof*. Try playing Horton in *Seussical* and you'll soon discover the major scenic element you deal with is a **rolling tree** you sit on for almost half the show. These will affect your performance significantly, so it behooves you to include scenic elements in your creative process.[41]

While Deer and Dal Vera identify that object-using humans will affect an actor's performance, they are not able to describe how an object-using human will affect the actor's performance. In their example above, if the "means by which" is a "rolling tree," there is an assumption that the rolling tree will affect the actor, but the actor will not affect the rolling tree. Latour's materialistic symmetry understands that it is just as important to think about how the actor will affect the "rolling tree" as the "rolling tree" does the actor. Actors that are using objects he calls "quasi-subjects," but for objects that are using human agents, he calls "quasi-objects." While Kenneth Burke preceded Latour by over fifty-years and Deer and Dal Vera by almost seventy-five, he describes a similar situation:

> In the first place, it is important to note any source of ambiguity that has great bearing upon the structure of language in all its levels: Grammatical, Rhetorical, and Symbolic. Thus, our concern with the ways of characterization, summarization, and placement requires us to not a point so critical as that watershed moment dividing the dramatistic from the operationalist. The realm of motion is now par excellence the realm of instruments. No instrument can record or gauge anything in the realm of action ('ideas') except insofar as the subject-matter can be reduced to the realm of motion.[42]

In other words, Burke describes Deer and Dal Vera's rolling log as an instrument, yet because Deer and Dal Vera limit that "instrument" to its function only as a prop to be manipulated by the actor using it, it cannot "record or gauge anything in the realm of action," it is only a log "in motion," at this point. These differences are stark, since Burke's pentad analysis complicates, or rather multiplies the dramatic options within the agent-agency ratio. While Deer and Dal Vera reduce those options, Burke always wants us to consider how complicated a dramatic situation can be made to be. Burke knew there would be doubters to this approach, even raising the objection himself, "But it may be asked, why make so much of the turn from action to motion in the vocabularies of human motivation when in the same breath we testify to the ways in which the distinction is continually being obliterated or obscured?"[43] For Burke, the most important difference between motion and action was a question of agency, "the means by which" the act occurred. An act is characterized by a "means by which," whereas a motion is not, yet at the same time we are trying to clarify those distinctions, Burke warns us against such oversimplifications. The gaps between action and motion that Burke described are seen here in Deer and Del Vera's advice to actors when working with physical action:

> Make a large physical commitment to each idea to intensify the physical impulse toward the action underlying every idea. Go over the top. Get feedback to see whether the show requires large physical action or if you should take the large physical impulse and pull it back in to a more naturalistic expression. In general, because songs are more heightened than text sections they will ask for a larger physical commitment.[44]

As Deer and Del Vera utilize Stanislavski's "Given Circumstances," they are still left with telling student actors to "get feedback to see" what effects their blocking will have. By utilizing Burke's dramatistic pentad, students will have already seen the effects their "means by which" will have on the other actors or scenes

involved. In the second chapter, we utilized Burke's concept of scene to complicate Stanislavski's "Given Circumstances" to include characterization of the actor's
"when and where the act occurred" by the characters. For example, the stage notes
that were given regarding the grandness of the fabric as affecting stage presence.
By using dramatistic pentad from the point of view of the objects themselves, they
are able to see the effects of their "means by which" on the other objects involved.

Staging Object Agencies

In following the advice of Deer and Dal Vera to "research previous productions,"
the actor portraying Cinderella would read the following critique from Jack Viertel:
"Cinderella, returning from her first encounter with the Prince in *Into the Woods*,
comes to a dead halt somewhere on the path home to ponder her fate. She's
been to the ball, but we haven't, so she needs to tell us what happened—or at
least what's happened to her."[45] In other words, Cinderella finds herself among
the "woulds" of her future after the ball. For Viertel, the exigence for her singing
the song "Steps of the Palace" is the essence of narrative storytelling itself, and
her "rhetorical situation" seems most closely allied with Lloyd Bitzer's—the
speaker steps into a situation to meet the needs of that situation, i.e., there is
a narrative void for the audience and Cinderella must fill that void. The actor
portraying Cinderella would also read the following from Viertel, "Cinderella
has to portray certainty and wisdom in a situation where she may actually pos-
sess neither."[46]

We quote Viertel's reasoning through this particular scene in order to establish the limitations of taking a complex musical number and simplifying it for the
audience. For Viertel, the "means by which" Cinderella must decide is to "appear
decisive." However, the second reason for examining this passage at length is to
demonstrate the limitations of conviction or argument as a basis for staging in
this scene. For example, if the student actor portraying Cinderella follows Viertel's
analysis of Cinderella here, then her "means by which" she solves her dilemma
is "by means of appearing decisive." But if you follow the lyrics that Viertel has
himself provided, that is not the case at all. The "means by which" she solves her
dilemma is not by appearing decisive, but "by means of a shoe."

In "Steps of the Palace," the dichotomy of Cinderella and her shoes stuck in
tar, all the while singing a rushed patter song to a busy accompaniment intensifies
the necessary decisions and questions to the audience that Cinderella has to face.
The agency of the stuck shoe is the "means by which" that helps her realize that her
"super objective" of "making a decision," is the full circle of dramatism, for in this

case, there is minimal stage motion, for it is the fast music, and the object of the shoe, rather than a person, that is the "means by which" she is able to deliver this message to the Prince.

In Act I Scene 5, Cinderella says that she won't decide but will leave behind her shoe instead. As a "means by which," Cinderella's shoe becomes a "quasi-object," meaning that it is the shoe that delivers Cinderella's message to the Prince. The prince then becomes a "quasi-subject," since he is now a "shoe-using Prince," which is different than a non-shoe-using Prince. The student actor portraying Cinderella now does not have to "deliver an argument," or "appear decisive." Rather, the "means by which" the actor portraying Cinderella can decide is through the "shoe-using" Prince. And by changing the agency from "appearing decisive" to "a shoe-using Prince," we have changed the nature of the rhetorical situation from one more closely allied with Bitzer's notion to that of Vatz's, that the speaker has created a new rhetorical situation—the "means by which" Cinderella makes a decision, the shoe, is now in the hands of the Prince.

The problem with utilizing argument as a "means by which" is that it can become a default mode for staging, often when that is not the optimal movement on stage. For example, just before the Baker's Wife sings "Moments in the Woods," she has just kissed the Prince and realizes what this means for herself and her family. For Deer and Dal Vera, the "means by which" the act occurred is through "the argument that the character is making." They write the following:

> Find and anchor the argument, physically. Start by identifying the argument the character is making. What is the essential question or persuasive point being made? Simplify and paraphrase that argument. Look for contrasting or antithetical ideas (not this, but that). Look for ideas that repeat and intensify (ladders, or this plus that). Find places to anchor the antithetical ideas and places to build the ladders. Decide how your character feels about each idea. Sometimes characters are torn between two opposing things that they want. Sometimes they are repulsed by one thing and drawn to another.[47]

However, again in the case of another character in *Into the Woods*, the character does not know which argument to make. In Act II Scene 2, the Baker's Wife has been kissed by Cinderella's Prince along her journey to find Jack.

As Kimberly contemplated how to stage this song—a repetitive, strophic number—she thought about the Baker's Wife's super objective and her struggle to find her purpose. Becoming a mother is still not enough. Yet she is singing about her moment in the "woulds" with the Prince. Placing her center stage with the Prince referenced on one side and the Baker on the other side depicted her struggle with which one to choose, debating the merits of each. The actor portraying the Baker's Wife was given center stage as home base and then her movement stage right to stage left highlighted the indecision she is faced with movement so many steps to the right and left on particular verses. Dramatism came full circle once she associated the movements with the text and used center as neutral.

In contrast to "The Steps of the Palace," the motion in "Moments in the Woods" was created by the actor, not the quasi-object, the shoe. For example, we used center stage to illustrate her space of rhetorical refusal; but she moved stage left on the word "and," referring to the Prince, and moved stage right on the word "or," referring to the Baker.

Our pentad theme does adjust a bit in Act II—all the objects have been attained and made useful for their intended purpose. The Act is to save themselves from the Giant, the Agency becoming the how—the woods themselves became the "means by which" the act occurred, and the "means by which" they were able to carry out their objective—the rhetorical refusal. In other words, argument as a "means by which" the actors stage themselves becomes a "trained incapacity" when the actors must avoid making argument in the first place, when they must avoid making a decision, when they must refuse a rhetorical response, and when they must create a new rhetorical situation.

Director's Notes

Why This Show

Into the Woods provided the students with an opportunity to explore what they thought were "children's stories." I myself have always connected to the Cinderella narrative, only because I had previous experience playing Cinderella in a community theater production. Not only had I played the role of Cinderella before, but I had a respect for the complicatedness of this show as I had also been behind the keyboard for many rehearsals throughout the years. The music is difficult, not your typical emotional rendering of a fairy tale—either musically or theatrically. However, I believe because of our focus on intensifying the intellectual challenges of our production, we were nominated for Excellence in Directing by the Kennedy Center American Theater Festival and represented the school in a performance of scenes at the 51st Annual Region IV Festival.

Variables

For a show like *Aida*, we needed to cut costs with our staging budget since we were also "in rep" with the play being staged by our theater department. For this show, we needed to cut musical costs. Like many music departments, we were at a crossroads—to pay or not to pay the student musicians in the pit. While we all seemed to agree to stop paying the student musicians and make it part of the curriculum, actually following through on those plans proved more of a challenge. Even though it takes some extra patience on the part of the production team, I love to use students as much as possible in every aspect of a show—it is part of their education. However, I had not been happy with the quality of the student-hired musicians on my last show, and so we decided to pick a show that I could either use tracks or OrchExtra as an accompaniment. *Into the Woods* offered both, and in spite of the uninspiring nature of making budget decisions like this, *Into the Woods* did inspire scene, lighting, and costume design.

Into the Woods maintains a myopic focus on objects—how to get them, who is going to get them, where they will find them, etc. However, just like the more traditional, easy-going fairy tale renditions of Disney where the wardrobe, clock, teapot, and cup and saucer of *Beauty and the Beast* talk and have stakes in the plot, we also discover in *Into the Woods* a perfect example of what we call "materialism." Stated earlier in this chapter, materialism is the principle that "human and non-human agents are treated alike when considering how controversies are settled. This symmetry involves keeping constant the series of competencies, of properties, that human and nonhuman agents are able to swap by overlapping with one another."[48] While this particular definition was especially difficult for students to understand, our examples of red tide here in Florida or how Disney films operate provided easier to utilize examples. In our production of *Into the Woods*, the line between human and nonhuman actor is often very blurry. For example, some directors actually choose to cast the Cow as a person, an interesting choice and one that I respect. This production, however, decided to make the cow a technical, inanimate design feature of the show, a nonhuman object that served to complicate to materialistically complicate the drama rather than simplify it. To characterize the cow by casting it as a person seems to simplify rather than complicate the drama.

Materialism as a Theme

We even incorporated materialism into the theme statement for our production:
"Every journey *Into the Woods* shows us that wishes are not always pure, good and bad are not that different, and only togetherness can get us through." The "togetherness" we imply does not just involve human actors, but a "togetherness" of human and nonhuman actors will get us through. We developed this human and nonhuman togetherness through our table work.

Table Work

We focused on the taking of the objects from the perspective of the actors first:

- Act—taking the Hair
- Scene—woods, between 2nd and last midnight, Milky-White is dead
- Agent—Witch, for purposes of her own, jealousy over the Prince
- Agency—Sings Stay with Me, manipulates Rapunzel to submit
- Purpose—to punish Rapunzel for disobedience, keep her plan in place

- Act—taking the Hair
- Scene—Rapunzel's tower, in the woods, dusk
- Agent—Baker's Wife, 3 of 4 things, almost there!
- Agency—Rapunzel's Prince, Witch—she studied the routines
- Purpose—no impediments, Rapunzel believes her, for a child of her own

- Act—taking the cape
- Scene—Granny's house, evening, inside the wolf
- Agent—Wolf—he eats little girls
- Agency—LRRH lured off the path, gave the wolf time
- Purpose—so the Baker could rescue them, getting the cape as a gift in return

- Act—taking the cow
- Scene—the woods, early afternoon, time to get all 4 things, energized by getting this 1st thing
- Agent—Baker, from Jack, because his mother didn't want it and needed money $
- Agency—a trade for beans
- Purpose—to do what they're told to do to end the curse

- Act—taking the slipper
- Scene—outside the palace, last Festival
- Agent—Baker's Wife, tired, the last thing she needs
- Agency—the sound of the Prince approaching
- Purpose—Cinderella can run faster with two shoes

Then we focused on pentad from the perspective of the object. This particular exercise was fun as we imagined what these objects would be saying back to us as actors or directors given the elements of the pentad.

- Act—hair getting cut
- Scene—attached to a girl in a tower who is traumatized, confused, and spoiled
- Agent—Witch
- Agency—scissors (I have never been cut before)
- Purpose—to separate

- Act—cape getting taken
- Scene—on LRRH
- Agent—Baker
- Agency—stolen
- Purpose—I'm not sure, but everyone loves a red cape

- Act—cow getting sold
- Scene—the scary woods where I get lost
- Agent—Baker, I mean the Butcher
- Agency—I got sold for beans?
- Purpose—I am worthless

- Act—slipper getting given away
- Scene—I'm full of tar and have no mate
- Agent—Cinderella
- Agency—Baker's wife traded her two shoes
- Purpose—Cinderella doesn't need pretty shoes anymore, especially only one

Scene by Scene: Materialism

The beans provide an especial place in pentad work for this show. They are both given and taken as a means to acquire all the other objects in the plot. They buy the cow, they barter for the slipper, and they grow the beanstalk. How they are exchanged, i.e., the Act involving the beans becoming the Agency of the scene in How they are exchanged, bears analysis. At the point of changing hands from the Baker and his Wife, this scene with the beans allows observation of materialism in all its forms—objects (the beans and the cow) and the scenic elements of the woods:

In Act I Scene 2, Jack encounters the Baker and his Wife who offer to buy Milky White for a sack of beans instead of money. At the point of viewing the scene materialistically, the beans have feelings as does Milky White. To the extent that Milky White is not cast as a person, Jack can respond to the animal as if it does have feelings.

If the beans are eager to be exchanged for the cow, maybe the Baker struggles holding onto them, dropping them and being clumsy with them. If the beans want to stay with the Baker, he struggles letting them go. The options are fun to play with and totally up to the director.

Jack sings goodbye to his cow with the same materialism. Per the previous pentad from the cow's perspective:

- Act—cow getting sold
- Scene—the scary woods where I get lost
- Agent—Baker, I mean the Butcher
- Agency—I got sold for beans?
- Purpose—I am worthless

As he sings, Jack can physically embody trying to get the cow to go with them and let go of him. Additionally, the Baker and the Baker's Wife can react with subtext inspired by this pentad from the cow's perspective. When Jack determines he will purchase him again, his subtext is "How can we do this to you?" since he is still mistaken that the Baker is a butcher.

Our work on pentad from the perspective of the object really helped the actors as they interacted onstage with them. The actors personified their objects and treated them like fellow characters, bringing interesting actions and reactions to those scenes. One of my favorite relationships was Jack with his cow, treating Milky White as if she could hear conversations, petting her, talking to her, referring to the Baker as the Butcher. This relationship of Jack with his cow is reinforced in Act II Scene 1. When Jack calls the baker "the butcher," the Baker's subtext is "I'm offended." This subtext creates a consubstantiality with the cow that is necessary for the Baker in motivating his action to save the cow.

"Our Little World" is a number that is sometimes not performed, but this song really helps establish the complexity of Rapunzel and her relationships with her hair and her mother. In Act I Scene 2, at the point her hair gets cut at the end of "Stay with Me," there are audible reactions from the audience. We can only surmise how the hair feels about being cut, but "Our Little World" firmly establishes how Rapunzel feels about her hair and how the Witch sees Rapunzel's hair in their relationship. This was the primary reason I wanted to include "Our Little World" in our production—it reinforced the materialistic pentad in a very strong way.

Scene by Scene: Motion

Because dramatism is not just a linguistic analysis, but also tied to movement, staging becomes a tool of the director to be able to dramatize the story for an audience.

Figure 4.1 *Into the Woods*: "Rapunzel." Photo credit: Candace Dickens

Utilizing the pentad system gives the director and the actors multiple choices to make, all of which can be strong and effective. On the side of linguistic analysis, I still like to utilize super objectives for a character throughout a show. For *Into the Woods*, I had the following to work with:

- Jack—I want to be THE MAN
- Jack's Mother—I want Jack to stay a little boy forever
- Cinderella—I want to find my home
- Narrator—I want to tell the story
- Mysterious Man—I want resolution
- Baker—I want to please my wife
- Baker's Wife—I want to discover my purpose
- LRRH—I want to find family
- Stepmother—I want to be in charge
- Florinda—I want to feel valued
- Lucinda—I want attention
- Witch—I want to start over
- Cinderella's Prince—I want to do whatever I want with no consequences
- Rapunzel's Prince—I want to find happiness
- Rapunzel—I want freedom

- Wolf—I want to survive
- Steward—I want to keep my job

Super objectives are arrived at through a thorough reading of the script, more than once, and discussions about everything from backstory to the writing of the show to musical analysis. At the point of musical analysis, decisions about movement first come into play. Is the stage direction going to work with or against the music? A lot of emotions can be evoked through a character's blocking turning frantic over a simple song, or calm and still amidst a busy underscore. You can also emote effectively by complimenting the music with action rather than contrasting with it. If language is drama, as in how "words shimmer," music as a language can also function the same way, as in "pitches shimmer," or "rhythm shimmers." In the scene "Steps of the Palace," we contradicted the "dialect" of the "patter song," but in "Your Fault," the blocking intensifies the drama of the up tempo ostinato structure of the pitches and rhythms, which both intensifies and is intensified by the staging.

"Your Fault"

We conclude this chapter with perhaps a penultimate experiment in dramatism and in materialism. When one thinks of *Into the Woods* and the numbers that are considered "hard," "Your Fault" immediately comes to mind. For an opera singer it is the equivalent to, say, the *Carmen* quintet. This is an example of when materialism helped complicate the staging in some very productive ways. Nathaniel Rivers's example on gun control provided the clearest example of object agency: "Perhaps the most familiar invoking of the humanist notion of agency is the old National Rifle Association defense: guns don't kill people, people kill people. Materialist symmetry shows us that a gun being held and a person holding a gun are distinct from an unarmed person and an unheld gun."[49] This example of gun control served us well as we staged, "Your Fault," since the objects themselves and their rhetorical circulation are a "means by which" fault is being passed around. After our staging of "Your Fault," students came to realize that they themselves could create an even more specific example themselves. We hope that however you are using this book, you find our example of staging in "Your Fault" a way to help students understand how the objects are responsible for the actions of the characters, not the characters themselves.

Another great example of the "means by which" in this scene is in the music. The staging can intensify the music, not simplify it. Although the music maintains a rhythmic intensity, a careful examination of which lines are directed to each character will lead a director to some fairly obvious crosses the actors can make while they pass the blame around. The scene before is the revelation that the Baker's Wife is dead and Jack has buried her in the Giant's footprint. The Baker has wandered downstage and away from the others as he contemplates how this possibly could have happened. The Witch has reiterated that the only thing left is to get Jack to the Giant. As the Witch lunges for Jack, and Cinderella and Little Red protect him, the Baker agrees with her and the song begins. After much consideration and debate among the cast members in this scene, it was decided that the baby could play an important role as an object. Treating the baby as an object created a material symmetry of the baby's human and nonhuman actor status, since the baby could not effectively act on stage. The actors holding the baby became quasi-subjects—baby-using actors—and the baby became a quasi-object, an actor-using baby. This suggestion was actually made by the actor who played the Witch, and since she takes the baby from Cinderella and gives it back to the Baker, it is symbolic of her authority and control in the last scene in which she appears.

The Baker begins the scene, blaming Jack right away for the fact that there is a giant among them and his wife has died as a result. Little Red and Cinderella protect Jack from the distraught Baker, taking a stance on the opposite side of the stage.

At this point, Jack states "it isn't my fault…you persuaded me to trade away my cow for beans" as he makes his way through LRRH and Cinderella in order to face off with the Baker who is all the way stage left. The Baker takes him on, moving toward center. The Witch peels off to let the back and forth begin and watches from the sidelines. LRRH stays center stage as she weighs in on the Baker and Jack.

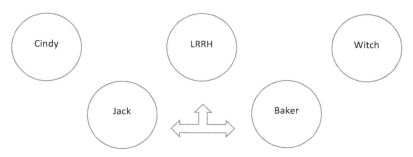

As each character passes blame here, there, and everywhere, we get deliberate movement on stage that is motivated completely by the *receiver* of the blame: in receiving blame from someone else the receiver becomes the giver. LRRH continues to play the analyzer, always getting in the middle of the primary argument, other actors becoming observers. Jack remembers that he only stole the gold to get his cow back—from the Baker—prompting Little Red to join the "blame the Baker" team.

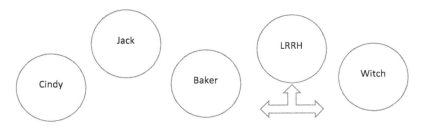

After an argument about the gold and the cow, it becomes an argument about the beans. The Witch places confusion about it being "his father's fault" his house was cursed, and Little Red moves aside to ponder that possibility, all the while the Baker begins to retrace his steps trying to remember. His retreat upstage creates a hole for Jack to fill. The Witch gradually retreats, hinting at the fact that she really knows everything. She routinely migrates upstage once she says something that places doubt and fear among the other characters.

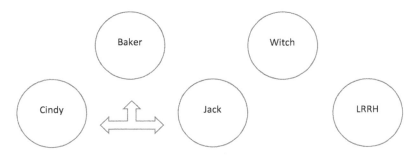

The continued back and forth brings us various pairings as each character remembers more and more about how they got to where they are. As the Baker remembers pocketing the other bean that he gave to his wife, he confronts Cinderella. Her position moves to a middle position between Jack and the Baker in an effort to defend herself from the two of them—motion motivated by her receiving the blame from the Baker. Little Red continues to observe.

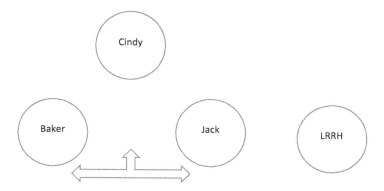

As the last phase of the argument unfolds, Cinderella mentions the harp, and Jack finally turns some blame on LRRH for daring him to get it. The Baker follows suit, the three of them tighten their position on the stage, and Little Red is isolated in their joint attack.

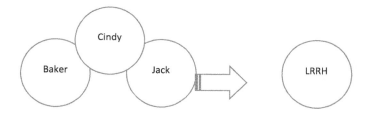

Cinderella finally crosses to Little Red as her anger motivates her on the line "if you hadn't dared him to," leaving Jack and the Baker stage right.

Gradually the group unifies in directing all of the blame toward the Witch as the one who "raised [the beans] in the first place." The Witch has been calmly observing the group as they argue and we have hardly noticed her with everything going on. But, as the Witch realizes they have figured it out, she makes her way downstage center, seemingly out of nowhere, for "Last Midnight." As she makes her way downstage, we realize she has the baby. We aren't exactly sure when the

Witch obtained the baby, but she definitely has it at the beginning of this number. There is a certain amount of shock value to extort from your audience with the object of the baby in this scene. Play around with this aspect of the scene in your own performance of this show. There are many options to consider!

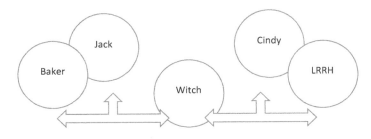

Figure 4.2 *Into the Woods*: "Last Midnight." Photo credit: Candace Dickens

As "Last Midnight" commences, the motivation for movement is to avoid the Witch at every turn. She is able to direct specific lines at specific characters, forcing them to receive her condemnation and respond accordingly—with movement. They are all receivers of her blame. This scene was improvised every performance, empowering the Witch to deliver her lines as if it were the first time, although patterns of reception and response emerged after several rehearsals.

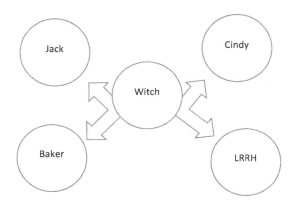

The characters begin to gravitate towards each other as the Witch singles them out. She starts with the Baker ("Told a little lie") to Jack ("Stole a little gold") to Cinderella ("Broke a little vow") and finally to Little Red ("Did you?"). The characters retreat with each accusation from the Witch, gravitating stage left just in time to make a human shield to protect Jack. The baby gets passed to Cinderella at the point the Witch focuses attention on Jack, a relief for the audience as we comprehend where this scene is going.

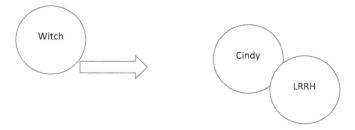

As a final attempt at intimidation, the Witch circles around behind the group, again forcing them apart before she begins throwing the beans, at which point they all scatter.

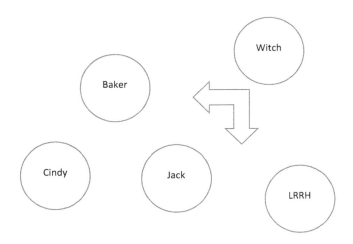

The Witch needs to keep them apart, and succeeds at different points in this scene, especially with the scattering of the beans all over the stage, each character frantically trying to retrieve them. She succeeds in getting them to question their actions even after she departs. However, the visualization of these four characters exhibiting the theme of the show with their movements, "only togetherness can get us through," is a poignant segue out of this number and into "No More" and "No One Is Alone."

> In this case, the characters are moving from certainty to uncertainty. They begin with "a point of view or an argument … because every character is pursuing an objective."[50] However, the staging of "Your Fault" in this musical becomes a penultimate experiment in dramatism, since it is not persuasion that becomes the "means by which" they learn to accept their own responsibility, but by being "in motion." We have discussed how Deer and Dal Vera define rhetoric, but after our staging of "Your Fault," it bears repeating:

> Rhetoric is the name applied to the persuasive devices writers and speakers use to carry their arguments. The way characters use words to push for their ideal outcome is their specific form of rhetoric. You might have a tendency to think of rhetoric as something rational. Actually, most arguments are a struggle between feeling and reason. Rhetoric is most persuasive when it appeals to the emotions (an explanation for why we have a paucity of reasoned political debate—it doesn't move people).[51]

For Deer and Dal Vera, emotions precede movement, but for Burke, movement precedes emotions, since dramatism is a "mind helping a body think." In our staging of "Your Fault," the characters move from conviction to "identification," and the "means by which" this is accomplished is through the continual movement of the actors, not by "anchoring" their emotion on set. The movement becomes a "means by which" new rhetorical situations are created every single time an actor moves in this particular number, and we hope that through the combination of Burke's dramatistic pentad and Bruno Latour's materialism, you can utilize our analysis of *Into the Woods* for your own experiments in rhetorical performances. Below we have provided a worksheet that we utilized in our table work.

Handout on Dramatism and Materialism

Dramatism and Materialism in *Into the Woods*

Dramatism—the invitation to "consider the matter of motives in a perspective that, being developed from the analysis of drama, treats language and thought primarily as modes of *action*." Kenneth Burke, *A Grammar of Motives*

"You must have a description that names the **act** (describes what took place, in thought or deed), and another than names the **scene** (the background of the act, the situation in which it occurred); also, you must indicate what *kind* of person (**agent**) performed the act, what means or instruments were used (**agency**), and the **purpose**."

ACT (a *description* of what happened):	"Florida's Toxic Red Tide is Spreading North Up the Gulf Coast"
SCENE (a *description* of where and or when it happened)	Protected coastal areas of the Gulf Coast known for fishing, swimming, and wildlife
AGENT (a *description* of the person or object which performed the act)	human polluters who do not care for clean water
AGENCY (a *description* of the means by which the act was accomplished)	state policies which allow corporations to dump harmful pollutants in coastal waters
PURPOSE (a *description* of the ends or why the act happened)	in order that corporations will give campaign donations to state lawmakers that allow them to dump harmful pollutants in coastal waters.

Discussion: In this example, my answers might differ from someone else that does not believe that human pollution is causing red tide. That's where this work gets fun. You find out other characters' motives for their actions. The more detailed the answer, the more you'll get out of it.

ACT: Taking the _____ (beans, cow, hair, cape, etc.)
SCENE (a description of where and or when it happened)
AGENT (a description of the person who performed the act)
AGENCY (a description of the means by which the act was accomplished)
PURPOSE (a description of the ends or why the act happened)
Based on your answers, which has the greatest effect on the Act? The scene, agent, agency, or purpose? Why?
Materialism—the principle that "human and non-human agents are treated alike when considering how controversies are settled. This symmetry involves keeping constant the series of competencies, of properties, that human and non-human agents are able to swap by overlapping with one another." Bruno Latour

"Perhaps the most familiar invoking of the humanist notion of agency is the old National Rife Association defense: guns don't kill people, people kill people. Materialist symmetry shows us that a gun being held and a person holding a gun are distinct from an unarmed person and an unheld gun." Nathaniel Rivers

This symmetry means that there are object-using humans (quasi-subjects), and human-using objects (quasi-objects). In *Into the Woods*, there is a cow-using Jack, who is different from a bean-using Jack. There are Jack-using beans, but those beans are different from baker's wife-using beans.

While it might seem strange to treat humans, nonhumans, and objects alike, Disney films operate on such a basis. The mice save Cinderella and sing. Candlesticks talk and sing. Clocks talk and sing, etc.

Objects are important in *Into the Woods*. You've just completed pentad on the Act of taking the _____ from the point of view of your character. Now, let's try to complete a pentad from the point of view *of the object itself.*

ACT: Taking the _____ (beans, cow, hair, cape, etc.)

SCENE (describe the setting from the point of view of the object).

AGENT (describe the person taking the object from the point of view of the object).

AGENCY (describe the means by which the object is taken from the point of view of the object).

PURPOSE (describe the reason why the object was taken from the point of view of the object).

Based on your answers, what has the greatest effect on the Act here, the scene, agent, agency, or purpose? Why?

So, you can see how your character feels about the person taking your object, and also how the objects themselves might change your characters different times throughout the show. That should give you lots of motivations for your scenes.

Notes

1 Kenneth Burke, *A Grammar of Motives* (Berkeley: University of California Press, 1945), 129.

2 Kenneth Burke, *A Grammar of Motives* (Berkeley: University of California Press, 1945), 287.

3 Clay Spinuzzi, "Symmetry as a Methodological Move," in *Thinking with Bruno Latour in Rhetoric and Composition*, ed. Paul Lynch and Nathaniel Rivers (Carbondale: Southern Illinois University Press, 2015), 23.

4 Paul Lynch, "Composition's New Thing: Bruno Latour and the Apocalyptic Turn," *College English* 74, no. 5 (2012): 471.

5 Levi Bryant, "Dark Objects," *Laval Subjects Blog* (May 25, 2011), Online.

6 James Beasley, "Materialist Rhetoric and For Us(e) Assessment," *Enculturation* 25 (2018), Online.

7 Kenneth Burke, *A Grammar of Motives* (Berkeley: University of California Press, 1945), 283.

8 Ibid., 228.

9 Ibid., 278–279.

10 David Ostwald, *Acting for Singers: Creating Believable Singing Characters* (Oxford: Oxford University Press, 2005), 29.

11 Ibid., 30.

12 Ibid., 34.

13 Jaclyn Olson, "Our Bodies and the Language We Learn: The Dialectic of Burkean Identification in the 1930's," *Rhetoric Review* 38, no. 3 (2019): 259.

14 Joe Deer and Rocco Dal Vera, *Acting in Musical Theatre: A Comprehensive Course* (New York: Routledge, 2008), 38–39.

15 Ibid., 247. Italics emphasized.

16 Aristotle, "Rhetoric," in *The Rhetorical Tradition: Readings from Classical Times to the Present*, ed. Patricia Bizzell and Bruce Herzberg (New York: Bedford St. Martins, 2001), 237.

17 Joe Deer and Rocco Dal Vera, *Acting in Musical Theatre: A Comprehensive Course* (New York: Routledge, 2008), 247.

18 Ibid., p.88.

19 Kenneth Burke, "Rhetoric—Old and New," *Journal of General Education* 5, no. 3 (1951): 203.

20 Joe Deer and Rocco Dal Vera, *Acting in Musical Theatre: A Comprehensive Course* (New York: Routledge, 2008), 88.

21 Ibid., 88–89.

22 Ibid., 93.

23 Jack Viertel, *The Secret Life of the American Musical* (New York: Farrar, Strauss, and Giroux Publishers, 2016), 89.

24 Barry Singer, *Ever After: The Last Years of Musical Theater and Beyond* (New York: Applause Books, 2004), 47.

25 All quotations from *Into the Woods* are from Stephen Sondheim and James Lapine, *Into the Woods* (New York: Theatre Communications Group, 1989).

26 Joe Deer and Rocco Dal Vera, *Acting in Musical Theatre: A Comprehensive Course* (New York: Routledge, 2008), 88.

27 Barry Singer, *Ever After: The Last Years of Musical Theater and Beyond* (New York: Applause Books, 2004), 47.

28 Ibid.

29 Mikhail Bakhtin, *The Dialogic Imagination: Four Essays* (Austin: University of Texas Press, 1983), 8.

30 Ibid.

31 Ibid.

32 John Bereton and Cynthia Gannett, "Review: Learning from the Archives," *College English* 73, no. 6 (2001): 677.

33 Tony Straiges, *Into the Woods* Lighting Design (New York: New York Performing Arts Library, September 29, 1987), Boxes 57–69.

34 Barry Singer, *Ever After: The Last Years of Musical Theater and Beyond* (New York: Applause Books, 2004), 48.

35 Henry David Thoreau, *Walden* (Boston: Beacon Press, 1997), 85.

36 Joe Deer and Rocco Dal Vera, *Acting in Musical Theatre: A Comprehensive Course* (New York: Routledge, 2008, 88.

37 Ibid.

38 Ibid.

39 Kenneth Burke, *A Grammar of Motives* (Berkeley: University of California Press, 1945), 231.

40 Bruno Latour, *Assembling the Social: An Introduction to Actor-Network Theory* (Oxford: Oxford University Press, 2007), 144.

41 Joe Deer and Rocco Dal Vera, *Acting in Musical Theatre: A Comprehensive Course* (New York: Routledge, 2008), 128.

42 Burke, *A Grammar of Motives* (Berkeley: University of California Press, 1945), 234.

43 Ibid.

44 Joe Deer and Rocco Dal Vera, *Acting in Musical Theatre: A Comprehensive Course* (New York: Routledge, 2008), 257.

45 Jack Viertel, *The Secret Life of the American Musical* (New York: Farrar, Strauss, and Giroux Publishers, 2016), 89.

46 Ibid.

47 Joe Deer and Rocco Dal Vera, *Acting in Musical Theatre: A Comprehensive Course* (New York: Routledge, 2008), 257.

48 Clay Spinuzzi, "Symmetry as a Methodological Move," in *Thinking with Bruno Latour in Rhetoric and Composition*, ed. Paul Lynch and Nathaniel Rivers (Carbondale: Southern Illinois University Press, 2015), 23.

49 Paul Lynch and Nathaniel Rivers, "Introduction," in *Thinking with Bruno Latour in Rhetoric and Composition*, ed. Paul Lynch and Nathaniel Rivers (Carbondale: Southern Illinois University Press, 2015), 6.

50 Joe Deer and Rocco Dal Vera, *Acting in Musical Theatre: A Comprehensive Course* (New York: Routledge, 2008), 85.

51 Ibid., 93.

Bibliography

Aristotle. "Rhetoric." In *The Rhetorical Tradition: Readings from Classical Times to the Present*. New York: Bedford St. Martins Publishers, 2001.

Bakhtin, Mikhail. *The Dialogic Imagination: Four Essays*. Austin: University of Texas Press, 1983.

Beasley, James. "Materialist Rhetoric and for Us(e) Assessment," *Enculturation* 25 (2018). Online. http://enculturation.net/materialist_rhetoric_and_assessment.

Bitzer, Lloyd F. "The Rhetorical Situation." *Philosophy and Rhetoric* 1, no. 1 (1968): 1–14.

Brererton, John and Cynthia Gannett. "Review: Learning from the Archives." *College English*, 73, no. 6 (2001): 672–681.

Burke, Kenneth. *A Grammar of Motives*. Berkeley: University of California Press, 1945.

_____. "Rhetoric—Old and New," *Journal of General Education* 5, no. 3 (1951): 202–209.

Bryant, Levi. "Dark Objects." *Larval Subjects Blog*, 25 May 2011. Online. https://larvalsubjects.wordpress.com/about.

Deer, Joe and Rocco Dal Vera. *Acting in Musical Theatre: A Comprehensive Course*. New York: Routledge, 2008.

Latour, Bruno. *Assembling the Social: An Introduction to Actor-Network Theory*. Oxford: Oxford University Press, 2007.

Lynch, Paul. "Composition's New Thing: Bruno Latour and the Apocalyptic Turn." *College English* 74, no. 5 (2012): 458–476.

Olson, Jaclyn S. "Our Bodies and the Language We Learn: The Dialectic of Burkean Identification in the 1930's." *Rhetoric Review* 38, no. 3 (2019): 258–270.

Ostwald, David. *Acting for Singers: Creating Believable Singing Characters*. Oxford: Oxford University Press, 2005.

Rivers, Nathaniel. *Thinking Along with Bruno Latour in Rhetoric and Composition*. Carbondale: Southern Illinois University Press, 2015.

Singer, Barry. *Ever After: The Last Years of Musical Theater and Beyond*. New York: Applause Books, 2004.

Sondheim, Stephen and James Lapine. *Into the Woods*. New York: Theatre Communications Group, 1989.

Straiges, Tony. *Into the Woods* Lighting Design. September 29, 1987. Tony Straiges Designs. New York Performing Arts Library. New York: New York.

Vatz, Richard E. "The Myth of the Rhetorical Situation." *Philosophy and Rhetoric* 6, no. 3 (1973): 154–161.

Viertel, Jack. *The Secret Life of the American Musical*. New York: Farrar, Strauss, and Giroux, 2016.

CHAPTER FIVE

Purpose in Motion: Dramatism in Stephen Schwartz's *Children of Eden*

In the fourth chapter, we focused on the agent ratio and its use in writing, in interpretation, and in musical theater staging. In this fifth chapter, we focus on Burke's purpose and the purpose ratio. For what purpose did the act occur? This might seem obvious, but describing the purpose for which the act occurred has important consequences on how we view student writers, how actors can create motivations for interpretation, and how directors can motivate purpose-directed staging.

Writing with a Purpose

In his analysis of the dramatistic pentad, Burke continues with purpose, or for what purpose did the act occur? In our example of red tide in Florida, we might describe the purpose of this act as "in order that corporations will give campaign contributions to state lawmakers that allow them to dump harmful pollutants in coastal waters," or we could describe this act as "in order to naturally cleanse the water of different impurities." One description supports a position that human pollution is the cause of red tide, while the other description does not. In our example of President Kennedy's assassination, we could describe the purpose of this act as "to retaliate against the anti-Soviet policies of the President," or we could describe this act as "to retaliate against the Soviet appeasement policies of the President." One description supports the lone gunman theory while the other supports a government conspiracy theory. How we describe the purpose concludes our journey of understanding the act.

As a student, you might be thinking about your next assignment you have for a class. Does this assignment ask you to think about the purpose of the assignment, or does it pretend that the purposes for your assignments are self-evident? That your instructor isn't needing your assignments for assessment artifacts? That those assessments won't have any consequences for her tenure or promotion? That the production of your assignment has far more consequences for your instructor than it probably does for you? While we want our students to think about how to create goals in their writing and in their other schoolwork, how often do we encourage this kind of openness regarding the many kinds of purposes for their writing assignments?

What are students' purposes in completing their writing assignments? If we describe the purpose of our writing assignment as "to get a good grade," then that is a different purpose than "to convince others of our closely-held position." If we describe the purpose of our writing assignment as "to convince others of our closely-held position," then that is a very different purpose than "to get others to hear me and validate my experiences." If the student writer's purpose is to "get a good grade," then the agency would then seem to be important, the "means by which" that good grade is achieved, such as following directions in a rubric or adhering to the correct number and format of source materials. If however, the student writer's purpose is to "get others to hear her voice and validate her experiences," then that student writer might not be so eager to follow a rubric or adhere to the correct number and format of source materials. As instructors, we often do not care what our students' purposes in writing often times are, yet this might be one of the most important questions to ask before we ask students to write in the first place.

The parlor: Discuss with your classmates your purposes in writing the assignments you've been given. Are there any similarities? Differences? Keep track of the differing purposes for the many kinds of assignments you've been given and discuss with your instructor.

Despite this lack of attention to the writing purposes of our student by teachers and by the lack of attention to the purpose of writing assignments by students, Burke's dramatism and the history of its adaptation in writing pedagogy is important in understanding how purpose figures into the writing situation. When Burke wrote *A Grammar of Motives* in 1945, he had already been making those pivots from dramatism in poetry and literature and toward motives and action in society. Part of this move away from dramatism in poetry was due to his teaching jobs at the University of Chicago and his relationship with a group of scholars there known as the neo-Aristotelians. For Burke, neo-Aristotelianism differed from dramatism in that it focused on the extrinsic characteristics of a text, rather than the intrinsic characteristics of a text, which the neo-Aristotelians championed. However, one important way in which both of them connected was on a writer's purpose. In his 1942 essay, "The Problem of the Intrinsic," Burke made the following contrast and comparison with neo-Aristotelianism:

> Mr. Crane gives us a choice between the poem as 'exemplar' and the poem as 'object'— and as though these alternatives had exhausted the field, he discusses no other. But if we begin by explicitly recognizing the dramatistic nature of the vocabulary, then looking at our pentad, we may ask ourselves: "What about the poem considered [sic] as an act?" Thus, when Mr. Crane says that the poem is to be considered 'as a product of purposive activity on the part of its author,' we would agree with him, only more intensively than he would want us to.[1]

For the neo-Aristotelians, the proof of a writers' purpose was to be found in the characteristics within the text, but for Burke, the proof of a writer's purpose was in its construction, in its extrinsic components outside the text. The point here is that though they differed in where those components came from, they both agreed on the fact that a reader should be interested in the purpose an author had for writing the piece in the first place. This differed from the New Critics, who believed that readers should ignore the intentions of the writer and see the poem or the writing as a work of art. The purpose that a writer has in writing any text is one of the most important concepts in the history of writing instruction, and several important writing texts have utilized the writer's purpose as having the greatest influence on the act of writing itself, most noticeably, James McCrimmon's *Writing with a Purpose*, whose first edition was written in 1950 and might be a text you have even adopted or had to purchase for a writing class. In *Writing with a Purpose*, McCrimmon seems awfully close to utilizing Burke's purpose ratio for exactly this reason. He wrote, "For example, if your motive is to complete the assignment with a good grade, then you will define your purpose in terms of the requirements of your teacher's writing assignment. If your motive is to publish your writing, then you will have to define your purpose in terms of the editor's assumptions about the publication's audience, purpose, and tone."[2] McCrimmon's direct appeal to Burke's purpose ratio demonstrates the impact of the combined efforts of the neo-Aristotelians and Kenneth Burke to bring a writer's purpose out from the shadows and into the forefront of literary criticism.

Purpose Ratios

As we come to the last chapter, it is perhaps fitting that Burke himself says less about his purpose ratio than any other. Perhaps that it is because purpose as the last ratio forces a kind of closure on the pentadic process. As a method, he often closed his chapters with discussions of purpose, as we are doing in this chapter here. At the end of the introduction to *A Grammar of Motives*, Burke wrote, "It is not our purpose to import dialectical and metaphysical concerns into a subject that might otherwise be free of them. On the contrary, we hope to make clear the ways in which dialectical and metaphysical issues necessarily figure in the subject of motivation."[3] But perhaps his lack of writing on the act-purpose ratio specifically is also due to the confluence of all the pentadic ratios coming together at once, so much so that it becomes harder and harder to tell them apart. Burke himself wrote that "The margins of overlap provide opportunities whereby a thinker can go without a leap from any one of the terms to any of its fellows,"[4] and most rhetorical scholars who utilize the pentad for their own analysis often confess their lack of distinguishability of the ratios. In their application of the dramatistic pentad to archival research, Cheryl Glenn and Jessica Enoch wrote the following:

> In taking this excursus among the ratios of Burke's pentadic terms, we have also been especially conscious of our central metaphor: the drama in the archives. For us, the metaphor has been most powerful in its quiet reminder that the ratios of the pentad shift and overlap; their tensions inevitably weaken and collapse before rising again in a different iteration. Despite our attempts to keep the ratios separate, such categories always overlap and sometimes leak. Such leakage reminds us that any categories or ratios that we have set out continue to be sites of theoretical struggle.[5]

For Glenn and Enoch, their purpose for applying Burke's dramatistic pentad to archival research was to "invigorate our understanding of historiographic methods and to open up new possibilities for future historians of rhetoric and composition."[6] Similarly, we use Burke's dramatistic pentad as a "means by which" we hope to "invigorate our understandings" of character, scene, and staging analysis and to "open up new possibilities for future" student actors and academic directors. As such, we are only part of a tiny fraction of scholars who have utilized Burke's dramatistic pentad as a "means by which" for purposes that are even more far ranging than either Glenn and Enoch's or our own. Some of the earliest articles on Burke's dramatistic pentad applied them to the writing classroom, including those of Phillip Keith in 1977, Joseph Comprone in 1978, and Charles Knuepper in 1979. However, in the 1980s and 1990s, scholars began expanding the use of Burke's pentad beyond the writing classroom in such articles as David Birdsell's "Ronald Reagan on Lebanon: Flexibility and Interpretation in Burke's Pentad," and Jeffery Thomas Higgins's "Examining Technical Reports Using Kenneth Burke's Pentad."

As the 2000s rolled along, scholars turned to Burke's dramatistic pentad for even more wide-ranging purposes, including Jeroen Bourgonjon's "From Counter Strike to Counter-Statement: Using Burke's Pentad as a Tool for Analysing Video Games," Elizabeth Dickinson's "The Montana Meth Project: Applying Burke's Dramatistic Pentad to a Persuasive Anti-Drug Campaign," and even Andrew Famiglietti's "The Pentad of Cruft: A Taxonomy of Rhetoric Used by Wikipedia Editors Based on the Dramatism of Kenneth Burke." These are just a sampling of the many purposes which scholars have utilized Burke's dramatistic pentad as a "means by which" to accomplish their specific and varied purposes. We invite students and teachers to participate in the following exercise in Burke's dramatistic pentad and the purpose ratio.

> The parlor: Now that you have seen many examples of Burke's dramatistic pentad at work, and you have written many of your own, discuss with your classmates the various purposes you might have for them in your own lives. Perhaps you might apply Burke's dramatistic pentad to help improve communication in your student government meetings, or perhaps you might apply Burke's dramatistic pentad to help generate better strategies on your athletic teams. Whatever your purpose, Burke's dramatistic pentad will open up new ways of thinking and help you understand how all the members of your group are approaching the particular problem or issue you have before you. After discussing these purposes with each other, share them with your instructor.

Like Glenn and Enoch, we also wish "to keep the ratios separate," even when "such categories always overlap and sometimes leak," but this is easier said than done. In fact, it is in the purpose ratio that even Burke described how this leakage muddles the very power of the purpose ratio itself:

> All told, of the five terms Purpose has become the one most susceptible of dissolution. At least, so far as its formal recognition is concerned. But once we know the logic of its transformations, we can discern its implicit survival; for the demands of dramatism being the demands of human nature itself; it is hard for man, by merely taking thought, to subtract the dramatist cubits from its stature. Implicit in the concepts of act and agent there is the concept of purpose. It is likewise implicit in agency, since tools and methods are for a purpose—and one of the great reasons for the appeal of pragmatism today, when the materialist-behaviorist reduction of scene has eliminated purpose, may reside in the fact that it retains ingredients of purpose in the very Grammatical function that is often taken as substitute for it.[7]

Like Glenn and Enoch, we also attempt to separate Purpose from the other ratios as long as possible in order to distinguish Burke's concept of purpose from that of the most influential method in character, scene, and staging analysis, the essential feature of Stanislavski's method, the actor's "I want." In other words, while purpose is last in Burke's dramatistic pentad, it certainly is not least for the student-actor. Understanding the difference between Stanislavski's "I want" and Burke's "for the purpose of" is essential for creating motives for action and for dramatic staging.

Acting with a Purpose

The purposes for students' writing assignments are not the only way students are asked to consider the purpose of their actions, either. In order to help students understand their writing assignments or acting roles, an analysis of the purpose ratio is Burke's final step in this particular journey. The final phase for Stanislavski's "as if" is in the character's purpose as well. Ostwald described this final phase the following way:

> What does my character want? Your character's want distills the need that drives her to do what she does. What is your character's want for the entire piece? This is called your character's super-objective. What is your character's want for each scene or stanza? These are called your character's objectives. Why does she want it? For the entire piece? For each scene or stanza?[8]

Ostwald's emphasis on Stanislavski's "I need" drives his focus on character, scene, and staging analysis through super objectives, objectives, and in beats. Kimberly has discussed how utilizing super objectives, objectives, and beats have helped her and her students discover a character's purpose effective in her own directing, as have many others. Deer and Dal Vera make use of Ostwald's super objectives, objectives, and beats as well in their own acting for musical theater text:

> Seen from the perspective of the whole story, characters usually want one important overarching thing. We call this the superobjective. The character proceeds in the direction of the superobjective through a series of smaller objectives. Every act, scene and song—right down to the smallest action—has its own objective, but they all point toward the big important thing your character wants.[9]

What is important to focus on in these descriptions, here, is the focus, often a myopic focus, on the "one, main objective," that "controls" all the other objectives. While both Ostwald and Deer and Dal Vera make room for competing objectives, they both are allied in the belief that there is a "hierarchy of objectives."[10] We have discussed the apparent similarities between Burke's dramatism and the literary theory known as neo-Aristotelianism, that both are interested in the writer's purpose. However, where Burke's dramatism and neo-Aristotelianism differ is in how they ascribe intent to these purposes. For the neo-Aristotelians, every aspect inside the poem or novel works to develop the writer's purpose. For Burke, it is those extrinsic characteristics, and we have provided examples of this difference throughout this text. Here, however, we can see how these differences can affect how actors prepare for their roles on stage. Let us consider what Ostwald has to say about discovering the playwright's purpose, "Start with the conviction that everything in a piece makes sense, and you will find sense in everything in it."[11]

So, as we read the descriptions of purpose in Ostwald and in Deer and Dal Vera, we start to see some very close similarities between their conceptions of character, scene, and staging analysis and the characteristics of the literary theory of neo-Aristotelianism. "As discussed earlier, you can count on the fact that the composer and librettist had a reason for each note and word that they included in their score, that if you can figure out their logic it will help you to make informed choices, and that one effective way to explore their logic is to question every piece of information in the score."[12] Following the advice of Deer and Dal Vera to "research the production history of your show," student actors will discover the book by Carol de Giere, *Defying Gravity: The Creative Career of Stephen Schwartz from Godspell to Wicked*. The answers to Ostwald's questions are readily available in this book for student actors in a production of *Children of Eden*. The questions that Ostwald asks based on the playwright and the librettist's purpose are many. His first question, "Why did the composer or librettist choose this particular title?,"[13] can be easily answered in de Giere's history. While the working title for *Children of Eden* was entitled *Family Tree*, de Giere explained how the change came to be, "Everything for the new musical started to change, including the title. Inspired by the title of the French film *Les Enfants du Paradis* (Children of Paradise), [John] Caird thought *Children of Eden* would be a more suitable name for their show."[14] Other questions on the composer's purpose that Ostwald asks are "Why did the composer choose this particular tempo or mood marking at the beginning of the piece? Why did the composer choose this particular form?"[15] A student conducting research on the history of *Children of Eden* in performance would find that de Giere records Stephen Schwartz on the answers to these questions, as well. "The second act, which takes place several thousand years later during the Noah story, is more pop and contemporary in style." He also included world music and Gospel music, so that collectively the musical numbers of Act II would represent the growing diversity for the human population."[16] A student conducting research on the performance history of *Children of Eden* would also find Stephen Schwartz's answers to Ostwald's questions "Why did the composer choose this particular time signature? Why did the composer choose this particular key?"[17] in de Giere's text:

'My thought was that when they were in Eden,' Schwartz comments, 'everything was going to be extremely simple…and with very pure chords. That's why 'The Naming' is basically A minor—no sharps or flats.' When the Snake makes its entrance in a scene with Eve, the music begins to get more harmonically complex with the introduction of the 7th chords.[18]

Students following the advice of Deer and Dal Vera to "research the performance history" of Stephen Schwartz's *Children of Eden* will find ample descriptions of Schwartz's purpose in composing the musical, everything from the title to the tempo and key signatures of specific songs. But what next? When the students have found these answers through a quick search in production histories, both Ostwald and Deer and Dal Vera do not give any advice on what is to be done with these histories. Should these purposes be followed or rejected? Burke analyzes this situation, when finding "what the author really means," has been completed, "Our investigation becomes complicated by the fact, in accordance with the paradox of substance, that a purpose as thus conceived is so pure as to be much the same as no purpose at all, so far as everyday standards are concerned."[19] Discovering a composer's purpose without any advice on what to do with that information is just as good as not having any purpose at all. What student actors will not discover in conducting this research, using Stanislavski's "Given Circumstances" is any of the purposes of the director in choosing and producing this show for these particular students at this particular time, with these particular methods, for a purpose that student actors are generally unaware of. These research questions for student actors are nowhere to be found in either Ostwald or Deer and Dal Vera's texts, yet these might be the most important questions to ask of an individual production. In other words, by following Stanislavski's "I need" of the actor, Ostwald and Deer and Dal Vera ascribe to a theatrical neo-Aristotelianism. Burke wrote the following:

In our introduction we noted that the areas covered by our five terms overlap upon one another. And because of this overlap, it is possible for a thinker to make his way continuously from any one of them to any of the others. Or he may use terms in which several of the areas are merged. For any of the terms may be seen in terms of the others. And we may even treat all five in terms of one, by 'reducing' them all to the one or (what amounts to the same thing) 'reducing' them all from the one as their common terminal ancestor.[20]

Without Burke's dramatistic pentad as a guide, how often are students made aware of the purposes for the theater productions they are involved in? That the shows chosen for a given season have specific purposes outside of their popularity? That shows chosen are based on how they can save the department money? Why this show, why at this time, why with these students? That the shows chosen satisfy a faculty member's particular service or scholarship requirements? How would being involved in these discussions inform their performances and in ways different from not knowing these purposes? Stanislavski's "Given Circumstances" only applies to the characters that actors are portraying, it never applies to the directors who have chosen the production, the director who will oversee their character, scene, and staging analysis, or the director that must justify the curricular value, marketing opportunities, or financial expense of the production. If we utilize Burke's purpose ratio for the Stanislavski-using student portraying Noah in *Children of Eden*, it might look something like this:

PURPOSE: to get Father's favor
ACT: emoting loyalty in scenes with Father

But, if we start to include the director's "Given Circumstances" for the actor portraying Noah, then Burke's purpose ratio might look something like this:

PURPOSE: to articulate musical theater directing as academic excellence
ACT: Preparing my scenes with further research and study

By involving students in the director's purposes in show choice; in character, scene, and staging analysis; and in how the show's curricular value, marketing opportunities, or financial expense can be articulated, we offer students more purposes than merely those of their characters, we enable them to engage our productions on more wholistic levels, enabling them to see how these decisions are made as they enter the professional worlds of working with students and actors themselves in their futures.

Staging with a Purpose

In the same way that a sole focus on purpose can have the same effect as having no purpose on character and scene analysis, that focus on purpose can also be a problem when it comes to staging, as well. As opposed to all the other productions examined in this text, Stephen Schwartz's *Children of Eden* was not created for a Broadway run and the accompanying staging spectacle. In fact, quite the opposite was true. *Children of Eden* is most often performed by regional theaters and smaller universities. According to de Giere's history, "Word of mouth spread and the show became a 'hit' with regional theatres, despite never having played Broadway. It consistently ranks among Music Theatre International's top 20 most frequently licensed titles."[21] Unlike other shows in this collection, our production of *Children of Eden* would not be challenging the production history of a show like Elton

John's *Aida*, for example, we would be staging *Children of Eden* for exactly the very reasons why the show was created. In so doing, our purpose for staging *Children of Eden* "is so pure as to be much the same as no purpose at all."[22] The challenge for staging *Children of Eden*, therefore, was to keep our purpose "on its toes," so to speak, by keeping it in relation to the other pentadic ratios. In other words, while we have been attempting to keep purpose separate from the other ratios as long as possible, perhaps now was the time to let them comingle with each other in as many indistinguishable ways as possible. Burke wrote that "Ironically, motivational schemes that call for [purpose] less, may feature it more."[23] In order to do this, we must consider all purpose ratios individually. We will start with the Act-Purpose ratio, and by choosing a scene from *Children of Eden* to examine, we will demonstrate how we can utilize the Act-Purpose ratio for staging. For example, let's take an example from Act I, Scene 9: "The Pursuit of Excellence." In this scene, Eve is approached by the snake who asks her many questions about where the sun goes after it sets and about what happens to our dreams when we are awake.

If the actors portraying the Snake were only utilizing Stanislavski's "Given Circumstances" here, they might focus on the linguistic persuasion inherent in the text, the questions, and the subsequent Act-Purpose ratio might look something like this:

ACT: The snake persuades Eve to eat the fruit from the Tree of Knowledge
PURPOSE: To prove our power

As helpful as this Act-Purpose ratio might be, it does not account for the other stage directions and the motion that this scene demands. For example, when the snake begins the song, "In Pursuit of Excellence," it begins to dance, but after a while it entwines itself around Eve and they dance together.

Throughout this text, we have repeatedly called attention to the scholars who have viewed Burke's identification through bodily action, and we believe Hawhee's description of this process complements the work that actors and directors can do in this scene specifically, "What Burke's meditations on verbal choreography produce, then, is an extension of Paget by which the linguistic dance develops in reciprocal, mimetic relation between and among biological, psychological, and linguistic processes as suggested in his use of identification above."[24] In the song, "Pursuit of Excellence," the snake does not want to get Eve to eat the fruit. The snake wants to get Eve to dance, and the physical dance in this scene is a "reciprocal, mimetic relation between" the linguistic dance of the snake. "The symbolic act," he writes, "is the dancing of an attitude," and in elaborating this point he mediates on the correlation between mind and body by suggesting that "the whole body may finally become involved in this attitudinizing of the poem."[25] Let us try another Act-Purpose ratio again, this time, utilizing the bodily movement as part of the "ways in which bodily movement can affect the development of linguistic expression":[26]

ACT: Getting Eve to dance
PURPOSE: Getting Eve to eat the fruit of the Tree of Knowledge

This Act-Purpose ratio differs from the previous one in that in the previous instance, both language and dancing might be considered under the Agency ratio, but in this instance, both language and dancing become part of the purpose of the act itself.

The next ratio we would like to consider is the Scene-Purpose ratio, and for this ratio we would like to use the example of "Clash of the Generations," which appears in Act I, Scene 21. In this scene, Cain continues to search for what lies beyond, making his own discoveries. Father's super objective also continues to be fulfilled, and his distrust in Cain evident as Cain fights against the wishes of his family. He returns home to tell them he has found a ring of stones, convinced there must be others out there besides just them. Eve is entranced and sides with Cain in his excitement over his discovery. Adam on the other hand, does not share in the excitement, for good reason, and a fight among them ensues. We choose to examine the Scene-Purpose ratio for this particular scene, for "In this formulation, the body becomes the primary vehicle for engagement with the environment and others—even the symbolic structures the mind erects are guided by the potentialities of its physical form."[27] In this scene, we can see how Cain's body "becomes that vehicle for engagement" with the stones, and how the stones become those "symbolic structures," which Olson described. The stones serve as a "representative anecdote" for the corruption of civilization in the "Clash of the Generations." As part of this clash, the stones would be the weapon that Cain will use to kill Abel. Fight scenes are always tricky, which is why many directors hire fight choreographers. Because we weren't using any weapons, though, Kimberly chose to choreograph it as far as movement and let the actors playing Cain and Abel decide what was comfortable for them. As part of the scenic elements, we had large, paper mâché rocks with enough framing underneath that you could both stand on them but easily move them for scene changes. Once Abel is struck in the head and falls, we made sure it was somewhat behind one of the largest rocks so Cain could bludgeon him further in the head without us really seeing how fake it was. What is interesting about these pages in the script is Eve's relative silence while her boys and their Father hash things out. She has become aware of Adam's inability to face the reality of their situation and does nothing to stop the fighting until it becomes physical.

For Eve, these scenes do not revolve around her—we are watching the boys fight it out. In this sense, the audience is able to witness Eve's identification with her sons and its subsequent consequences. Olson described this process in this way:

> By attending to Burke's continued wrestling with the materiality of his body, I argue that we can see identification in a new light—not only as the means by which an individual situates herself into a social texture, but also as the ultimate rhetorical human motive, one that must be understood as anchored in the material existence of the "symbol using animal."[28]

Watching the actress portraying Eve utilizing the Scene-Purpose ratio is fascinating. For Eve, she is "situating herself in a social texture," but that now becomes her purpose; her new super objective in helping everyone acclimate to the new social texture, a purpose that she carries over into Act I's finale, "Children of Eden." Using the pentad structure, here are some options for the actress who plays Eve: Choosing the Act conjures up feelings about what has taken place with a reaction to the event in either action and/or with emotion. For example, the act in this scene is the confrontation of Cain and Adam. Eve can choose her motivation for gestures and movement based upon her despair at the two of them fighting.

Choosing the Scene will motivate her to react to the location with her own perceptions and backstory about where she is. For example, the scene is the ring of stones that Cain found earlier and has now led them to. Eve, a mother interested in her son's discovery (something she herself has had to confront) convinced Adam to come along earlier in the scene, so she was at one point excited to see what Cain had found. However, what was once exciting and new becomes a scene of violence. Her physicality with the rocks can go from curiosity to needing them for shelter and hiding.

Choosing the Agent will lead the actor to explore her feelings about the other character, reacting to them with prejudice, "a preconceived opinion not based on reason or experience." For example, the agents of the act in this scene are Cain and Adam. Although focusing on the Act of the fight in general, focusing on Cain and Adam as agents of the fight provides Eve with even more nuanced movements and gestures depending on who is speaking.

Choosing the Agency answers the question about how the actor feels about how the act was accomplished, reacting to the individual *with* bias and opinions. For example, the agency in this scene could be why Cain and Adam are fighting—putting Abel in the middle of the mess. Cain and Adam are fighting because Abel cannot choose between them. Eve choosing to focus on Abel in this scene provides an element of suspense in that we know Abel dies, but at one point, it seems maybe she can protect him.

Choosing the Purpose focuses actors inward on whether the scene's outcome furthered or hindered their objective. The reaction is the motivation for that purpose. For example, the purpose of this scene is to demonstrate the failure of Adam as a father, putting Cain on a level playing field with him in that Adam strikes him first. Eve does not know how to choose between them once that happens. It is now the choice of breaking them up or protecting herself and Abel. In view of the purpose of the show motivating every scene, the consequences of free will are firmly established with the death of Abel. The fight between Cain and Adam has to happen and Abel has to die. Eve's recognition of this inevitability can be counter-acted by the actress playing her in allowing that foreknowledge to add to her despair at this chain of events.

The next ratio we would like to consider is the Agent-Purpose ratio, and for this ratio, we would like to use the example of "The Hardest Part of Love," which appears in Act II, Scene 38. In this scene, Yonah is about to be sacrificed, yet Noah spares her. This would be a contraction of Noah's purpose in pleasing Father. This purpose, then, is a purpose arrived at after the act, rather than before. What we hope to accomplish by examining this scene is to show a contrast to Stanislavski's "Given Circumstances," in that an actor internalizes a purpose before an act, but in this scene, Noah's act leads to a newfound purpose. "The Hardest Part of Love" is the culminating scene of the relationship between Father and humans in the show. This is the scene that makes Father human most of all. Yonah is discovered on board and Noah has a decision to make. Shem and Ham believe the rain hasn't stopped because Japheth has kept Yonah hidden on board. A fight ensues and Noah is confronted with a choice: sacrifice Yonah to end the rain or choose the happiness of his son and risk destruction. Because Noah's act leads to a newfound purpose, the actor's subtext reveals when this purpose is actually discovered. For example, when Mama says, "You must be the father now," the actor's subtext "you must choose" reveals how this purpose is revealed near the end of the scene, rather than at the beginning.

At this point, Noah begins to sing about Japheth, comparing him to his childhood, the sentiments reminding us of Adam and the song "Close to Home" from Act I. Father does not respond to Noah until several verses later when he tells Noah that "The Hardest Part of Love" is "letting go." We perceive that Noah is going to come to this conclusion, but that Father does in this moment is stunning and moving, since while they are both singing the same lines, they are doing so for very different purposes. Burke wrote, "Two men, performing the same motions side by side, might be said to be performing different acts, in proportion as they differed in their attitudes toward their work."[29] The emotional power of this duet is that the audience has been able to witness their development, and how these two characters have worked at cross-purposes, yet arriving at similar conclusions. Noah marries Japheth and Yonah and the family prepares for what they think will be the end of their existence. It does not come, however, because Father sends a dove with an olive branch. We hear from Father right before the final number with the words "Fare thee well, my precious children. In your hands I place the key to this prison made of gratitude which has held you close to me." The actor subtext in turn reflects his internal emotions apart from the rhythm and rhyming of the song lyrics—"It's your turn to choose. This is so bittersweet, but I've learned from you. I'm happy you're happy." Father's purpose has changed from "having my children show their gratitude toward me," to "helping them be happy." This change in the Agent-Purpose ratio might be expressed in this way:

> AGENT: a father who expects gratitude
> AGENT: a father who wants his children to be happy

Purpose here has redefined who the character is, and this demonstrates the potential that not naming the purpose in the "Given Circumstances" can have. For Noah in this second act, not deciding on a purpose early on, made his choices much easier later in Act 2 to discover what purpose he should have.

The final ratio we would like to consider is the Agency-Purpose ratio, and for this ratio, we would like to use the example of "Close to Home," which appears in Act I, Scene 19. Because we know Abel dies, this foreshadowing of Father's objective, to choose Abel as the next savior since Adam failed him, makes the next scene poignant. Scene 19, "Close to Home" is a look back at a Young Cain and Abel when they were innocent children. Adam, Eve, and Abel (Cain is still gone) mournfully sing the same song the young boys used to sing together, and this scene highlights the Agency-Purpose ratio, and this scene highlights the discrepancies between utilizing Stanislavski on the agency's role in purpose and Kenneth Burke on the agency's role in purpose. In the last chapter on agency, we highlighted the discrepancy between Stanislavski and Burke on agency: Stanislavski does not provide for one. Because this is the case, the Agency-Purpose ratio might be the most significant contribution that Burke's dramatistic pentad has on character, scene, and staging analysis. In other words, what makes motivation and purpose in musical theater different from straight theater? It is the music itself which becomes the "means by which" the purpose is carried out. Zachary Dunbar explained:

> Though the musical theatre acting literature fails to formally explain the modes of appropriation or varying legacies of Stanislavski's tenets (a task I will briefly cover), the pervasive reception given aspects of his systematic preparations may rest, in part, on the apparent logic of a methodology that enables actors, during the process of preparing for a role, to approach a song and its lyrics as though they would a play and its spoken text. Moreover the holistic way Stanislavski perceived the actor's process

(particularly in the latter part his career), reinforced the intrinsic coalescence of psychophysical work and active engagement with emotions (or broadly, components of affective and sense memory), and this approach resonates with the integrationist ideals in modern musical theatre actor training which seek to combine, in an emotionally invested way, the essential elements of acting, singing and movement. However, when preparing to act through song, the integrationist stance of psychophysical characterisation may be challenged by the vocal technical requirements of learning the music, which alongside musically affective experiences, may not necessarily cohere with a monological acting exercise of, say, speaking the lyric-text.[30]

For Dunbar, the vocal technical requirements serve as a dialogic act, rather than the monologic act of "speaking the text." According to Burke, the difference between poetry and the novel is the difference between the "psychology of form," and the "psychology of information."[31]

In the example of "Close to Home," it is the music itself that serves as the "means by which" the audience is affected by their words. The music is child-like, like a nursery rhyme: repetitive with a steady pattern, easy for a child to learn and sing. The rhyming pattern makes it easy for the audience to follow the form, even completing the tunes in their heads before the songs are even finished. As an example of the "psychology of form," this rhyme also functions as a way for the audience to foreground the current conflict, since the setting is a flashback as we see the Young Cain and Able in contrast now with their grown-up selves. Burke wrote the following description of this process of identification: "Once you grasp the trend of the form, it invites participation regardless of the subject matter."[32] If Stanislavski's method relies on the "psychology of information," then it is no wonder that his method will be inadequate when it comes to musical theater production, with its use of the "psychology of form" when it comes to the musical elements of the show. Burke's "psychology of form" creates the conditions for student actors, directors, and audiences alike to "turn the matter around," to understand character, scene, and staging analysis as the work that "comes before," in order to gain an "earned increment," which "goes after."

Director's Notes

Why This Show

Because *Children of Eden* never was produced on Broadway, it has always retained a kind of innocence that complements its themes. Often performed in churches, schools, and community theaters, *Children of Eden* serves one of my purposes as a director, choosing shows that involve the immediate community and that the public would want to come see. I knew that *Children of Eden* would be a great choice, not only for my roster of singers, but also for community involvement, and so we treated our production more like a community theater performance, with less research preparation such as the archival research I had done for previous shows. I did have musical experience with this show, playing Keyboard I in a previous production. I knew the power and the beauty of the music and was excited to present this production to JU and the Jacksonville community at large.

Variables

Because *Children of Eden* is so linked to community theater, there is a sense of responsibility to remain faithful to the script and storyline. When a show is based upon Bible stories, therefore, a director may feel they do not have license to manipulate meaning and intention, for the audience's sake, so to speak. Although my overall super objective for the show was embodied in our theme and could be applied to many facets of life, the stories of Cain and Abel, Noah and the Ark, and Adam and Eve have history. For example, most scholars believe that Genesis 1–2 was written in the 7th century BCE, while Genesis 3–12 was written in the 9th century, BCE.[33] This means that although the Noah story chronologically appears in the second act, it was actually written before the Adam and Eve story in the first act. Why this matters connects back to audience. The audiences for Genesis 1 and 2 were different from the audiences of the Noah story, and that means that they needed different stories for different experiences. Which story would our audience need? As we worked on our beats and objectives for this show, we strove to bring these stories off the page and into the theater in a way that made them new and relevant.

Table Work

As a community-theater focused show, I approached table work to focus on basics. I had a lot of young performers in this show, casting two sophomore girls as Eve, a freshman as one of the Fathers, a freshman as Noah, and an ensemble full of first-year students and sophomores. They were all talented and eager but new to this show and to the stage at JU. While this show is a good example of the necessity of the basics, it also demonstrated limitations of only using the basics for directing. I choose to divide up the process into the following segments:

- To Do
- Group Work
- Journal
- Homework

Once we worked through some initial questions and analysis, we created a flow chart to help us decide on key words and ideas for our theme:

Plot/conflicts Act I
FATHER – "worship me!"
Adam and Eve created
Animals created
EVE—"beyond"
Adam—bug list
Snake—BEYOND
EVE eats—1st sin
FATHER after fruit—punishment, no more Eden, children
Adam's choice—Eve
Abel and Cain parallels—no waterfall
Cain—BEYOND—leaving
Contrast of young and old Cain and Abel
Cain shows them other people
Abel stuck between parents and Cain
Abel's murder—2nd sin
Eve dies
Childlike innocence

Plot/conflicts Act II
Test of Noah—the Ark
No Cain descendants
Noah and Japheth—Adam and Cain parallels
Finding the animals
Eden's animals—pets
FATHER in Flood
Yonah and Japheth
Brother's fighting—Lesson learned for Japheth
Sacrifice of Japheth and Yonah
Parental love
Noah's choice—Japheth and Yonah
Olive branch

Overall larger concepts
Home/Family
Faith vs. safety and security
Punishment

Letting go of what you love—freedom
Innocence
Hope
Choices
Forgiveness
Abandonment
Humans in service to God—Does God need humans more than they need God?
Humans exploring and discovering—punishment/penalties?

We worked through all of the concepts and ideas over the course of a week. With a large cast, this is challenging as there are many opinions in the room about what story we want to tell. Coming up with the verb is the first hurdle, since the verb functions as the Act, and sets us on the journey that we will take. Some options we considered were:

1. Children of Eden teaches us...
2. Children of Eden is...
3. Children of Eden sparks...
4. Children of Eden challenges us...
5. Children of Eden inspires us...
6. Children of Eden empowers us...

Our choice of the word "sparks" was in response to the fact that Eve is a central figure and she sings the song "Spark of Creation," the theme of that song repeated in musical motives and reprises throughout the first Act. The selection of the object following that verb comes next followed by the how and the why. In other words, these are the Agent, the Agency, and the Purpose. To finalize the theme, we rejected a more internal focus on the show itself and its concepts of home, family, and love, and chose to focus outwardly in order to convey what we felt the purpose of the story was, what we wanted the world to hear. Our final theme was:

Children of Eden sparks a journey that inspires understanding in order to empower others with the freedom of discovery.

Scene by Scene

As a director, using pentads thematically can help you focus an actor, but in a way that gives them options and empowerment. Playing to the Purpose is perhaps an equivalence to Ostwald's theme idea in the sense that it is overarching. However, in *Children of Eden*, we have a religious purpose to the telling of this story—or do we. Burke refers to religion as the ultimate purpose for any story,[34] and *Children of Eden* definitely has found a home among houses of worship. Once you direct this show, you realize that it is not just a simple Bible story that Schwartz and Caird are telling:

> From musical theatre greats, Stephen Schwartz and John Caird, comes a joyous and inspirational musical about parents, children and faith... not to mention centuries of unresolved family business! An expansive and ambitious musical, the original production used a cast of sixty. Adam, Eve, Noah and the "Father" who created them deal with the headstrong, cataclysmic actions of their respective children. The show ultimately delivers a bittersweet. but inspiring. message: that "the hardest part of love... is letting go."[35]

The Bible stories definitely help, but the Purpose of the melding of these stories is to make a larger, epistemological point about free will: Father God has had to let go of mankind as part of loving him. Although this might be over the heads of a portion of the audience as they engage with the fight scenes, the flood, and the beautiful choral numbers, a director should definitely highlight the realization of the purpose: the power in the telling of origin stories. No matter what happens throughout the details of rehearsals, actors can always come back to their Super Objective to find their home base. And because the Super Objectives were based upon the questions surrounding the theme, there is always a superseding purpose for every actor in every scene regardless of variables.

Act I

- Storytellers—We, the storytellers, want our story to be understood.
- Snake—We, the snake, want to destroy innocence.
- FATHER—I, Father, want a generation I can trust.
- ADAM—I, Adam, want to keep my family together.
- EVE—I, Eve, want to make my own decisions.
- Cain—I, Cain, want to determine my own future.
- Abel—I, Abel, want to keep the peace.

Act II

- Noah—I, Noah, want to protect my family.
- Mama—I, Mama, want my family to be at peace.
- Japheth—I, Japheth, want to choose who I love.
- Ham—I, Ham, want to be a good husband.
- Aphra—I, Aphra, want to protect my baby.
- Shem—I, Shem, want respect.

- Aysha—I, Aysha, want recognition as a woman.
- Yonah—I, Yonah, want to be accepted.

There is an element of dramatism and perhaps materialism in that the actors are not just the tools for the retelling of these Bible stories, they are agents of the pentad in service of the purpose of explaining free will. You could break it down this way:

- Scene: The Middle East in the 9th and 7th centuries BCE.
- Act: Telling the Bible stories of Adam and Eve and Noah and the Ark.
- Agent(s): Actors playing Father, Adam, Eve, Cain, Abel, Noah, and his family.
- Agency: Humanizing Bible characters, including Father God, with relatable emotions.
- Purpose: Equalizing man and God in a demonstration of free will.

In any given scene, this pentad can apply and be used by the actors as a way to focus their fulfillment of the purpose of the show. Even the theme is in service to the Purpose in this pentad:

Children of Eden sparks a journey that inspires understanding in order to empower others with the freedom of discovery.

As you read through the selected scenes, you will notice the heightened human emotions being highlighted by the actors via their subtext, the result being a constant reminder that we are all Adam, Eve, Noah, and Father. According to Stephen Schwartz and John Caird, "The design of the show should rely as little as possible on-stage machinery or elaborate technical devices, and as much as possible on simple, imaginative storytelling."[36] We did not try to play Bible characters in a Bible story. We played actors in a real-life story relevant today.

"A World Without You"

With this in mind, the players in this scene include Adam, Father, and Eve. Once super objectives are established as the actor's Purpose, they inform the objectives for every scene which that character is in. Adam's need for family, Father's need for trust, and Eve's desire to make her own decisions are on display vividly in this scene. The actors humanized their characters with the following objectives and beats:

Character	Objective	Beat(s)
ADAM	Make the decision	Comparing Father and Eve
FATHER	To control the decision	Keep Adam in the Garden
		Appeal to his need for security, a wife, and a family
EVE	Defend my decision	Show no remorse

The scene prior is set up by the Storytellers after Eve has eaten the forbidden fruit. While the super objective of the Storytellers is to tell a story that is understood, the other characters frequently interrupt with their own meanderings. Their frustration is provided in their subtext, which humanizes them as they become co-actors with the other characters on stage. Since our overarching pentad element of Purpose for the show is an equalization of man and God in a demonstration of free will, this element of humanization gained by completing subtext only reinforces this element of the pentad. Again, think about the look and sound of the lines if acted in accordance with what the subtext says. For example, in Act I, Scene II, "Childhood's End," Father's objective to "control the decision" is demonstrated in his subtext of "I thought this might happen" when he confronts Eve over eating the fruit. Eve's objective in defending her decision to eat the fruit is demonstrated in her subtext of "I don't have to ask you questions anymore." Adam's objective of "make the decision" is demonstrated in his subtext of "How can this even be a choice?" This subtext then motivates Adam's fight for Father to "forgive Eve" when he ask Father not to make him choose between them.

At the conclusion of this powerful song, Adam eats the fruit too, and Father expels Adam and Eve from the garden. We have previously mentioned how Kenneth Burke helps us understand religion as an ultimate purpose, so much so that with religion as the ultimate purpose it appears as if there is none. But Burke helps us understand the origins of this difficulty, and his description is particularly important in this scene, as Father "expels" his children from the garden:

> His [Aristotle's] God, the origin of all motion, was conceived dramatistically, as the end of action. By the paradox of the absolute, such pure act is like no act at all, being that of an 'unmoved mover' in perfect repose. Also, in accordance with that same paradox, this pure act motivates as a passive. For Aristotle's God is not a creative of the world, which has existed from eternity. But he is the goal towards which all worldly forms strive, as the loved or desired (*eromenon*). But either as pure motionless act or as the loved, God is conceived in terms of action.[37]

For the actor staging the actions of Father, the Act-Purpose ratio seems to be the most important ratio for characterization and staging. Father acts, and the characters who strive to be like Father, or to have the same power or authority as Father, are the ones whose goal "towards which all worldly forms strive," they are those who also Act. Once living in the wilderness, Eve bears Cain and Abel and the next phase of the story is told.

"Lost in the Wilderness"

Cain keeps trying to explore, but has been told not to go beyond the waterfall. With Adam and Eve down at the river, Cain attempts to get Abel to go with him. Abel is praying, having brought his sacrifices to the altar. As Cain sings the popular "Lost in the Wilderness," we see several beats play out for Cain.

Character	Objective	Beat(s)
Cain	Convince Abel to come	Nobody cares We're alone Father is ignoring us
Abel	Calm Cain down	Reason with him Acknowledge Father
FATHER	Choose Abel as a savior	Ensure his sacrifice

For Deer and Dal Vera, beats also form the basis of their staging, "Let's pretend you've arrived at [your] beat breakdown for 'Lost in the Wilderness' from *Children of Eden*. Your objective is to get your brother to join you as an ally and leave your parents."[38] While this is true, Burke's Act-Purpose ratio in this scene demonstrates why this objective matters to the overall religious motive of God-like action. Deer and Dal Vera's description of the action motivated by their objective seems to ignore the God-like motives for action in their discussion of "anchor points."

> Once you've decided on anchor points, you can play your objective through a clear relationship with those places, things, and people, and in turn be affected by them. It will become natural for you to point or gesture offstage right as you blame your parents. You'll automatically see the eagle above and watch it fly past you (just over the orchestra seating). You will look to God [Father?] as you accuse him, and receive his judgment in return. And we in your audience will never notice these were choices. We will simply know what you know. You've built a set and peopled it with your mind. The audience will follow you with their own imagination.[39]

Deer and Dal Vera's phrase, "We will simply know what you know," can be understood differently than what they intend, since we really want to know more than "simply" here. Dramatism enters the interpretation if subtextualized beats are utilized in addition to anchor points on the stage that the actor has to react to. We enable the actor to be nuanced and possibly improvisatory as he moves about the stage to and from anchor points, empowered by his own feelings as a person, not just as a character, to emote. Not only are the stage movements personified with feelings, but the gestures take on these emotions as well. Cain walks around the altar, not because it is in his way, but because he needs to get into Abel's prayer space in order to enact his subtext. What gestures are implied as he moves? Below is the actor's subtext which may provide some clues.

CAIN:

> *This is ridiculous*
>
> *wasting our food*
>
> *hoping for rescue*
>
> *will we just whither away?*
>
> *now is the perfect time!*

He sets his bundle down so he can more adequately gesture about the world and the garden and the wilderness they now inhabit. If we break down the earlier analysis of this scene, we can see that if we ignore subtext as part of the motivation for movement, it places the need to feel an emotion on the other actor in the scene, not the actor delivering the lines. If empowered with subtext simultaneously with the actor that has the lines, the second actor is also able to move and gesture without having to react.

CAIN:

> *I didn't put us here.*
>
> *I didn't lose eden.*
>
> *I know they chose to leave.*

He constantly brings himself back to Abel's level on the stage in reaction to Abel trying at first to ignore him, but then to listen and engage with him. Abel is not just "front of You/Cain, slightly left of center." Abel has also done subtext for this scene for his non-verbal responses to Cain's enticement. Abel is moving as well, not simply an anchor point that is static.

ABEL: I can't believe that, Cain. *I think you're wrong.*
CAIN: *Why* can't you? *He hasn't helped yet.*
ABEL: Maybe I'm just not as angry as you are, Cain. *I'm not bitter, I'm hopeful.*
CAIN: You should be! *Look around.*

Once the nuance of subtext motivates movement, when pentad is now the final discovery process for a scene, several options exist for the actor in spite of or in addition to stage directions. Choosing the Act conjures up feelings about what has taken place with a reaction to the event in either action and/or with emotion. For example, the act in this scene is Cain needing to convince Abel he is right about their parents in order to get him to come with him beyond the waterfall. This focus as a motivation would draw him physically closer to Abel throughout the song.

Choosing the Scene will motivate you to react to the location with your own perceptions and backstory about where you are. For example, the scene is the wilderness, the house, and the altar that Cain cannot stand any longer. As he sings, his disdain for the setting can be a motivation for him.

Choosing the Agent will lead you to explore your feelings about the other character, reacting to them with prejudice, "a preconceived opinion not based on reason or experience." For example, the agent of the act in this scene is Cain. Cain being motivated by who he is, his relationships, and his determination gives the scene an internalized feel different even still in its expression.

Choosing the Agency answers the question about how you feel about how the act was accomplished, reacting to the individual *with* bias and opinions. For example, the agency in this scene is how Cain will accomplish the act of convincing Abel to join him. Agency is most closely aligned with the traditional beats of a scene, or "by means of."

Choosing the Purpose focuses you inward on whether the scene's outcome furthered or hindered your objective. Your reaction to that outcome is your motivation. For example, the purpose of this scene is to bring Cain and Abel together in one final effort at keeping this family together. Playing to the purpose of the scene motivates a tug of war throughout the song the keeps us hanging until the last "Finally, we'll be found." In view of the purpose of the show motivating every scene, Abel is most keenly confronting human's claim to free will. His struggle between choosing Adam/Father, and Cain is real, and his conflict is easily seen throughout the subtext the actors provided in the rest of their song. I have left the stage directions in the script in tact as they are provided by the writers to help the actors with motivation. Actor subtext is often in response to these directions in the script in tandem with the song lyrics.

CAIN:

Just like papa, you blindly follow false hopes.

We're barely getting by.

Make a change yourself, then.

Things can change.

What would beyond be like? Why just dream?

What's the worst that can happen?

I don't know what's beyond the waterfall, but it could be better. Imagine what we could discover.

"A Piece of Eight"

Act II introduces the story of Noah and the Ark to the audience. The student choreographer choreographed both the opening number, "Generations," and this one. As with all things academic, I try and use students in these roles as much as possible. JU has a wonderful dance department, and many of our musical theater majors are also wonderful dancers—they have to be! My student choreographer was happy to tackle this challenging number. We have a busy scene with the entire family, Yonah being the newest member as Japheth's fiancé. Each member has their own objectives and beats for this scene, both during the song and in the dialog that follows. What is always interesting to me as a director is the reactions of the cast members not talking, and we had a lot of fun with that in this scene, Aysha and Aphra especially! We started with the following objectives and beats:

Character	Objective	Beat(s)
Storytellers	Build anticipation	Introducing a potential new family member
Noah	Affirmation and consistency	Celebration Shunning Yonah Refusing Japheth
Yonah	Acceptance	Being a good servant girl
Japheth	Introducing Yonah as my fiancé	Overcoming fear Being confident Being positive

Character	Objective	Beat(s)
Mama	Diffusing conflict	Not revealing she knows about Japheth and Yonah Sitting the family down to dinner Happy and positive
Aysha	Get through dinner	Another glass of wine
Aphra	Welcome Yonah	Imagine my child in this situation

As Noah finishes the ark, the Storytellers take on the narration of this scene. The song proceeds with the seating of each member of the family. Suspense builds until all Japheth invites the servant girl, Yonah, to the table at which point the family realizes Japheth has committed himself to her. The stage directions imply that Japheth understands his family's disapproval, but the subtext from the characters provide a new level of consubstantiality with Japeth.

JAPHETH: My choice is Yonah. I want Yonah to be my wife. *We just sang about this!* [I
                liked this subtext from this actor! It was clever coming out of singing into the
                scene.]
NOAH: It's not possible. *Are you stupid?* [Imagine all kinds of vocal inflection here.]
JAPHETH: Why? I love her. *Uh, oh.* [Worry sets in.]
(turns to his brothers)
You know I love her. And she loves me. *Yonah, come here.* [Again, vocal inflection reveals
the depth of the subtext.]
YONAH: Japheth... *This isn't going well.* [In this case, the subtext can even stand in for
                the unfinished sentence.]
JAPHETH: **(to Yonah)** You don't deny it, do you? *Are you getting cold feet?*

Aysha and Aphra had subtext like "why are we here?" and "where's the wine" to affect their physicality on stage. Sometimes the actors not singing or talking can be the best storytellers of all. As a director or an actor, never ignore the non-speakers and non-singers in spite of working the lines and lyrics of the rest of the cast. You will miss out on some key opportunities to develop your pentad.

In the Beginning

The final number with the company brings home the theme of the show that the journey we all take inspires us to open our hearts to the journeys of others in order to empower further discovery in all of us. With the company on the stage, the actors are interacting with everyone possible.

Character	Objective	Beat(s)
FATHER	Letting go of pride	Changing is okay
Japheth	Yonah	Find Eden with her
Yonah	A hopeful future	Find Eden with Japheth Start a family
Noah	Start over	Let my sons go
Mama	Enjoy the success of my family	Let them find their way
Storytellers	Acknowledge free will	Remind us of the past and what has been learned and accomplished

As the dialog concludes, I had the cast circle the stage in a downstage semi-circle for the final number. It starts to dawn on the audience that this is the end of the story, and this musical was way more than a Bible story before bedtime. In being "wiser than before," the audience has "earned their increment," as Burke would say.

The journey of our pentad is over. The purpose has been intensified through the support of the scene, act, agents, and agency. While lessons have been learned by all the characters on the stage, even [Aristotle's] Father admits to the journey being "worth the taking."

Notes

1 Kenneth Burke, "The Problem of the Intrinsic as Reflected in the Neo-Aristotelian School," *Accent* 3 (1943): 93.
2 James McCrimmon, *Writing with a Purpose* (New York: Houghton Mifflin, 1984), 23.
3 Kenneth Burke, *A Grammar of Motives* (Berkeley: University of California Press, 1945), xxiii.
4 Ibid., xxii.
5 Cheryl Glenn and Jessica Enoch, "Drama in the Archives: Rereading Methods, Rewriting History," *College Composition and Communication* 61, no. 2 (2009): 331.
6 Ibid., 321.
7 Kenneth Burke, *A Grammar of Motives* (Berkeley: University of California Press, 1945), 289.
8 David Ostwald, *Acting for Singers: Creating Believable Singing Characters* (Oxford: Oxford University Press, 2005), 29–30.
9 Joe Deer and Rocco Dal Vera, *Acting in Musical Theatre: A Comprehensive Course* (New York: Routledge), 27.
10 Ibid.
11 David Ostwald, *Acting for Singers: Creating Believable Singing Characters* (Oxford: Oxford University Press, 2005), 74.
12 Ibid., 78.

13 Ibid.

14 Carol De Giere, *Defying Gravity: The Creative Career of Stephen Sondheim from Godspell to Wicked* (New York: Applause Books, 2008), 23.

15 David Ostwald, *Acting for Singers: Creating Believable Singing Characters* (Oxford: Oxford University Press, 2005), 79.

16 Carol De Giere, *Defying Gravity: The Creative Career of Stephen Sondheim from Godspell to Wicked* (New York: Applause Books, 2008), 208.

17 David Ostwald, *Acting for Singers: Creating Believable Singing Characters* (Oxford: Oxford University Press, 2005), 80.

18 Carol De Giere, *Defying Gravity: The Creative Career of Stephen Sondheim from Godspell to Wicked* (New York: Applause Books, 2008), 208.

19 Kenneth Burke, *A Grammar of Motives* (Berkeley: University of California Press, 1945), 288.

20 Ibid., 127.

21 Carol De Giere, *Defying Gravity: The Creative Career of Stephen Sondheim from Godspell to Wicked* (New York: Applause Books, 2008), 222.

22 Kenneth Burke, *A Grammar of Motives* (Berkeley: University of California Press, 1945), 288.

23 Ibid., 291.

24 Debra Hawhee, "Language as Sensuous Action: Sir Richard Paget, Kenneth Burke, and Gesture-Speech Theory," *Quarterly Journal of Speech* 92, no. 4 (2006): 342.

25 Ibid., 343.

26 Kenneth Burke, *A Grammar of Motives* (Berkeley: University of California Press, 1945), 348.

27 Jaclyn Olson, "Our Bodies and the Language We Learn: The Dialectic of Burkean Identification in the 1930's," *Rhetoric Review* 38, no. 3 (2019): 262.

28 Ibid., 259.

29 Kenneth Burke, *A Grammar of Motives* (Berkeley: University of California Press, 1945), 276.

30 Zachary Dunbar, "Stanislavski's System in Musical Theatre Actor Training," *Stanislavski Studies* 4, no. 1 (2016): 63.

31 Kenneth Burke, *Counter-Statement* (Berkeley: University of California Press, 1931), 33.

32 Kenneth Burke, *A Rhetoric of Motives* (Berkeley: University of California Press, 1950), 58.

33 M. Jack Suggs, Katherine Sakenfeld, and James Mueller, eds., *The Oxford Study Bible* (Oxford: Oxford University Press, 1992), 12.

34 Kenneth Burke, *Rhetoric of Religion* (Berkeley: University of California Press, 1966), 220–221.

35 Stephen Schwartz and John Caird, *Children of Eden* (New York: Music Theatre International, 1996), 1.

36 Ibid.

37 Kenneth Burke, *A Grammar of Motives* (Berkeley: University of California Press, 1945), 230.

38 Joe Deer and Rocco Dal Vera, *Acting in Musical Theatre: A Comprehensive Course* (New York: Routledge), 260.

39 Joe Deer and Rocco Dal Vera, *Acting in Musical Theatre: A Comprehensive Course* (New York: Routledge), 263.

Bibliography

Beasley, James P. *Rhetoric at the University of Chicago.* Peter Lang, 2018.

Birdsell, David. "Ronald Reagan on Lebanon: Flexibility and Interpretation in Burke's Pentad." *Quarterly Journal of Speech* 73, no. 3 (1987): 267–279.

Bourgonon, Jeroen. "From Counterstrike to Counter-Statement: Using Burke's Pentad as a Tool for Analysing Video Games." *Digital Creativity* 22, no. 2 (2011): 91–102.

Burke, Kenneth. *Counter-Statement.* Berkeley: University of California Press, 1931.

_____. *A Grammar of Motives.* Berkeley: University of California Press, 1945.

_____. *A Rhetoric of Motives.* Berkeley: University of California Press, 1950.

_____. "The Problem of the Intrinsic as Reflected in the Neo-Aristotelian School." *Accent* 3 (1943): 80–94.

_____. *The Rhetoric of Religion.* Berkeley: University of California Press, 1966.

De Giere, Carol. *Defying Gravity: The Creative Career of Stephen Schwartz from Godspell to Wicked.* New York: Applause Books, 2008.

Deer, Joe and Rocco Dal Vera. *Acting in Musical Theatre: A Comprehensive Course.* New York: Routledge, 2008.

Dickenson, Elizabeth. "The Montana Meth Project: Applying Burke's Dramatistic Pentad to a Persuasive Anti-Drug Campaign." *Communication Teacher* 23, no. 3 (2009): 126–131.

Dunbar, Zachary. "Stanislavski's System in Musical Theater Actor Training: Anomalies of Acting Song." *Stanislavski Studies* 4, no. 1 (2016): 63–74.

Familgelti, Andrew. "The Pentad of Cruft: A Taxonomy Used by Wikipedia Editors Based on the Dramatism of Kenneth Burke." *First Mind* 17, no. 9 (2012): Online.

Glenn, Cheryl and Jessica Enoch. "Drama in the Archives: Rereading Methods, Rewriting History." *College Composition and Communication* 61, no. 2 (2009): 321–342.

Hawhee, Debra. "Language as Sensuous Action: Sir Richard Paget, Kenneth Burke, and Gesture-Speech Theory." *Quarterly Journal of Speech* 92, no. 4 (2006): 331–354.

McCrimmon, James. *Writing with a Purpose.* New York: Hougton Mifflin, 1984.

Olson, Jaclyn. "Our Bodies and the Language We Learn: The Dialectic of Burkean Identification in the 1930's." *Rhetoric Review* 38, no. 3 (2019): 258–270.

Ostwald, David. *Acting for Singers: Creating Believable Singing Characters.* Oxford: Oxford University Press, 2005.

Schwartz, Stephen. *Children of Eden.* New York: Music Theatre International, 1996.

Suggs, M. Jack, Kathryn Sakenfeld, and James Mueller, eds. *The Oxford Study Bible.* Oxford: Oxford University Press, 1991.

Conclusion: "When in the World Are We?"

Ever paying attention to scene, Burke always asked his friends, "When in the world are we?" We started our introduction with how a call to gather can help us heal. As we write this conclusion at the beginning of our COVID-19 social distancing and self-quarantining, we are being told to avoid each other in order to heal. Over the last year, we have seen great social and political upheaval. During the writing of this book, our country has endured impeachment hearings, contentious elections, and the COVID-19 outbreak. We have transitioned all of our academic classes to online instruction, and the students we started with at the beginning of this year are now displaced all over the country and the world.

At the beginning of our introduction, we began with President Trump's travel ban from Muslim countries in the spring of 2017, and as we enter the spring of 2020, the xenophobic messaging coming from the current administration has not gotten better. In the midst of our COVID-19 outbreak, the President is insistent on speaking of the "Chinese virus," rather than its medical name. In our discussion of *chora* in our introduction, we had hoped that maybe we would see that the entertainment industry, including theater and musical theater, would be able to demonstrate the sustaining power of rhetoric, a "bargain between two people." If these two people must be gathered together, then how can rhetoric sustain its "coming together" function in a time of self-imposed exile, in a time of mandated quarantine? Is rhetoric still rhetoric if two people are not allowed to "come together"?

At the beginning of this book, we spoke of how musical theater can make our world a closer place. But in the midst of mandated quarantines, with theaters and Broadway itself abandoned, how can music theater make us a closer people? How can we fight against the savagery of the xenophobia that makes us distrust every person who is not like "us"? In many ways, the answers to these questions are harder than the ones we started with when we began this book, but if there is a time to try to answer them, it is now, and it is a journey (still) worth the taking.

While Kenneth Burke "went out on the town" as a New York music critic, one wonders what he would be doing during these current mandated quarantines. Burke never sat still, so we can almost see him walking around in his staccato way, mumbling and pacing back and forth in many of the itinerant dwellings he inhabited all over the country. If there was one thing Burke hated, it was to be restricted in his movement:

> Burke was incensed that Cowley should find it so damned poetic to picture me walled up at seventeen in the "Apprenticeship of the Arts" episode of *Exiles Return*. "So, Malcolm, who has made it his practice his whole life to bury me, who put me in a narrow house years ago, who once again sees me facing the wall, and who can imagine nothing prettier than a picture of me masturbating myself into extinction at the age of seventeen…He bows me out when I am just beginning." The episodes in *Exiles Return* were published as a book in 1934.[1]

There were points in Burke's life, of course, when he endured great isolation, as when his second wife, Libby, was ill and dying. His letters with friend Henry Sams describe many bouts of isolation and with own illness later in life.

The Solitary Writer

Burke's isolation as a writer is what he fought his entire life, and his dramatistic pentad is an effort to demonstrate how social our writing worlds actually are. In our discussions of the differences between intrinsic and extrinsic criticism, we highlighted the ability of extrinsic criticism to allow for the where and the when of student writing. In our new environment of online learning, these questions are becoming more obvious. If students don't have access to the internet, then how will they complete their coursework? If students don't have access to a desk or laptop computer, then how will they follow along in online chat sessions? What if students are only able to access their online learning courses through their phones? The "where and when the act occurred" seems more prevalent than ever in online learning environments, and intrinsic criticism of student writing seems woefully inadequate to address those concerns than ever before. Not only is this difference striking, but the relevance of intrinsic features of a text is even more in question. Paul Lynch wrote about these inadequacies in the face of global crises back in 2012:

> Do we really need close and careful readings to convince ourselves that we live in hard times? What can critique do for us now? "While most readers of the Great Eastern Garbage Patch have said that it's a bad idea to have a Texas-sized island of plastic floating in the Pacific, a close and careful reading shows ...." I do not mean to be glib, nor do I mean to be dismissive of Bartholomae's canonical essay. Of course, education ought to be a critical enterprise. Besides, all of the writers of the apocalyptic turn have, at least implicitly, made the "inventing the university" move: "While most teachers of composition have said that critique is the fundamental move, a close and careful reading shows that critique may become a trained incapacity." The problem is not a close and careful reading itself; the problem is whether a close and careful reading must always be positioned to undermine the realities we see around us.

We have addressed many "trained incapacities" in this book, starting from intrinsic criticism as a method for reading and responding to student texts to Stanislavski's "Given Circumstances" as a method for character development and staging. Lynch's question still lingers; however, "do we really need close and careful readings to convince ourselves that we live in hard times?" If we take this question and recast it for our own purposes here, it might read something like "do we really need intrinsic criticism to convince ourselves that writing is a difficult process for students?" And especially in the specific time of our writing, with students now having to fend for themselves in online environments, is intrinsic criticism even exacerbating the trained incapacities of student writing?

By the same token, we could also recast Lynch's question for the student-actor, "Do we really need Stanislavski's "Given Circumstances" to convince ourselves that acting is a difficult process for students?" If we already know that characterization and staging are difficult processes, then would not a method that exploits those moments of difficulty make it ultimately more rewarding for student-actors and directors?

Dramatism and Musical Theater

In the introduction, we address three audiences, the student writer, the student-actor, and the collegiate director. As we close out our discussions here, we hope to reemphasize our work for these three audiences. First, for the student writer, we hope that our section in the first chapter helps you understand how by making argument an act, rather than a method, an agency, you can question the instances in which your arguments are actually persuasive or not. In other words, anyone can make an argument, but it is more worthwhile to understand if your arguments are actually persuasive. In doing so, we write about how you understand you cannot change a problem, like red tide, by arguing about it, but you can exert change in society by changing the society itself.

If you are a student actor, we hope that from reading this text you are able to determine that, whether or not your director has chosen to use an aspect of the pentad as a focus or a theme, the pentad can help you direct yourself in a scene. If acting is reacting, you know have five options to react to, not just the other actor. In essence, you could also react to that actor reacting to any aspect of the pentad that they choose—the choices are limitless! For working with a director who wants you to "take five steps to the right on the word 'no'," pentad work can help you find that motivation that you are going to engage with above and beyond your blocking direction. If you are working with that actor, that just doesn't give you very much to work with, you can control your own characterizations, since you have four other ratios you can choose to react to, turning their non-reaction, non-objective acting into a scene you direct yourself.

- Choosing the ACT conjures up feelings about what has taken place with a reaction to the event in either action and/or with emotion.
- Choosing the SCENE will motivate you to react to the location with your own perceptions and backstory about where you are.
- Choosing the AGENT will lead you to explore your feelings about the other character, reacting to them with prejudice, "a preconceived opinion not based on reason or experience."
- Choosing the AGENCY answers the question about how you feel about how the act was accomplished, reacting to the individual *with* bias and opinions.
- Choosing the PURPOSE focuses you inward on whether the scene's outcome furthered or hindered your objective. Your reaction to that outcome is your motivation.

Conventional acting, or the traditional tools of objectives and beats and subtext, is foundational and necessary. However, they are subject to stage directions, focus only on the actor and one aspect of the scene, are highly individualized, and prescriptive rather than descriptive. To what extent are other aspects of the scene acting on each other simultaneously and to what degree? To what extent are the act, agent, scene, agency, and purpose act on each other and to what degree? If dramatism is language and thought as modes of action, and dare I add reaction, then there is a layer cake of options within the pentad system for these modes.

Physical actions/reactions are portrayed with posture, stance, movement, and gesture. Audible actions/reactions are delivered by variance in inflection and volume. The locus of those actions/reactions are upstage, downstage, offstage, center, right, or left. While each scene demands its own leaders, it is the balance of leaders to followers that reflects social values. Another maxim is that it isn't about whether an acting choice is right or wrong but whether it is effective or ineffective. However, with pentad analysis, the degree to which an aspect is influenced by another one, even if ineffective, is in and of itself a reaction and may to a greater/more effective degree work with any other aspect of the scene.

If you are a director, we hope that you will enable your cast to self-direct. You can either do pentad work with the cast or on your own. Decide on scene leaders together with your cast or on your own as a means to an overall aesthetic. When using the pentad thematically, actors are given a focus to their character's individuality that can give a show the dramatic aesthetic you are looking for.

- Choosing the ACT as the leader enables individual or group responses.
- Choosing the SCENE as the leader shifts the viewpoint.
- Choosing the AGENT as the leader highlights personalities.
- Choosing the AGENCY as the leader encourages dissenting opinions.
- Choosing the PURPOSE as the leader pulls out extremes.

Experiments in Rhetorical Performance

We have subtitled this book "Experiments in Rhetorical Performance," and these experiments exist on several levels: first, there is Kimberly's initial experiment using Burke's pentad with her students in the characterization and staging phases of her directing. Then, of course, writing of the accounts of these experiments. Rather than providing a chronological narrative of Kimberly's experiments, we have provided additional experiments, in other words, what if the account of Kimberly's experiments with Burke's dramatism is only the beginning of the experiment, not the end. In each chapter, we focus on what Burke's pentad can mean for student writers in general, then move outward to how Burke's pentad can help student actors find additional material for characterization, and then finally move further outward to help student-actors and directors find additional material for staging. By doing so, Kimberly was able to find greater material to use now in describing what she had done then. In other words, at the beginning of each chapter, there was a "goes before," and at the end of each chapter there was a "comes after" moment for Kimberly in her descriptions of her staging decisions. In this experiment, we follow the direction of Collin Gifford Brooke:

> For Latour's sociologist, the textual account is a laboratory, and the account itself can succeed or fail just as an experiment might. When that account "allows the writer to trace a set of relations defined as so many translations" among mediators, it is successful; by contrast, "in a bad text, only a handful of actors will be designated as the causes of all the others, which will have no other function than to serve as a backdrop or relay for the flows of causal efficacy."[2]

What we thought we had started with, a description of Kimberly's use of Burke's dramatism in her characterization and staging of the musical theater shows presented here, was only one experiment; or in Brooke's words, these actors "had no other function that serves as the relay for the flows of causal efficacy." Through the "tracing of the sets of relations" among mediators, we hope to demonstrate how our experiments, with other experiments, have been successful in each chapter.

In chapter one, one of the most important discoveries that we made was how describing argument as an act, rather than an agency, can help students discover whether their arguments are actually persuasive or not, and in doing so, see how their own languages serve as that agency which makes social change a reality. This discovery helped Kimberly describe her own staging from *Little Women: The Musical* by focusing on her staging of the attic scene with Jo March, "The Fire Within Me." While Jo is "alone" in the attic, the memories of her family are the languages, which are ultimately persuasive, which motivate her act of writing.

In chapter two, one of the most important discoveries we made was how describing the scene of the actor portraying the character, not just the scene of the character, could create an "ephemeral narrative" to subvert the "durable narrative" of slavery and power. This discovery helped Kimberly describe her own staging from Elton John's *Aida* by focusing on the scenes in motion, the motion of the fabric curtains and lighting to create a "scope and reduction" of the options available to Aida and Amneris on stage. This discovery also helped Kimberly describe the importance of the production in motion, from Broadway with its hyperbolic set design, to Jacksonville University, site of Anna Kingsley, princess turned slave, slave turned slave owner's wife, and wife turned social reformer, through the use of ever moving sets in motion.

In chapter three, one of the most important discoveries we made was that it was the languages of the agents that were in motion and that discovery allowed us to consider how those languages affected the actions of the antagonist, Frank Maurrant, in Kurt Weill's *Street Scene: An American Opera*. By describing Frank's hatred of his tenants through the differing languages, Kimberly was able to describe how some agents became "consubstantial" with the protagonists, Sam and Rose.

This discovery led to some innovative staging descriptions, such as how Kaplan, the Jewish immigrant, could interact with the other women of the tenement or even how Sam is a "body that learns language," in his commitment to Rose.

In chapter four, one of the most important discoveries we made was how the objects in motion created moments in the "woulds," The woods themselves became places on stage that actors moved to or behind in order to consider their options. This discovery helped Kimberly describe her staging in Stephen Sondheim's *Into the Woods* through the many "rhetorical refusals" that the characters utilize. These rhetorical refusals serve as an agency, a "means by which," the actors could create new rhetorical situations for other actors. This discovery helped Kimberly describe her staging of "Your Fault," a dizzying display of rhyme, music, and staging, as each rhetorical refusal moves each actor into a new position on stage.

In chapter five, one of the most important discoveries we made was how Burke's "psychology of form" contrasted with Stanislavski's "psychology of information" in the act-purpose ratio, and how that discovery helped Kimberly describe her staging in Stephen Schwartz's *Children of Eden*, especially in the scene, "Lost in the Wilderness." When the purpose of the scene is merely to provide information, the staging is limited to the providing of information. But when the purpose of the scene is to complete a psychologically derived need, the need for closure, then the staging can be expanded upon. Kimberly's description and visualizations of this scene are motivated by the actor's subtext as well as the need for bringing the act-purpose ratio to its dramatic conclusion.

One of the connections that we make throughout our book is how utilizing Burke's dramatistic pentad works against a kind of theatrical neo-Aristotelianism. What we mean by this is that in Stanislavski's "Given Circumstances," there is a focus on what is motivating a character in any given scene. This is similar to Burke's dealings with the neo-Aristotelians at the University of Chicago and their approach to literary interpretation, the importance of the writer's purpose, and how the writer goes about accomplishing that purpose. For Burke, purpose was only one of the five ratios, of course, and so therefore Burke's dramatistic pentad focuses on the extrinsic, rather than the intrinsic characteristics of writing, rhetoric, and theater production. What is interesting to note, in perhaps our last experiment here, is how Collin Gifford Brooke describes Wayne Booths' account of rhetoric. Booth was both a student of the neo-Aristotelians and a strong follower of Burke's extrinsic criticism, so to say that Booth was conflicted in what he saw in rhetorical study would be an understatement. Brooke's description here then serves as a final coda to our own experiments in rhetorical performance:

> This is perhaps the sharpest distinction to be drawn between Latour's work and Booth's: the ideal model of rhetorical interaction that Booth proposes is abstracted

from the empirical world that Latour asks us to engage with. And, yet, within Booth's account of rhetoric, there are some suggestive passages which may close this gap. While Booth restricts his description to human activity, those humans are not fully formed, discrete individuals; we are "in large degree what other men and women have created through symbolic exchange. Each of us 'takes in' other selves to build a self"[3]

We have gone to great pains to distinguish what Burke's dramatistic pentad can offer theater interpretation and dramatic staging that recent applications of Stanislavski's "Given Circumstances" cannot. In one such application, the writers remind student actors that their characters are not a "who, but an it."[4] Perhaps we are indeed our own characters, many "its" awaiting symbolic exchange to become "who's." In our time of temporary isolation, this symbolic exchange is what is necessary in order to "gather together," to participate in rhetoric.

Notes

1 Ann George and Jack Selzer, *Kenneth Burke in the 1930s* (Columbia: University of South Carolina Press, 2007), 245, note.
2 Collin Gifford Brooke, "Latour's Posthuman Rhetoric of Assent," in *Thinking with Bruno Latour in Rhetoric and Composition*, ed. Paul Lynch and Nathaniel Rivers (Carbondale: Southern Illinois University Press, 2015), 158.
3 Ibid., 161.
4 Joe Deer and Rocco Dal Vera, *Acting in Musical Theatre: A Comprehensive Course* (New York: Routledge, 2008), 135.

Bibliography

Brooke, Collin Clifford. "Bruno Latour's Posthuman Rhetoric of Assent. In *Thinking with Bruno Latour in Rhetoric and Composition*, edited by Paul Lynch and Nathaniel Rivers, 151–164. Carbondale: Southern Illinois University Press, 2015.

Deer, Joe and Rocco Dal Vera. *Acting in Musical Theatre: A Comprehensive Course.* New York: Routledge, 2008.

George, Ann and Jack Selzer. *Burke in the 1930's.* Columbia: South Carolina University Press, 2007.

Index